Politics and the Earthly City in Augustine's *City of God*

In this volume, Veronica Roberts Ogle offers a new reading of Augustine's political thought as it is presented in *City of God*. Focusing on the relationship between politics and the earthly city, she argues that a precise understanding of Augustine's vision can only be reached through a careful consideration of the work's rhetorical strategy and sacramental worldview. Ogle draws on Christian theology and political thought, moral philosophy, and semiotic theory to make her argument. Laying out Augustine's understanding of the earthly city, she proceeds by tracing out his rhetorical strategy and concludes by articulating his sacramental vision and the place of politics within it. Ogle thus suggests a new way of determining the status of politics in Augustine's thought. Her study clarifies seemingly contradictory passages in his text, highlights the nuance of his position, and captures the unity of his vision as presented in *City of God*.

Veronica Roberts Ogle is Assistant Professor of Philosophy at Assumption University, Worcester, Massachusetts.

T0351998

Politics and the Earthly City in Augustine's *City of God*

VERONICA ROBERTS OGLE

Assumption University

CAMBRIDGE
UNIVERSITY PRESS

CAMBRIDGE
UNIVERSITY PRESS

Shaftesbury Road, Cambridge CB2 8EA, United Kingdom

One Liberty Plaza, 20th Floor, New York, NY 10006, USA

477 Williamstown Road, Port Melbourne, VIC 3207, Australia

314–321, 3rd Floor, Plot 3, Splendor Forum, Jasola District Centre, New Delhi – 110025, India

103 Penang Road, #05–06/07, Visioncrest Commercial, Singapore 238467

Cambridge University Press is part of Cambridge University Press & Assessment,
a department of the University of Cambridge.

We share the University's mission to contribute to society through the pursuit of
education, learning and research at the highest international levels of excellence.

www.cambridge.org
Information on this title: www.cambridge.org/9781108294496

DOI: 10.1017/9781108903639

First published 2021
First paperback edition 2022

A catalogue record for this publication is available from the British Library

ISBN   978-1-108-84259-4   Hardback
ISBN   978-1-108-82949-6   Paperback

For Nicholas and Peter

He refused to be subject to his Creator, and in his arrogance supposed that he wielded power as his own private possession and rejoiced in that power. And thus he was both deceived and deceiving because no one can escape the power of the Omnipotent. He has refused to accept reality and in his arrogant pride presumes to counterfeit an unreality.

Augustine, *City of God* 11.13

Contents

Acknowledgments

I would first like to thank Mary Keys for being a model of Augustinian humility and a trusted advisor far beyond the years of graduate school. She and Ashleen Menchaca Bagnulo were my first companions in the conversation with Augustine, and I continue to learn much from their insights, as well as those of so many Augustinian friends. I am also deeply indebted to John Cavadini for enriching my understanding of Augustine's theological vision and to Peter Brown for the myriad of references and insights he provided me during my year at Princeton. I am grateful to both for comments made on early drafts of chapters.

This project would not have been possible without the financial support of Princeton's James Madison Program, the University of Notre Dame, and Assumption University. Thanks go in particular to Michael Zuckert, whose invitation to return to Notre Dame for a postdoctoral fellowship was not only significant for my life path but also allowed me two years to work on the project with little distraction. Of course, the project would not have gone anywhere without a press. Therefore, I am particularly grateful to Beatrice Rehl at Cambridge University Press for taking an interest in the project, sending it to such thoughtful reviewers, and shepherding it though the entire process. To these anonymous reviewers, I also owe much.

Finally, significant thanks are due to my family: to my sister-in-law, Allison Ciraulo, for being a careful editor of the whole work; to my mother-in-law, Ellen Ogle, for providing such loving childcare in the project's final days; and above all, to my husband, Nicholas Ogle, for his gracious criticism, loving patience, and steadfast encouragement. I could not have done it without him.

Deo Gratias.

Abbreviations

In what follows, I have used the abbreviations of *Augustinus-Lexicon* (Basel: Schwabe, 1986–). The Latin critical editions consulted are those gathered together by Dr. Cornelius Mayer in the *Corpus Augustinianum Gissense* (Basel: Schwabe, 1995). For English translations of Augustine's works, I have mostly drawn from the ongoing *The Works of Saint Augustine: A Translation for the Twenty-First Century* (WSA) (New York: New City Press, 1990–).

SERIES CONTAINING CRITICAL EDITIONS

CCSL = *Corpus Christianorum. Series Latina*. Turnhout, 1959–.
CSEL = *Corpus Scriptorum Ecclesiasticorum Latinorum*. Vienna, 1866–.
PL = *Patrologiae cursus completus*, Series Latina (ed. J. P. Migne). Paris, 1844–64.

TEXTS

ciu. = *de ciuitate Dei* (CCSL 47–48). *The City of God against the Pagans*. Trans. H. Bettenson. New York: Penguin, 2003.
conf. = *confessiones* (CCSL 27).*The Confessions*. WSA, vol. I/1. Trans. M. Boulding, OSB. Ed. J. E. Rotelle, OSA. New York: New City Press, 1997.
ep. = *epistula* (CCSL 31, 31A, 31B; CSEL 44). *Letters*. WSA, vol. II/1–4. Trans. R. Teske, SJ. Ed. J. E. Rotelle, OSA. New York: New City Press, 2001–5.

doct. chr. = de doctrina christiana (CCSL 32). *Teaching Christianity.*
WSA, vol. I/11. Trans. E. Hill, OP. Ed. J. E. Rotelle, OSA. New York:
New City Press, 1996.

en. Ps. = Enarrationes in Psalmos (CCSL 40). *Expositions of the Psalms,*
121–150. Vol. III/20. Trans. Maria Boulding. Ed. Boniface Ramsey,
OP. New York: New City Press, 2004.

ep. Io. tr. = In Epistulam Iohannis Ad Parthos Tractatus Decem (PL 35).
Homilies on the First Epistle of John. WSA, vol. I/14. Trans. B. Ramsey.
Eds. D. Doyle, OSA and T. Martin, OSA. New York: New City Press,
2008.

Gn. litt. = de Genesi ad litteram (CSEL 28). *On the Literal Meaning of*
Genesis. WSA, vol. I/13. Trans. E. Hill, OP. Ed. J. E. Rotelle, OSA.
New York: New City Press, 2002.

Io. eu. tr. = In Iohannis euangelium tractatus CXXIV (CCSL 36).
Homilies on the Gospel of John 1–40. WSA, vol. I/12. Trans. E. Hill,
OP. Ed. A. Fitzgerald, OSA. New York: New City Press, 2009.

s. = Sermones (CCSL 41, 41Aa, 41Ab, 41 Ba, 41Bb). *Sermons.* WSA, vol.
III/1–11. Trans. E. Hill, OP. Ed. J. E. Rotelle, OSA. New York: New
City Press, 1997–2006.

trin. = de trinitate (CCSL 50). *On the Trinity.* WSA, vol. I/5/ Trans.
E. Hill, OP. Ed. J. E. Rotelle, OSA. New York: New City Press, 1996.

Introduction

In *City of God*, Augustine famously writes that the two cities are created by two kinds of love: "the Heavenly city by love of God (*amor Dei*) carried as far as contempt of self," and the earthly city "by self-love (*amor sui*) reaching to the point of contempt for God" (*ciu.* 14.28).[1] Significantly, the grammar of these two loves betrays their difference: one is relational, the other is not. That is, looking at *amor Dei* grammatically, we can read the "of" contained therein as, at once, the subjective genitive and the objective genitive; both speak of the same love, the former referring to God's love for us, carried as far as the cross, the latter referring to our return of this love, carried as far as the martyr's witness.[2] While *amor Dei* bears the relationality of its love in its very grammar, *amor sui* betrays its narcissism. Collapsing the subject and object into one, it is the verbal image of a self loving itself.[3]

Taking this as but one instance of the symbolic richness that Augustine's language affords us, if we examine it with his vision of the two cities in mind,

---

[1] Throughout, I quote the Bettenson translation, unless otherwise noted. Augustine, *City of God*, trans. Henry Bettenson (London: Penguin, 2003). For the Latin, I use the critical edition of *De Ciuitate Dei* that can be found in the *Corpus Christianorum, Series Latina* (CCSL 47–48). Since I refer to the text so frequently, I merely refer to the chapter and book in in-text parentheses. All Latin references stem from the critical editions collected in the *Corpus Augustinianum Gissense* (Basel: Schwabe, 1995).

[2] There is some debate over this reading of the term "*amor Dei*" in Augustine. Burnaby argues that Augustine distorts St. Paul's meaning by reading *amor Dei* solely as the objective genitive, or our love for God, in *Amor Dei: A Study of the Religion of St. Augustine* (New York: Harper and Row, 1972), 99. I, however, follow Oliver O'Donovan's reading in *The Problem of Self-Love in Augustine* (Eugene, OR: Wipf and Stock, 1980), 130. O'Donovan's reading, I believe, fits better with the ontological framework presented in *City of God*.

[3] See again O'Donovan, *The Problem of Self-Love in Augustine*, 142.

this book explores the relationship between the earthly city and the political sphere as it is presented in *City of God*, asking whether Augustine's decision to call both by the same name (*ciuitas terrena*) bears any intelligible significance. In brief, I will argue that it does, and that this relationship is best described as hegemonic: for Augustine, the earthly city *covets* the political sphere, claiming it for itself, and so gaining its name from its earthly orientation.[4] This, however, does not mean that the earthly city invents politics, only that it co-opts the political project for its own ends. Yet, because Augustine never expressly unpacks how the two meanings of *ciuitas terrena* relate, this interpretation is not immediately obvious from the text. Instead, his word choice has posed difficulties for many seeking to understand the status of politics in his thought.

Currently, there are two dominant theses about this linguistic overlap: either Augustine uses the term *ciuitas terrena* indiscriminately because the two meanings amount to the same thing – that is, the political sphere *is* "the realm of sin" – or, his indiscriminate use of *ciuitas terrena* is merely literary, and no precise relationship between the two meanings can be found.[5]

---

[4] I mean hegemonic in the negative sense, as in when a hegemonic force occupies a conquered territory, it declares its rule legitimate, while the truth of the matter is that the territory belongs to another – in this case, God. Setting its eyes on the political realm as a prize worth having, the members of the earthly city have staged a coup, claiming the political sphere for their own and attempting to shape it in their own image.

[5] John Milbank, *Theology as Social Theory: Beyond Secular Reason* (Oxford: Oxford University Press, 2006), 411. For the former thesis, see Herbert Deane, *The Political and Social Ideas of St. Augustine* (New York: Columbia University Press, 1963); Reinhold Niebuhr, "Augustine's Political Realism," in *The Essential Reinhold Niebuhr*, ed. Robert McAfee Brown (New Haven, CT: Yale University Press, 1986), 123–141; Peter Kaufman, *Incorrectly Political: Augustine and Thomas More* (Sound Bend, IN: University of Notre Dame Press, 2007); Milbank, *Theology as Social Theory*, and William Cavanaugh, "The City: Beyond Secular Parodies," *Radical Orthodoxy: A New Theology*, ed. John Milbank, Catherine Pickstock, and Graham Ward (London: Routledge, 2002), 182–200. For the latter thesis, see Weithman, who writes, "No visible society or institution can be identified with either the City of God or the earthly city. The distinction between the two cities is an eschatological rather than a political one." Paul Weithman, "Augustine's Political Philosophy," in *The Cambridge Companion to Augustine*, ed. Eleonore Stump (Cambridge: Cambridge University Press, 2001), 237. Though acknowledging an overlap between the two meanings of *ciuitas terrena*, Harrison similarly argues that Augustine "writes within a tradition of rhetoric which was not at all constrained by matters of general consistency." Carol Harrison, *Christian Truth and Fractured Humanity* (Oxford: Oxford University Press, 2000), 216. To be sure, I agree that the two meanings of *ciuitas terrena* are not synonymous, but that is not to say that there is no consistency of vision behind his word choice. Wetzel sidesteps the difficulty by translating the term in two ways, using "secular city" to describe the mixed city and earthly city to describe the city of self-love. James Wetzel, "Splendid Vices and Secular Virtues: Variations on Milbank's Augustine," *Journal of Religious Ethics* 32, no. 2 (2004):

Neither of these alternatives, however, is satisfactory. On the one hand, the conflation of the two meanings takes his pessimism about politics too literally and on the other, few of Augustine's linguistic decisions are *merely* literary.[6]

Indeed, I will argue, a literalistic interpretation Augustine's pessimistic tone is out of sync with the work's genre. As Pierre Hadot ably demonstrates, one cannot read the ancient philosophers as if they were merely pouring their emotions onto the page.[7] Instead, one must interpret their rhetoric in light of its overarching purpose. Describing the genre of writing known as psychagogy – the art of leading souls to a state of health – Hadot explains that the ancient philosophers believed the human condition was marked by a sickness of soul which prized material things above their true worth; seeking to achieve "the sought-after therapeutic and psychagogic effect" for their readers, they meticulously crafted the "formulations necessary" to cure them of such mistaken beliefs.[8] The same can be said of Augustine. Christianizing the genre, to be sure, Augustine attributes our distorted vision to sin and argues with a view to religious conversion.[9] Yet, like all other authors writing works of psychagogy, he seeks to correct the vision of his readers by carefully crafted rhetorical arguments.

---

275. This is helpful for clarifying which *ciuitas terrena* he is referencing, but does not resolve the problem of the relationship between the two entities. Again, I think only a sacramental semiotics provides a conceptual framework that adequately addresses the question.

[6] Many scholars read Augustine as a pessimist. See the previous footnote. Niebuhr, for example, calls Augustine the "first great realist." Niebuhr "Augustine's Political Realism," 124. Peter Brown famously characterized Augustine's pessimism as a loss of worldly hope in his great biography's chapter "The Lost Future." Peter Brown, *Augustine of Hippo* (Berkeley: University of California Press, 2000), 139–150. For a critique of the realist reading of Augustine, see James V. Schall, SJ, "The 'Realism' of Augustine's 'Political Realism': Augustine and Machiavelli," *Perspectives on Political Science* 25, no. 3 (1996): 117–123.

[7] Michael Lamb has also invoked Hadot as a fitting guide for interpreting Augustine's political rhetoric in his recent article "Beyond Pessimism: A Structure of Encouragement in Augustine's *City of God*," *Review of Politics* 80 (2018): 591–624.

[8] Pierre Hadot, *Philosophy as a Way of Life* (Malden, MA: Blackwell, 1995), 201. Citing Marcus Aurelius's *Meditations* as an example, Hadot shows how its author sought to counteract his readers' gluttony by reminding them that even the best gourmet dishes really comprised "dead fish, birds and pigs" (185).

[9] Letters that explicate Augustine's intention in writing *City of God* include *ep.* 184A and *ep.* 10*. Using Hadot, Kamimura explores the difference between Christian spiritual training in *City of God* and its philosophic forerunners. Naoki Kamimura, "Scriptural Narratives and Divine Providence: Spiritual Training in Augustine's City of God," *Patristica*, suppl. vol. 4 (2014): 43–58.

Situating *City of God* within this framework, it becomes clear that our interpretation of its political passages must begin with the recognition that the work is psychagogic. Viewed in this way, Augustine's pessimistic rhetoric about Roman politics emerges as curative; applying the medicinal art of contraries, Augustine aims to liberate his readers from an excessive attachment to Rome so that they might express a proper allegiance to the city of God.[10] Accordingly, in speaking of Rome's faults and failings, he does not cast it as the "realm of sin" *per se*; rather, he does what is necessary to resituate the Roman *ciuitas* within an eschatological worldview.[11] Reading the political passages of *City of God* in this light, I will argue that Augustine's goal is to help us see the world, even the political world, anew: as part of a created order that is *good*, but that points beyond itself all the same.

What is more, I will argue, Augustine's decision to give the term *ciuitas terrena* a dual meaning is not accidental, but reflective of his overarching theological and metaphysical commitments. In what follows, I will demonstrate that Augustine's writings are shot through with a grammar that reflects his Christianized notion of Platonic participation – what I call a *sacramental* grammar. Indeed, as Robert Markus has noted in his excellent work on Augustinian semiotics, sacramentality – the quality of acting as a sign that points to God – is at the center of Augustine's whole worldview.[12] Developing this thought, E. J. Cutrone comments on the expansiveness of this notion of sacramentality: for Augustine, the material world as a whole points beyond itself toward a "deeper, inner reality" and

[10] In a similar vein, von Heyking has argued that Augustine's antipolitical rhetoric has obscured the degree to which he agrees with the ancient political philosophers, though ultimately von Heyking's study finds deeper agreement than mine. John von Heyking, *Politics as Longing in the World* (Columbia: University of Missouri Press, 2001).

[11] Milbank, *Theology and Social Theory*, 411.

[12] Robert Markus, "St. Augustine on Signs," *Phronesis* 2 (1957): 60. For other work on signs in Augustine, see Clifford Ando, "Augustine on Language," *Revue d'Études Augustiniennes et Patristiques* 40, no. 1 (1994): 45–78, and "Signs, Idols, and the Incarnation in Augustinian Metaphysics," *Representations* 73, no. 1 (2001): 24–53; B. D. Jackson, "The Theory of Signs in St. Augustine's *De doctrina Christina*," *Revue d'Études Augustiniennes* 15 (1969): 9–49; Mark D. Jordan, "Words and Word: Incarnation and Signification in Augustine's *De doctrina christiana*," *Augustinian Studies* 11 (1980): 177–196; Giovanni Manetti, *Theories of the Sign in Classical Antiquity*, trans. Christine Richardson (Bloomington: Indiana University Press, 1993); Robert Markus, "Augustine on Magic: A Neglected Semiotic Theory," *Revue d'Études Augustiniennes et Patristiques* 40, no. 2 (1994): 375–388. For a reading of Augustine's sacramental worldview that ultimately counters my position, see Phillip Cary, *Outward Signs: The Powerlessness of External Things in Augustine's Thought* (Oxford: Oxford University Press, 2008).

is thereby "revelatory of the divine mystery."[13] By paying attention to the way in which *City of God* reflects the sacramental cosmos in which Augustine finds himself, I find that Augustine shows us how politics is related to the earthly city, even if he does not explicitly tell us.

To be sure, Augustine's writings as a whole are full of such signs waiting to be read – allusions, word plays, and double entendres – all these are designed to reflect the rich, meaning-laden world he inhabited.[14] As Gertrud von Le Fort has aptly explained,

> Symbols are . . . the language of an invisible reality becoming articulate in the realm of the visible. This concept of the symbol springs from the conviction that in all beings and things there is an intelligent order that, through these very beings and things, reveals itself as a divine order by means of the language of its symbols.[15]

In Augustine, this conviction reaches its apex in his reading of creation as a divine speech act. This belief is not only the root of his deep sense that created things speak of God by virtue of their createdness, it is also why he considers rhetoric to be a divine art – a way of beckoning to the human heart written into the very fabric of creation.[16] However, to borrow from von Le Fort yet again, while the fecundity of symbols is central to the way Augustine thinks, speaks, and writes, "The language of symbols, once universally understood as an expression of living thought, has largely given place today to the language of abstract thinking."[17] If we are to truly understand the place of politics in Augustine's *City of God*, we must recover this older language, this *sacramental* language.

Therefore, what I develop in this book is a reading of *City of God* that reflects the sacramental ethos of the text. According to this reading, a proper understanding of the relationship between politics and the earthly city is rooted in Augustine's way of speaking about the earthly city; in particular, it pays attention to the fact that the earthly

---

[13] E. J. Cutrone, "Sacraments," in *Augustine through the Ages: An Encyclopedia*, ed. Allan Fitzgerald and John C. Cavadini (Grand Rapids, MI: Eerdmans, 1999), 741. Cf. Dodaro, *Christ and the Just Society*, 117n6, where he writes that "the term *sacramentum* may well be the most semantically dense term in Augustine's theological vocabulary," explaining that its "range of meanings . . . extends far beyond its vastly more limited usage within modern Christian theology."

[14] Cf. Dodaro, *Christ and the Just Society*, 152.

[15] Gertrud von Le Fort, *The Eternal Woman* (San Francisco: Ignatius Press, 2010), 3.

[16] By virtue of their createdness, they participate in the qualities of the God who created them, and so point to God as their origin. Again to call on von Le Fort: created things are "signs or images through which ultimate metaphysical realities and modes of being are apprehended, not in an abstract manner but by way of likeness." Ibid.

[17] Ibid.

city is consistently presented as a *simulacrum* (counterfeit imitation) of the heavenly city. For our purposes, the central implication of this presentation is as follows: while the city of God receives its eternal home as a gift, the earthly city grasps at the world to make it its home. Thus, while Augustine believes that the world has a sacramental meaning, in that it naturally points beyond itself to God, he also believes that the earthly city imposes an antisacramental meaning on it: one that reorients the significance of earthly things back to itself, political life included. For Augustine, then, the earthly city is defined by its perpetual attempt to edit the original meaning of reality – to erase meanings it does not like, and to reenforce illusions in which it has a stake. Much of what he says about politics is informed by this insight.

This, I will argue, is why a careful reading of Augustine's political analysis shows that the earthly city's activity within the political sphere does not define political life, but only corrupts it. In other words, on Augustine's reading, the earthly city recasts the political project in a way that undermines its true essence, precluding the possibility of genuine political community. Importantly, Augustine's sacramental language also reflects this insight; in the end, the dual use of the term *ciuitas terrena* turns out not to be a concession of politics to the earthly city, but symbolic shorthand for the relationship between a tyrant people and the world they covet.

CONTEXTUALIZING THE PROJECT WITHIN THE EXISTING LITERATURE

To reiterate, then, this monograph takes two facets of *City of God* seriously in order to explore its presentation of the relationship between politics and the earthly city: these are its psychagogic character and its sacramental ethos. The book begins by laying out Augustine's vision of the earthly city, proceeds by tracing out his psychagogic strategy, and ends by articulating his sacramental vision and the place of politics within it. By showing how Augustine's political pessimism fits into this psychagogic strategy and considering the place of politics in the vision to which it leads, I hope to open up conceptual space between the antisocial practices presented by the earthly city as political, and the underlying social endeavor that is, for Augustine, truly political. More than this, I hope to show how Augustine encourages his readers to participate in this underlying social endeavor.

I am, however, hardly the first to explore Augustine's understanding of the relationship between politics and the earthly city. For interpreters of Augustinian political thought writing in the first half of the twentieth century, what seemed to be at stake in this question was its implications for a Christian society in postwar Europe.[18] Increasingly, however, the concern of scholars turned to the question of church–state relations.[19] Most notably, what we see as the twentieth century unfolds is a reaction against what Arquillière has called "political Augustinianism" – the medieval absorption of the political realm into the jurisdiction of the Church.

For advocates of political Augustinianism, however, the subordination of political authority to the Church opened up the possibility of a new era

[18] Major works on Augustine's political thought during this period include John Neville Figgis, *The Political Aspects of St. Augustine's "City of God"* (London: Longmans, 1921); Gustave Combès, *La Doctrine Politique de Saint Augustin* (Paris: Plon, 1927); Henri-Xavier Arquillière, *L'Augustinisme Politique. Essai sur la Formation des Théories Politiques du Moyen Âge* (Paris: Librairie Philosophique J Vrin, 1933), and Henri-Irénée Marrou, *Saint Augustin et La Fin de la Culture Antique* (Paris: E. De Boccard, 1938).

[19] In the Straussian world, there has been a steady stream of publications on Augustine's political thought. However, situated in the discipline of political theory, this tradition tends to focus on the status of Augustine in the history of political thought rather than the status of politics in his theological worldview. In many ways, the conversation has occurred quite apart from that in religious studies and theology, though that is beginning to change. The father of this tradition, of course, is Ernest Fortin, and his most influential works include "St. Augustine," in *History of Political Philosophy*, ed. Leo Strauss and Joseph Cropsey, 3rd ed. (Chicago: University of Chicago Press, 1987), 176–205, and "The Political Thought of St. Augustine," in *Classical Christianity and the Political Order*, ed. Brian J. Benestad (Lanham, MD: Rowman and Littlefield, 1996), 1–30. Other helpful studies in the Straussian tradition pertaining to Augustine include Pierre Manent, *Metamorphoses of the City*, trans. Marc LePain (Cambridge, MA: Harvard University Press, 2013), and *The City of Man*, trans. Marc LePain (Princeton, NJ: Princeton University Press, 2000); Douglas Kries, "Augustine's Response to the Political Critics of Christianity in the *De Civitate Dei*," *American Catholic Philosophical Quarterly* 74, no. 1 (2000): 77–93; Michael Foley, "The Other Happy Life: The Political Dimensions to St. Augustine's Cassiciacum Dialogues," *The Review of Politics* 65, no. 2 (2003): 165–183; Mary Keys, "Augustinian Humility as Natural Right," in *Natural Right and Political Philosophy: Essays in Honor of Catherine Zuckert and Michael Zuckert*, ed. Ann Ward and Lee Ward (South Bend, IN: University of Notre Dame Press, 2013), 97–116; Daniel Burns, "Augustine on the Moral Significance of Human Law," *Revue d'Études Augustiniennes et Patristiques* 61, no. 2 (2015): 73–98; and all the essays in *Augustine's Political Thought*, ed. Richard Dougherty (Rochester, NY: Rochester University Press, 2019). Arguably, Jean Bethke Elshtain is also in this tradition. For her work on Augustine, see *Augustine and the Limits of Politics* (South Bend, IN: University of Notre Dame Press, 1998); "Augustine," in *The Blackwell Companion to Political Theology*, ed. Peter Scott and William T. Cavanaugh (Oxford: Blackwell, 2004), 35–47; and "Why Augustine? Why Now?," *Theology Today* 55, no. 1 (1998): 5–14.

of virtuous politics. For its critics, this solution was no solution at all, as politics with a powerful Church turned out to be just as corrupt as before. Here, it must be noted that the real disagreement between the two parties was over the relationship between the institutional Church and the city of God. For the political Augustinians, the Church was equated with the city of God to such an extent that it could be counted upon to heal politics. For their critics, the Church was no guarantor of such healing and, therefore, could not be the morally pure city of God that the former had supposed. Though an extensive foray into the question of their relationship and its political implications is beyond the scope of this book, my reading of *City of God* does suggest that a truly Augustinian answer would not side with either camp; rather, it would conceive of both the Church and the relationship between the Church and the city of God sacramentally.[20] That is

[20] The question of the relationship between the Church and the city of God in Augustine's thought is a fraught one. In *City of God* itself, it is not clear that he makes a strong distinction between the two, but many recent readers have wanted to draw a line between the *corpus permixtum* that is the institutional Church and the pure city of God. Cf. John Rist, *Augustine: Ancient Thought Baptized* (Cambridge: Cambridge University Press, 1995), 245; Harrison, *Christian Truth and Fractured Humanity*, 220; von Heyking, *Politics as Longing in the World*, 37, inter alia. This solution is attractive because it avoids the obvious error of maintaining the Church's perfection and yet still maintains the distinction between the two cities. Following this line of thought, Weithman, for example, has argued that because the members of the two cities are intermingled in the Church, there cannot be an identification of the Church with the city of God: Weithman, "Augustine's Political Philosophy," 236. Yet, I think the dichotomy between identification and equivocation is the wrong distinction to make if we are to be true to Augustine's own thought. Furthermore, for Augustine, each member of the pilgrim city is as yet imperfect – in the process of being healed. While some partake of the sacraments with ill intention, Augustine writes that it is the "City of God" who "has in her midst some who are united with her" in this way – this is not how he differentiates between the Church and the city of God (*ciu.* 1.35). As Dodaro has rightly argued, Augustine does not conceive of the Church institutionally, as moderns do, but as the body of Christ made visible. Cf. Robert Dodaro, "*Ecclesia and Res Publica*: How Augustinian Are Neo-Augustinian Politics?," in *Augustine and Postmodern Thought: A New Alliance against Modernity?*, ed. L. Boeve, M. Lamberigts, and M. Wisse (Leuven: Peeters, 2009), 238. This being so, the most we can say is that certain persons show up to church without *amor Dei* and that some who participate in its sacraments will not "join her in the eternal destiny of the saints." Ibid. Nevertheless, not all members of the former group will be part of the latter because human beings are capable of conversion. Accordingly, the real distinction, if we are to follow the distinction between the mixed and the pure, is between the city of God on pilgrimage and the city of God triumphant. The former is a *corpus permixtum*, both as a whole, and in each heart, and the latter has been brought to perfection. All this said, in recovering Augustine's sacramental use of language, we find that there is a way to distinguish between the Church as the visible body of Christ and the city of God; viewed from a sacramental perspective, we can say that the visible Church is a sacramental sign of the city of God: not a mere symbol, and yet not strictly speaking identical either, in that

to say, because Augustine conceives of the visible Church as the community bound together by the sacraments – and not primarily in terms of its hierarchy, and because he conceives of the visible Church as a synecdoche of the city of God – and not as identical or equivocal to it, he is not forced into the terms set forth by the abovementioned debate. For him, participation in the sacraments facilitates participation in *amor Dei* but does not guarantee it; this belief lays the groundwork for a very different conversation about the role the Church can have in healing politics.

Just as the relationship between the Church and the city of God remains in the background of the debate over political Augustinianism, so too, does the relationship between politics and the earthly city. Turning to the modern critics of the view, we find two predominant interpretations of Augustine's thought: first, that most famously promoted by Deane, in which Augustine the realist sees politics as the realm of the earthly city *per se*; and second, that most famously promoted by Markus, in which Augustine the proto-liberal presents the political sphere as a neutral space in which the two cities are inextricably intertwined.[21] In the former, the state is the earthly city; in the latter, the state is neutral.[22]

While Rowan Williams's influential essay "Politics and the Soul" sought to resolve the abovementioned debate by denying the de facto neutrality of the political sphere and, at the same time, refusing to concede politics to the earthly city, it did not provide a definitive answer as to what view of politics held both positions together. After all, Williams argued, Augustine is not a political thinker; "we cannot really say that he has a theory of *the* state at all."[23] Confronted with this difficulty, scholars

---

what we do not see is greater than what we do. Cf. Charles Mathewes, "A Worldly Augustinianism: Augustine's Sacramental Vision of Creation," *Augustinian Studies* 41, no. 1 (2010): 338–340.

[21] Deane, *The Political and Social Ideas of St. Augustine*, and Robert Markus, *Saeculum: History and Society in the Theology of St. Augustine* (Cambridge: Cambridge University Press, 1970). Both, in other words, worry that in the past politics has been absorbed under ecclesial jurisdiction and that a misreading of Augustine provides no theoretical arguments against this absorption. Accordingly, both readings of Augustine, despite their serious differences, want to emphasize the autonomy of secular institutions over and against any political claims of the institutional church. The first responds to political Augustinianism by relegating the two cities to their own separate arenas, the second by depicting the political sphere as a neutral space in which the two cities, interpreted as the religious and the nonreligious, meet.

[22] In this literature, the state, rather than the political community, is equated with politics. I will address this aspect of the scholarship in Chapter 6.

[23] Rowan Williams, "Politics and the Soul: A Reading of the City of God," *Milltown Studies* 19/20 (1987): 57–58. Reprinted in *On Augustine* (London: Bloomsbury, 2016), 110.

after Williams have either focused on the way Augustine conceives of Christian statesmanship or turned to constructive projects, using Augustinian ideas to think about contemporary issues.[24] It remains to be seen a precise relationship between politics and the earthly city can be found in *City of God*.

Meanwhile, the debate about the status of politics has reached a stalemate.[25] As Michael Bruno has pointed out in *Political Augustinianism*, the field can be divided into two camps: the pessimists and the optimists.[26] The pessimists continue to cast the political sphere as the "realm of sin," describing the work of the statesman as "damage control."[27] The optimists, on the other hand, continue to

---

[24] For the best of the former, see Robert Dodaro, *Christ and the Just Society* (Cambridge: Cambridge University Press, 2004); for the best of the latter, see Eric Gregory, *Politics and the Order of Love: An Augustinian Ethic of Democratic Citizenship* (Chicago: University of Chicago Press, 2008).

[25] Earlier studies that either touch or focus on the status of politics in *City of God* include Peter Brown, "Political Society," in *Augustine: A Collection of Critical Essays*, ed. Robert Markus, 311–335 (New York: Doubleday, 1972); Peter Dennis Bathory's *Political Theory as Public Confession the Social and Political Thought of St. Augustine of Hippo* (New Brunswick, NJ: Transaction Books, 1981); George Lavere, "The Political Realism of Saint Augustine," *Augustinian Studies* 11 (1980): 135–144, and "The Problem of the Common Good in Saint Augustine's *Civitas Terrena*," *Augustinian Studies* 14 (1983): 1–10; Oliver O'Donovan, "Augustine's City of God XIX and Western Political Thought," *Dionysius* 11 (1987): 89–100; Peter Burnell, "The Problem of Service to Unjust Regimes in Augustine's City of God," *Journal of the History of Ideas* 54, no. 2 (1993): 177–188, and "The Status of Politics in St. Augustine's City of God," *History of Political Thought* 13, no. 1 (1992): 13–29.

[26] Michael Bruno, *Political Augustinianism: Modern Interpretations of Augustine's Political Thought* (Minneapolis, MN: Fortress Press, 2014), 230–244. Bruno's book is the best available resource for understanding the development Augustinian political thought in the twentieth and twenty-first centuries.

[27] Milbank, *Theology as Social Theory*, 411; Kaufman, *Incorrectly Political*, 4. Ultimately, Milbank's view of Augustinian politics *is* that of Niebuhr, though this concession of politics to the earthly city leads him to present the Church as the new realm of politics. To my mind, this is simply a restatement of a position equating the state with the earthly city and the institutional Church with the city of God triumphant. Other notable works in this movement that draw on Augustine include Graham Ward, *Cities of God* (London: Routledge, 2000), and the work of William Cavanaugh, especially "From One City to Two: Christian Reimagining of Political Space," *Political Theology* 7, no. 3 (2006): 299–321, and "The City: Beyond Secular Parodies," 186. While Cavanaugh follows Milbank in declaring the political order to be sinful and the Church to be the new realm of politics, Graham Ward seeks a renewal in the political sphere through the Christian engagement. For Dodaro's critique of Milbank's stance on politics and the Church, see Dodaro, "*Ecclesia* and *Res Publica*," 256–270. Though Dodaro is somewhat more favorable to Kaufman's brand of pessimism in the essay, he still argues that Kaufman "misreads Augustine's intention" and that Augustine offers what he thinks is needed: "a set of religious practices through which Christian statemen undergo

cast the political sphere as a sphere of engagement, marking the *saeculum* as a neutral arena where Christians and non-Christians ought to work together for earthly peace.[28] Though scholars interested in the historical Augustine have made great strides in other areas, in reality, the question of the status of politics must be addressed because it is foundational to Augustine's thought: it can tell us whether and in what way Augustine thinks we can hope for positive political change, how he thinks we ought to participate in our political communities, and why and in what way the two cities participate in the drama of political history.[29]

Yet, as I have suggested, addressing this question in light of Augustine's own sacramental worldview, a clear relationship does emerge: the earthly city covets the political sphere and frequently dominates political life, but it does not create the political project.[30] Another way to put this is that Augustine does not concede politics to the earthly city. Instead, he opens up a new way of viewing our political communities; they are wounded, stunted by *amor sui*, but capable of being improved by *amor Dei* nonetheless. This view, in turn, invites a new way of serving our political communities; we, who are wounded and stunted by *amor sui* are capable of serving them in *amor Dei* nonetheless. Remarkably, then, Augustine's sacramental vision manages to delegitimate the earthly city's claim on politics without underestimating the hold *amor sui* has both on politics as we know it and on our own hearts, and more than this, does so in a way that invites us into *amor Dei*.

transformation through a deepening of their love of God that results in a gradual deepening of their political wisdom." Ibid., 246.

[28] See, for example, the work of Paul Weithman, especially his essay "Augustine's Political Philosophy," which follows Markus in his interpretation of the *saeculum*. Markus himself modified and somewhat moderated his position in *Christianity and the Secular* (South Bend, IN: University of Notre Dame Press, 2006), 64–66. Dodaro's aforementioned essay also addresses his newly stated position. Dodaro, "*Ecclesia* and *Res Publica*," 247–256.

[29] In a way, Fortin's essay on political idealism attempts to answer some of these questions, but as with other works in the Straussian tradition, it does not delve far into the theological foundations of his position. Ernest Fortin, "Political Idealism and Christianity in the Thought of St. Augustine," in *Classical Christianity and the Political Order*, ed. Brian J. Benestad (Lanham, MD: Rowman and Littlefield, 1996), 31–64. Lamb also addresses the question of hope in "Beyond Pessimism," esp. 594n20.

[30] That is, because Augustine thinks that the earthly city's speech and action are designed to grasp at what is given and claim them for its own, he also recognizes that the earthly city claims political life for its own. Furthermore, because human beings tend to act out of *amor sui*, he also grants that the logic of the earthly city has a significant effect on political life as we know it.

CHAPTER OUTLINES

Above, I suggested that a correct reading of the status of politics in *City of God* must be grounded in a careful study of Augustine's way of speaking about the earthly city. Accordingly, the first chapter is devoted to this theme, looking to books 11–14 for his account of the earthly city's origin and essence. Reading Augustine's exegesis of John 8:44 as the true origin story of the earthly city, I argue that he uses the devil's fall to highlight the irony of the earthly city's rebellion: the devil, as he puts it, is "both deceived and deceiving" (*ciu.* 11.13). Showing that the earthly city only exists by falling away from communion with God, Augustine reveals it to be a counterfeit rival: a parody of the city of God that has no originality beyond its capacity to distort and destroy. Turning to the psychological reasoning that defines the earthly city, I argue that Augustine's goal in presenting his readers with the logic of *amor sui* is psychagogic: by developing a psychology that his readers cannot but find in their own thoughts and behaviors, he chastens them. Implicating his readers in the dynamics of the earthly city, he aims to move them toward humility: toward the need for God.

In Chapter 2, I follow up on this analysis by tracing the trajectory of Augustine's psychagogic project through book 1. Based on a close reading of the preface, I argue that Augustine sets up *City of God* as a work designed to teach his readers to see the world anew: not simply as it fits into the Roman story, but as it fits into God's story: the story of the two cities. I then trace this endeavor throughout the rest of book 1, showing how he presents facets of the Roman perspective as distortions generated by *amor sui*. Approaching his response to the sack of Rome in this light, I find that Augustine is especially sensitive to the way in which pride has fostered judgmentalism among the Romans. Playing with Roman conceptions of friendship, civilization, and the prerogatives of empire, he highlights the way in which pride has vitiated their culture, creating customs all too marked by *amor sui*. In order to combat these distortions, Augustine models a stance of compassion rooted in humility and points to *amor Dei* as the source of true cultural renewal. In this way, I argue, he begins the process of correcting his readers' distorted vision.

In the third chapter, I follow Augustine's psychagogic argument through the first half of *City of God*, finding that books 1–9 in particular are constituted by Augustine's attempt to undercut ever more compelling, but similarly premature solutions to the problems generated by *amor sui*. Beginning with the promises offered by civilization, I trace the challenges

Augustine makes to Roman *consuetudo* (custom) and its ability to yield just politics. Turning to his treatment of the philosopher-statesmen, I show that these, too, are incapable of undoing the political damage done by the earthly city, willing as they are to endorse falsehoods for the sake of political stability. Finally, I turn to Augustine's treatment of the philosopher, wherein he argues that no one can cultivate a just soul independent of God's help, only an impassible one. Ultimately, I argue, Augustine leaves his readers with no way to solve the problem of *amor sui* on their own. Sealing them in at all sides, Augustine points to one way out: through the Mediator.[31]

Having traced out this arc of Augustine's psychagogic argument, in the fourth chapter I situate his retelling of Roman history within it. Here, I argue that Augustine's engagement with the Roman *literati* – those invested in the project of making Rome just through myth-making – has an important function within his argument: it helps detach his readers from an excessive attachment to Rome so that he can later resituate patriotic love within its proper context. Zeroing in on books 2–5, I argue that Augustine's retelling of familiar Roman stories is designed to highlight the distortion in the way they were originally told. Examining his subsequent retelling of the whole Roman story, I argue that his objective is to underscore the presence of *amor sui* in all stages of Roman history, even as its increase led to greater decline. Yet, in doing this, Augustine leaves us with problem: are we to read this retelling as proof that the political sphere is the realm of sin? Reading the history in light of its psychagogic purpose, I argue that the answer is no. Rather, Augustine thinks that the dysfunction that exists must be revealed, lest people succumb to the myth that Rome is the eternal city.

And yet, this reading of Augustine's political history must be defended. Read out of context, books 2–5 do tell the tale of a city mired in sin. In order to demonstrate that *amor sui* is not the solitary feature of Augustine's view of politics, it is necessary to further develop our understanding of the sacramental vision to which *City of God* leads. Accordingly, in Chapter 5, I embark on an analysis of this vision, approaching it by way of the sign theory laid out in *De Doctrina Christiana*. Exploring the sacramental worldview undergirding this theory, I find that Augustine considers the reality of created things to be

---

[31] Dodaro has an exhaustive account of how Augustine conceives of the "just and justifying" Christ as the Mediator. Dodaro, *Christ and the Just Society*, 107. Compellingly, Dodaro argues that Christ stands at the center of Augustine's whole worldview, so that in him, humanity is offered a new path toward virtue "freed from the pretensions of moral self-reliance." Ibid., 71. In brief, Christ comes to cure our ignorance and weakness by teaching us to rely on him and helping us to rely on him.

endowed with a given meaning that points to their Creator – a meaning that the earthly city replaces with its own antisacramental meaning. Returning to *City of God*, I find the battle between the sacramental and the antisacramental worldview to be at the root of Augustine's psychagogic strategy; looking at key passages from the second half of the work, it becomes clear that the *telos* of the text is a sacramental vision in which we can see two opposing economies at work in the world, one a parody of the other.[32] With this in mind, I conclude that *City of God* is designed to help us see through the false claims of the earthly city and ultimately to resist them.

Finally, in Chapter 6, I consider the status of politics within this sacramental vision. Finding that Augustine's ultimate goal is to help us see the world anew, I argue that he also helps us see politics anew. In other words, when it comes to politics, his deconstructive treatment of Rome in the early books is only half of his strategy; he also resituates it within the vision he spends the second half of *City of God* articulating. This is where book 19 comes in. Here, Augustine's profound sense that the earthly city overstates its claim on the world translates into a different vision of politics: one in which our political communities are wounded. Making conceptual space between natural political community, postlapsarian political necessity, and sinful political behavior, the Augustine of book 19 does not concede the political sphere to the earthly city. Instead, he urges us to participate in our political communities without participating in the earthly city. Thus, I conclude, when it comes to politics, the psychagogic goal of *City of God* is that we participate as pilgrims, striving to be a healing presence within our political communities while seeking a good beyond them all the same.

A NOTE ON THE TWO CITIES PARADIGM

Before beginning our inquiry in earnest, it is fitting to say a few words about the source of Augustine's two cities paradigm. While there is much scholarly speculation about the Platonic, Stoic, and Manichean influences on his conception of the two cities, Van Oort concluded in his 1991 book that the idea is fundamentally scriptural. There has been a more or less general consensus that, *at bottom*, it is Augustine's meditation on

---

[32] Figures within Radical Orthodoxy have focused on the theme of parody in Augustine with great fruitfulness: see especially Graham Ward, *Cities of God*; John Milbank, *Theology and Social Theory*; Catherine Pickstock, "Music: Soul, City and Cosmos after Augustine," 261; and William Cavanaugh, "The City: Beyond Secular Parodies."

Scripture that leads him to speak of the two cities – first in *De Catechizandis Rudibus* and, in its fullest expression, in *City of God*.[33] My concern in this book is not to examine the origins of the two cities paradigm. Rather, it is to understand how Augustine thinks in terms of the two cities in *City of God* so that we can understand the relationship between the earthly city and political life. For our purposes, it is enough to say with Van Oort that "Augustine speaks of two cities because in his opinion the Scriptures themselves already do so."[34]

Thus, when Augustine writes in *City of God* 15.1 that the two societies can be called two cities "*mystice,*" what he means is that God has used the symbolic quality of Jerusalem and Babylon to reveal that there are, in the end, only two societies of rational creatures.[35] Scripture, for Augustine, is the communication of eternal vision translated into time. As such, it can only be translated into an eschatological vision – the kind of vision that we penetrate "through a glass darkly" (1 Cor. 13:12).[36] Thus, when these two cities are revealed, they are revealed as eschatological realities – societies made visible in light of their destiny and destination. This is a perspective that must be received as gift, and, fundamentally, as mystery.

And yet, Augustine believes, by seeking to understand this obscure vision, we are able see more clearly than we could on our own. For Augustine, Scripture is designed to cultivate and nurture a posture of

[33] J. van Oort, *Jerusalem and Babylon: A Study into Augustine's City of God and the Sources of His Doctrine of the Two Cities*, Supplements to Vigiliae Christianae 14 (Leiden, 1991), 199–360. In addition to Oort's study, Harrison's brief overview of the idea's sources is a helpful summary. Harrison, *Christian Truth and Fractured Humanity*, 200–202. Within this literature, there is also a discussion of the influences Tyconius had on Augustine's thought. Cf. Gerard O'Daly, *Augustine's City of God: A Reader's Guide* (Oxford: Oxford University Press, 2004), 57–58. Significantly, Crantz situates the relationship between the empire and the earthly city in the shift in emphasis between *De Catechizandis Rudibus* and *De Ciuitate Dei*. F. Edward Crantz, "Society before the Donatist Controversy," *Harvard Theological Review* 47, no. 4 (1954): 384.

[34] Van Oort, *Jerusalem and Babylon*, 117. While it is true that Oort also thinks that Augustine read the idea of the opposition of the two cities back into Scripture from the tradition, he does cite numerous places in scripture where the character of the two cities are depicted (356). For a thorough and lucid overview of Augustine's take on scripture, see Michael Cameron's essay "Augustine and Scripture," in *A Companion to Augustine*, ed. Mark Vessey (Malden, MA: Wiley-Blackwell, 2012), 200–214.

[35] Van Oort, *Jerusalem and Babylon*, 314–318. In Bettenson, *mystice* is translated as "allegorically." Henry Bettenson, *City of God*, 595.

[36] Cf. Kamlah's argument as relayed by Van Oort in *Jerusalem and Babylon*: "Instead of a theocratic, an empirical or a purely idealistic interpretation [of the predestined members of the city of God], Kamlah presents an eschatological view." Van Oort, *Jerusalem and Babylon*, 126; cf. ibid., note 586.

humility, of faith seeking understanding.[37] In arguing for this hidden power of humility in the preface of *City of God*, Augustine trades on the words of Christ: "I give praise to you, Father, Lord of heaven and earth, for although you have hidden these things from the wise and the learned you have revealed them to the childlike" (Mt 11:25). With this having been said, we can return to *City of God* 15.1 with a greater sense of why Augustine begins his meditation with the premise that Scripture reveals two societies understood "*mystice*" as cities (*ciu.* 15.1). Because Augustine reads Scripture through Christ – that is, through the Incarnation – he views the Scriptures as a way in which God condescends to speak to the human community in ways human beings can understand, albeit "through a glass darkly."[38]

Here, I hope, we begin to glimpse the distinctly premodern way that Augustine views the relationship between the visible and the invisible. Augustine does not think of the visible as real and the invisible as ideal. Rather, the visible bears witness to the invisible; it points toward it by its very existence. Yet, in Augustine, we are not merely dealing with a strictly Platonic ascent from material image to immaterial reality.[39] For Augustine,

---

[37] See, e.g., *trin.* 1.2.4–1.3.5 for Augustine's hermeneutic of humility. Augustine, *The Trinity*, trans. Edmund Hill, OP, series ed. John E. Rotelle, OSA (Brooklyn, NY: New City Press, 1991), 68. Similarly, Rowan Williams describes "the difficulties of Scripture as a kind of parable for our condition," given that we are in "constant danger of premature closure," that is, tempted to think "the end of desire has been reached and the ambiguities of history and language behind us." Rowan Williams, "Language, Reality and Desire: The Nature of Christian Formation," in *On Augustine* (London: Bloomsbury, 2016), 47.

[38] As Carol Harrison writes, "for Augustine, Scripture is *par excellence*, an example of language and rhetoric being used to address fallen man in terms he will be able to apprehend in order to lead him to divine truth. . . . It is likened (as are those who preach) to an eyesalve, or a lamp for fallen man's darkened sight and reason. Like the flesh of Christ, it enables man to be lifted up to His divinity. Like the heavens, it provides authority, like a forest, a place to contemplate divine mysteries." Carol Harrison, *Beauty and Revelation in the Thought of Saint Augustine* (Oxford: Oxford University Press, 1992), 81 and 83. Given this, it is important to note the status of Scripture in Augustine's thought. As one of the foremost scholars of Scripture in Augustine has argued, "as majestic as it is, Scripture is nevertheless not in itself God's eternal Word, who is Christ alone. Scripture is rather a part of God's massive rescue program to save humanity and to return it to right reason. Augustine calls that program the "temporal dispensation" (*dispensatio temporalis*: *Vera rel.* 7.13, *Fid. et symb.* 4.8). Other elements of this program include the church, the sacraments, and even the flesh of Christ." Michael Cameron, "Augustine and Scripture," 205. In this way, Scripture in Augustine's thought is best understood as a vehicle through which Christ speaks to humankind.

[39] Rowan Williams puts this well: "God's *nature* is such as to produce beauty; it is in this way that the world's beauty tells us something of what it is to be God – not because God stands at the summit of an ascending scale of beautiful things, but because we grasp that, whatever God's life is (and we can never catch it in a concept), it is what makes for

the starting point is always the givenness of Scripture – for him, it is Scripture that provides perspective, and it is by following *its* lead that the visible sheds light on the invisible.[40] Accordingly, there may be ways in which visible cities, such as Rome, manifest or reveal something about the earthly city, but it is only from the perspective afforded by Scripture – what I am calling the sacramental worldview – that Augustine thinks these similarities may be parsed.[41]

Before we continue, it should be noted that the invisibility of the earthly city besets the task of this book with some difficulties. If our goal is to become acquainted with Augustine's understanding of the relationship between politics and the earthly city, the very fact that Augustine cannot point to the earthly city in the same way that he can point to Carthage or Rome already indicates this challenge. We cannot verify what he says about the earthly city simply by locating it and scrutinizing it ourselves. This is the difficulty that goes along with Augustine's hermeneutic of faith. While the vision afforded by Scripture makes sense of life in the *saeculum*, it is not a vision that could have been achieved any other way. It could not have been achieved, for example, through a meditation on political history alone, though it can be read back into it.

harmony." Rowan Williams, "Good for Nothing? Augustine on Creation," in *On Augustine* (London: Bloomsbury, 2016), 64. For the differences between a Platonic ascent from the *peras* (the finite) to the *apeiras* (the infinite) and Augustine's view, see Richard Avramenko, "The Wound and Salve of Time: Augustine's Politics of Human Happiness," *The Review of Metaphysics* 60, no. 4 (2007): 779–811. Finally, for the difference in attitude toward the visible, see Carol Harrison, *Beauty and Revelation*, 180: the "temporal, created realm is therefore not simply to be left to one side until man has purified himself, but is instrumental in his purification and needs to be turned towards and used by fallen man, in the faith, hope, and love which are inspired by God's revelation within it, and by the confession of sin and confession of praise which this revelation brings about." Cf. Hans Urs von Balthasar, *The Glory of the Lord: A Theological Aesthetics*, vol. 2 (Edinburgh: T& T Clark, 1982), 121–143.

40 Cf. D. J. MacQueen, "The Origin and Dynamics of Society and the State According to St. Augustine," *Augustinian Studies* 4 (1973): 81.

41 As Carol Harrison puts it, it is Scripture's "mysteries, enigmas, allegories, parables, and miracles" that "are the glass through which man must look and by them the mind is gradually exercised and cleansed and brought to the truth from which it had fallen. Its veils of obscurity and imagery serve to protect the weak eyes of fallen man from what would otherwise be the blinding light of truth, and yet its mystery also evokes a search for knowledge or sight of it. Meanwhile, the eyes of the mind are covered with the healing salves of the double commandment of love, by which Scripture might be interpreted, even though its difficult passages and lessons are not understood." Harrison, *Beauty and Revelation*, 181.

Furthermore, the fact that the earthly city is only eschatologically visible means that we cannot say who is part of it here and now.[42] It is for this reason that Augustine's account of the earthly city resists a certain kind of application. It resists becoming a rubric by which we can justify imputing the basest of motives – the motives of the earthly city – to our enemies. It is not designed to help us prematurely sift the wheat from the chaff. Rather, as Peter Kaufman puts it, Augustine's point is to give an "extended sermon" that invites and draws each reader toward and into the *ciuitas Dei*.[43] To put it another way, what Augustine has to teach his readers about the earthly city makes the most sense when it is viewed as part of an attempt to liberate the reader from the seductive clutches of the earthly city. It does not make sense when it is viewed as a weapon to be leveraged against what one translator has called "the heathens."[44] When Augustine writes that all people are born into the earthly city, but no one need remain there, he writes in a pastoral register (*ciu.* 15.1). Indeed, he explains, no one should want to remain in the earthly city because its "good" is passing away (*ciu.* 15.4). As long as this world remains, the earthly city might maintain some semblance of cohesiveness, but, Augustine teaches, this will not always be the case, and the earlier one realizes this, the better.

[42] For a thought-provoking meditation on this aspect of *City of God*, see James Wetzel, "A Tangle of Two Cities," *Augustinian Studies* 43 (2012): 5–23.
[43] Kaufman, *Incorrectly Political*, 228.   [44] I.e., Marcus Dods.

I

The Parodic City

Augustine's Account of the Earthly City and Its Logic of Self-Love

Our present inquiry seeks to clarify the relationship between the political sphere and the earthly city in *City of God,* asking whether Augustine's decision to call both by the same name (*ciuitas terrena*) bears any intelligible significance. As I suggested in the introduction, this investigation must begin with Augustine's construal of the earthly city, for unless we understand what he means by the earthly city, we risk misunderstanding the relationship in question. Moreover, because *City of God* is a psychagogic text, written to cure its readers of the distorted vision that results from *amor sui,* it has a distinctive structure; broadly speaking, the first half aims to divest readers of the logic of *amor sui* by calling the worldviews it generates into question, while the second half offers a sacramental worldview in their stead – a worldview, that is, in which all created reality points to the God who sustains it in being.[1] Accordingly, while the books from the first half do provide a window into the way the earthly city and its logic shapes political life, it is not until the second half of the work that we get a robust account of the earthly city's origin and essence. For this reason, it is fitting to begin our inquiry with the latter half of the text, homing in on books 11–14 in particular. Doing so, we will discover that the earthly city is the antisocial result of that-which-is-lacking in the fallen heart: the rendering visible of self-centeredness *as* lack. Worse, we will discover, it has been brought into being by creaturely

---

[1] As Robert Markus has noted, sacramentality – the quality of acting as a sign that points to God – is at the center of Augustine's whole worldview. Markus, "St. Augustine on Signs," 60. For a fuller explanation of the notion of sacramentality employed here, see the introduction.

choice – our choice. Because the earthly city would not exist apart from *amor sui*, we who live out of *amor sui* bear responsibility for its very existence. We sustain it in being.

For our purposes, this view will be important to understand because it undergirds the way Augustine talks about the earthly city throughout the entire *City of God*. If the earthly city serves an explanatory function in his analysis of political life, it matters that his focus on "that-which-is-lacking" in the ethos of the earthly city is rooted in a metaphysical claim about the earthly city. As we will discover, it is not Augustine's goal to reify the concept of depravity. Rather, his goal is to undermine the legitimacy of the earthly city's claim on the world. In order to do this, he needs to distinguish between the boasts the earthly city makes about its own power and effectiveness and the phenomena that are actually due to its principal love. He needs to show that the logic of the earthly city only bears independent responsibility for evil.

THE EARTHLY CITY'S ORDO AMORIS

It is well known that Augustine defines a *societas* by its shared love (*ciu.* 19.21). In the case of the earthly city, this love is *amor sui*: the kind of self-love that implies the preference of the self over God (*ciu.* 14.13). Yet, Augustine also indicates that the earthly city is bound together by its love of the world. This, after all, is why it is called the earthly city. Augustine is able to reconcile these two teachings through his theory about the rational creature's *ordo amoris*, or order of loves.[2] Simply put, the members of the earthly city love the world out of *amor sui*. They do love the world, but as something *for* themselves. Yet, one might ask, if *self*-love is the most fundamental love of this society, why does Augustine call it the earthly city? That is, if names are so important, why does he pick a derivative love as its titular feature? Not only is Augustine making a Platonic contrast between the earthly and the heavenly – the community dragged down by the weight of its earthly loves over and against the community drawn

[2] Burnaby's work *Amor Dei* remains the most exhaustive treatment of love and the *ordo amoris* in Augustine. Most importantly, he argues against Nygren's position in which *caritas* and *cupiditas* are intrinsically opposed. For Burnaby's Augustine, *eros*, or desire, finds its fulfillment in *agape* or charity. Anders Nygren, *Agape and Eros*, trans. Phillip Watson (Chicago: University of Chicago Press, 1982). Hannah Arendt also reads Augustine as opposing *eros* and *agape* in her dissertation on Augustine: Hannah Arendt, *Love and Saint Augustine* (Chicago: University of Chicago Press, 1996).

upward by Love,[3] he is also taking his cue from Scripture.[4] Augustine's earthly city is what Christ, John, James, Paul and Jude call "the world."[5]

In order to get a better sense of how Augustine is thinking about the earthly city in *City of God*, it is helpful to begin with an excerpt from a sermon on the first epistle of John.[6] In it, Augustine unfolds John's linguistic logic and reveals its influence on his own thought by asking "What is the world?"

When it is understood in a bad sense, it is the lovers of the world (*dilectores mundi*).[7] When it is understood in a praiseworthy sense, it is heaven and earth and the works of God that are in them. Hence it is said, And the world was made through him (*et mundus per eum factus est*) (Jn 1:10). Likewise, the world is the fullness of the earth, as John himself said, He is the propitiator not only for our sins but also for those of the whole world (*non solum autem nostrorum peccatorum propitiator est, sed et totius mundi*) (2:2). World (*mundi*) refers to all believers scattered throughout the earth. But in a bad sense the world is the lovers of the world (*amatores mundi*). Those who love the world cannot love their brother (*qui amant mundum, fratrem amare non possunt*). (ep. Io. tr. 5.7)[8]

Here, Augustine is explaining why John uses the phrase "the world" (*mundus*) in two very different ways.[9] Across the board, Augustine's interpretation of Scripture is characterized by the belief that it bears mystery in its very word choice. John's decision to call the earthly city "the world," for example, reveals an important truth about how the members of the earthly city love the world. Venturing an explanation as to what makes a person part of the world in the bad sense, Augustine suggests that it is to act as a lover (*dilector, amator*) of the world. Clearly, given that the world is good, and therefore lovable, Augustine thinks that John must mean something very particular when he disparages the lovers

---

[3] See, e.g., *s.* 65A.1.   [4] E.g., see *en. Ps.* 141.6–147.15.

[5] One might ask why Augustine does not just call the earthly city the world; perhaps this is because he thinks the term bears too much of a multiplicity of meanings, none of which are related. We see him working through this difficulty in *s.* 96.5–9. There, he differentiates between the world as the heavens and the earth, and the world as people, and then, within the world as people, he distinguishes between the world as condemned and the world as reconciled.

[6] See, e.g., Augustine's use of 1 Jn 2:16 in *City of God*: "If anyone has become fond of the world, there is no fondness in him for the Father" (*ciu.* 14.7). Augustine also takes this language from Paul, who advises the Romans not to be conformed to this world (Rom 12:12). Cf. *ciu.* 19.8.

[7] PL 35, 2017.

[8] Augustine, *Homilies on the First Epistle of John*, trans. Boniface Ramsey, ed. Daniel E. Doyle, OSA, and Thomas Martin, OSA (Hyde Park, NY: New City Press, 2008), 84.

[9] John 1:10 is an excellent case in point.

of the world. To be a lover of the world, Augustine explains in another homily, is to prefer to remain in the world rather than to strive "toward him who created the world" (s. 81.7).[10] To love the world in this way, he warns elsewhere, "is a serious pollution of the soul, and a heavy weight holding down the soul that is longing to fly" (s. 65A.1).[11]

Yet, one might still ask, where does *amor sui* fit into this notion of loving of the world? I have already suggested that Augustine finds particular significance in John's use of language; there is something in the earthly city's name that reveals its members' *ordo amoris*. This is the hiddenness of *amor sui*. Thus, while *amor sui* is the fundamental love of the earthly city, it is a love that is only revealed by its fruits – by the actions it brings into being. *Amor sui* is revealed *in* love of the world. In fact, *City of God*'s interpretation of the Fall hinges on this insight. In trying to understand how Adam and Eve could have been seduced by the snake's promise of a god-like existence apart from God, Augustine reasons that it was only possible because they had already abandoned "the basis on which the mind should be firmly fixed" (*ciu.* 14.13). It was "in secret that the first human beings began to be evil" (ibid.).

In other words, unless Adam and Eve had already become self-pleasers (*sibi placentes* – a phrase Augustine takes from 2 Peter 2:10), they would never have entertained a scenario that involved breaking the one rule God had given them. What is more, to find it plausible that God was hindering their pursuit of happiness, Augustine reasons, they must have already somehow distanced themselves from God. They must have forgotten who God is: the source of their true happiness. Analyzing the story figuratively, he concludes, "the will itself was the evil tree which bore evil fruit, ... or rather it was the man himself who was that tree, in so far as his will was evil" (*ciu.* 14.11).[12] This, however, can only be inferred from the fact that they later sinned openly. It is, nonetheless, why Scripture calls pride the "beginning of all sin" (*ciu.* 12.6; Eccl. 10.13).

Returning to the passage on John, we discover that here, in the same way, the lovers of the world manifest behaviors that can only be explained by *amor sui*. In wanting to rest in the world, that is, in wanting to find happiness in it here and now, the lovers of the world treat it as something

---

[10] Augustine, *Sermons, (51–94) on the Old Testament* (New York: New City Press, 1991), 364. Cf. *s.* 96.5, where Augustine again is trying to parse out John's language.

[11] Augustine, *Sermons, (51–94) on the Old Testament*, 199. This sermon is on Matthew 10:37.

[12] Somehow, Adam's will is Adam himself; it is not an abstract faculty that developed a flaw. There is no getting around our responsibility in Adam here.

it is *not*, namely, our final home. To treat the world as something one wishes it were, over and against what it is, implies a certain resistance to reality; and this, Augustine thinks, can only be explained by a hidden commitment to one's own will as the final arbiter of meaning. Thus, while lovers of the world focus their attention on the world, this love can only spring from a prior devotion to oneself.

The symbolic value of John's language, however, does not end here. By layering the negative sense of the "world" on top of its original meaning, John highlights the chasm between the lovers of the world and the world they claim to love. While the lovers of the world wish to become one with their object of love, in founding their project on a denial of the original meaning of the world – the world *as* God's creation – they actually end up rejecting the world they claim to love.[13] By covering over the original meaning of the world with their own interpretation, they (or we, insofar as we do this) only end up using it – and, not in the way that Augustine famously praises. Rather, they *abuse it*, treating the world as material to be reimagined into something desirable.[14] Underneath this makeover, the world quietly remains what it is, bearing witness to the God who created it. By choosing to call the lovers of the world "the world," John reveals the derivative meaning of "the world" to be a charade.

Furthermore, because this way of loving the world is not a genuine love of the world at all, it creates discord among its lovers. Because the members of the earthly city have come to believe that it must choose between God and the world if they are to have what they want, they exhibit a willingness to resignify reality in a way that creates a chaotic scramble over the power to do this with impunity. The tragedy here is that they are entirely mistaken (cf. *ciu.* 14.4). The members of the earthly city cannot have what they want from the world because the world cannot give them what they want, not because God has made himself an obstacle to their desires. While the created world really *is* good, the consolations it can offer are subject to change; at best, the love of another mortal being, at worst, the possession of material things entirely ephemeral (cf. *conf.* 4.10).

---

[13] Often, Augustine plays on the marital metaphor of the unity of lover and beloved actually brought to fruition in Christ and the Church – and the way in which the earthly city's orientation toward the world is a parody of this.

[14] In Balthasar's discussion of Platonism's skepticism toward the imagination, he writes that Augustine accepts this skepticism to a degree, but modifies it since he "knows that it is not the imagination which sins, but the free rational person, but the sin lies in taking the buffoonery of the imagination for truth and in becoming attached to it." *Glory of the Lord II*, 124.

Because the members of the earthly city share the belief that the world is the locus of their happiness, they are all engaged in the pursuit of ultimate peace in the created realm (*ciu.* 19.17). Whether due to the anxiety that the pursuit of contingent things evokes, the urgency one experiences as a need to secure one's hold on them, or the feeling of starvation that comes from feeding on things that do not satisfy, the commonality of this pursuit yields competition instead of community.

Moreover, Augustine thinks that even when the members of the earthly city do work together for a common goal, insofar as they are motivated by *amor sui*, they will only do so for as long it is in their particular interests to do so. Of course, a contemporary reader might ask whether there is a third way between *amor sui* and *amor Dei*. In other words, does Augustine think human relationships themselves can draw people out of a selfish disposition, such that they come to love another *not* out of *amor sui* but truly for the other? Can interpersonal love inspire people to work together for a truly common good?

Simply put, Augustine is adamant that love of neighbor is made perfect *by* loving God as God (*ciu.* 19.14). This is because the hole that the absence of God has left in the human heart constantly demands to be filled.[15] Without God, all we have to fill it with are the products of our own imagination, or, the things in the world that have captured our imagination. The logic of his argument is as follows: *insofar* as we refuse to accept God's divinity, we refuse to accept the meaning of reality, and, insofar as we refuse to accept the meaning of reality, we become inclined to refashion those who inhabit our world into creatures of our own design. We reorder everything in reference to our wishes.

All this said, Augustine's thought is complex, and, as anyone who has read his *Confessions* knows, the intertwining of human and divine loves in a particular person's life resists easy formulation. All Augustine can say is that the created world bears witness to God such that allowing it to be what it is draws us out of ourselves (and our imaginary worlds) and points us toward the Creator. Yet, insofar as we are animated by *amor sui*, we become disposed to reinterpret the world according to what we wish it were. We tend to filter our experience of reality through these wishes. This is why our love for others is not always able to overcome *amor sui*.

---

[15] If one can even call it an absence of God, given Augustine's observation in his famous "late have I loved you" hymn that "You were with me, but I was not with you" (*conf.* 10.27.38).

This means that until God fully fills and heals the hole in our hearts, we will continue to exhibit at least some of the earthly city's patterns of behavior. Indeed, Augustine is certain of this precisely because of the insight behind his famous adage: "our heart is unquiet until it rests in You" (*conf.* 1.1).[16] Because we are created for eternal happiness, he asserts, it is impossible for us to completely stifle our desire for it (*ciu.* 12.1; 12.6; 14.4, inter alia). We are compelled by our very nature to seek peace somewhere (*ciu.* 19.11).[17] Thus, an orientation to the world that hopes to find in it absolute peace, regardless of whether this hope is explicitly understood, leads to a perception of the other as relative to *our* happiness.[18] This objectification of the other, regardless of whether as an obstacle, a tool, or an idol, is, for Augustine, the social upshot of loving the world. It is why *amor sui* generates what John Cavadini calls "a community that is no community."[19]

WHAT IS THE EARTHLY CITY?

And yet, who are the members of the earthly city?[20] Is there really anyone entirely motivated by selfishness, who does not in some way try to accommodate a *genuine* consideration of others' welfare into his or her own pursuit of happiness? Augustine does not think so – this is why Cacus is a monster (*ciu.* 19.12).[21] Here, then, we should ask what exactly Augustine is doing in working out what the earthly city is, especially given that he says it is the city into which we are all born (*ciu.* 15.1). If this is true, we might ask, can the earthly city really be so bad? People, after all, are generally mixed in their motivations. No one is wholly depraved – few are even as bad as Sulla or Cataline. The question, then,

---

[16] Augustine, *The Confessions*, trans. Maria Boulding (Hyde Park, NY: New City Press, 1997), 39.

[17] This goes along with Augustine's famous dictum "*pondus meum amor meus*" (*conf.* 13.9.10), which draws upon the classical sense that the natural movement of all things follows from their desire to be in the right place.

[18] For Augustine, we can be devoted to many conflicting ideas of happiness, both at once and over time. The one commonality underlying them is our commitment to what *we* want. The only constancy in a self-pleaser is the commitment to pleasing oneself.

[19] John Cavadini, "Spousal Vision," 144n49, and "Ideology and Solidarity," 106.

[20] Frequently, I will use the term *earthly city* as shorthand to describe the collective of creatures bound together by self-love. Because the earthly city has no existence apart from its members – those who act out of self-love – it is important to read it as a synecdoche, not an entity with independent agency.

[21] Cacus was a figure in Roman mythology who lived alone in cave and is famed for his savage nature.

arises: is the earthly city merely a warning – an exaggerated depiction of *amor sui* taken to its radical antisocial conclusion? Is it, in other words, merely an idea?

While some have pursued this line of argument, to conclude this would contradict the observations we have already made about Augustine's way of thinking about Scripture, metaphysics, and mystery. Augustine really does think that the two cities exist. In fact, based on the testimony of Scripture, he thinks they are more fundamental than the visible societies in which we find ourselves (*ciu.* 11.1). Not only does Scripture teach us that we *already* belong to one or another of the two cities, it also shows us what they are. By trying to integrate and make sense of the various things Scripture says about the earthly city, Augustine is not caricaturing or radicalizing the behavior of the unbaptized. Rather, he is showing us *what it means* to participate in the earthly city (*ciu.* 1.35). He is showing what kinds of behavior and what kind of community *amor sui* generates.

This, however, is not the same thing as abstracting the essence of *amor sui* into an idea and imagining what a society entirely governed by that idea would look like. If, as I will argue, the earthly city is the society that need not exist – the society whose very existence is dependent upon the participation of the rational creature *in it* – then the discussion of the earthly city in terms of what it means to participate in it is entirely apt. It is how Augustine spells out which behaviors (and, before that, which loves) sustain the earthly city in existence. It is how he separates the earthly city's claims about its achievements from its actual achievements.

Ultimately, Augustine's teaching on the earthly city contains three central tenets: first, that the society called the earthly city really does exist, second, that we do (or did) belong to it, and third, that we all participate to some degree in its patterns of behavior. While this is a complex vision, it is the only way Augustine can adequately capture the interwoven dynamics of the two cities phenomenon. To treat the members of the earthly city as the sole causes of sin in the world would be to misunderstand the nature of God's city on pilgrimage; to treat the members of God's city as the sole recipients of grace would be to reduce God's sphere of activity to the sphere where it is recognized; to treat the two cities as two poles of a spectrum upon which most people lie in the middle would be to miss the point of God's revelation. Avoiding these errors, Augustine manages to pair the belief that God is constantly extending His love to everyone (*ciu.* 1.8) with the fact that everyone struggles with "fleshly" loves (*ciu.* 15.15) *without* dissolving the difference between the two cities (*ciu.* 1.*praef*).

Essentially, Augustine accomplishes this by distinguishing the question of participation from the question of citizenship. By saying that each person *participates* in the earthly city to the degree that *amor sui* shapes his or her actions, Augustine reminds us that we all bear some responsibility for the hold the earthly city has on the world. The question of participation, then, becomes a question of how far we allow *amor sui* to guide our choices in a way that pits us against others and against God. Alongside this question, however, there is also the question of citizenship. This is a matter of a person's *ordo amoris*.[22] At each point in time, Augustine thinks, each person has an *ordo amoris*, which is to say that at each point in time, in a hidden way known only to God, each person is either clinging to God, or, at bottom, turned away from Him (*ciu.* 14.4). Through the orientation of our hearts, we secretly pledge allegiance to one or the other of the two cities, whether we are on the outskirts of one, or even on our way out of the other.

With these points in mind, we can return to the question with which this section began: what is Augustine doing in working out what the earthly city is? In short, Augustine is working out the temporal and eternal consequences of choosing the self over God. This, for Augustine, is an unnatural choice, and, the degree to which it is embraced is the degree to which a person gives himself or herself permission to rewrite reality – or, as Augustine puts it, to "counterfeit an unreality (*simulare quod non est*)" (*ciu.* 11.13).[23] By drawing out the effects of the absence (or, better, the exclusion) of God in our attempt to build a social life, Augustine defines

---

[22] This statement has to be qualified by a few theological points, lest it come across as Pelagian. According to Augustine, every human being is born into the earthly city because of original sin. Though God's grace works beyond the city of God's borders, Augustine does believe that a person joins the city of God through baptism, even though not everyone who is baptized remains a part of the city of God. The desire to be joined to God, therefore, is always situated within a theological context wherein God has set out a certain *sacramentum* by which sins are forgiven and human beings are reconciled to God. For Augustine, true *amor Dei*, the genuine desire to be with God, involves accepting baptism as the gateway into the city of God that God has set up. Nevertheless, baptism does not guarantee *amor Dei*; even after receiving baptism, a human being is capable of rejecting grace, and therefore also capable of rejecting God as his or her foundation. This is why there are members in the Church who are not, in Augustine's mind, true members. In sum, when it comes to the question of citizenship, the orientation of our hearts is the matter at hand, but there is a sort of divinely ordained infrastructure undergirding it as well.

[23] CCSL 47.334. In other words, the degree to which a person chooses to rewrite reality cannot be predicted from the fact that a person seizes and reserves the right *to* rewrite reality. The decision to pilgrimage with the heavenly city is the constant relinquishing of this right.

the essence of belonging to the earthly city as the refusal to be in harmony with God's will (*ciu.* 12.3). Everything that seems to belong to the glamor of *amor sui* is borrowed capital. To grasp this is to enter the realm of mystery, not the realm of abstractions.

THE EARTHLY CITY'S ANTICREATION STORY

To see why, for Augustine, the derivative status of the earthly city is not merely an idea but an ontological fact, and why the earthly city is only independently responsible for evil, it is helpful to turn to books 11–14 of *City of God*, where Augustine begins to flesh out his account of the two cities. That these two cities exist, Augustine writes, is "vouched for by those Scriptures whose supremacy over every product of human genius does not depend on the chance impulses of the minds of men, but is manifestly due to the guiding power of God's supreme providence, and exercises sovereign authority over the literature of all mankind" (*ciu.* 11.1). In a world of stories forged from the partial perspective of the fallen creature, Augustine sees Scripture as speaking with unique authority about the two cities.

Unfolding what it tells us, Augustine explains that the earthly city is primarily defined by its members' shared attempt to shield themselves from God's love (*ciu.* 14.28). As such, its human members have preferred to worship "those who are deprived of his changing light which is shed upon all alike" (*ciu.* 11.1).[24] They are less threatening (*ciu.* 15.7). For Augustine, these so-called gods are actually fallen angels, at once great and pathetic. Shadows of their former selves, they engage "in a kind of scramble for their lost dominions," clamoring to gain "divine honors from their deluded subjects" (*ciu.* 11.1). Here is the original meaning of the fall from grace.

Because Augustine conceives of not four societies but two, each comprising a "fellowship of men and angels," his discussion of the Angelic Fall sheds light on the dynamic of whole earthly city (*ciu.* 12.1). The story is familiar. Created to "live in wisdom and bliss," some of the angels "turned away from this illumination" (*ciu.* 11.11). Augustine spends a good deal of time wondering how this is possible, and how, *if* part of the consolation of eternal bliss is to know its eternality, those who forsook it could have ever experienced this bliss to the same degree as those who did not.

---

[24] This is a striking phrase: how can one be deprived of a light that is shed upon everything?

Ultimately, Augustine leaves the question unresolved, only noting that it is probably "intolerable to believe" that the angels who fell were created without foreknowledge of whether they persevered, while the rest were created with it (*ciu.* 11.13). This being so, we are left to conclude that "all were created at the beginning with equal felicity" (ibid.).[25] Though Augustine does not say so, perhaps the question of confirmation did not even arise until *after* those who fell made denying God into an option. That is, in choosing to fall away, perhaps they opened a door that was not previously *lacking* even though it had not yet been proposed.[26] This possibility raises an interesting question: was the choice of responding yes or no to God always on the table? Are they ever on the table as two equally valid responses? In pondering this, we glimpse how the perspective of the earthly city secretly reshapes the way we conceive of freedom.

Above all, the Angelic Fall shows how the earthly city spins its own story as a result of its drive to be like God apart from God. Exegeting John's comment about the Devil, "He was a murderer from the beginning and did not stand fast in the truth" (Jn 8:44), Augustine highlights the disjunction between what the earthly city claims to be and what it actually is. First, he steers his readers around Manichean dualism by explaining that the phrase "from the beginning" does not imply that the Devil was always evil. In fact, Scripture denies this: regardless of whether he fell at the beginning of his creation or at a later point, Christ's own words in Luke 10:18 make it clear that the Devil was a creature who fell "from the truth" (*ciu.* 11.13). The answer as to when he fell, Augustine seems to think, lies beyond what Scripture offers us for our own edification (*ciu.* 10.32).

What Scripture does offer, Augustine thinks, is a way to see through the illusions that the Devil both represents and perpetuates.[27] These are the illusions that constitute the earthly city.[28] While it is true that Augustine thinks that the strange unity of the earthly city can only be seen clearly from the eschatological perspective afforded by Scripture – not, in other

---

[25] Here Augustine takes the same tentative approach that has marked his entire approach to scriptural interpretation in book 11. Of this he *is* certain: "it would be much more intolerable to suppose that the holy angels are now uncertain of their future" (*ciu.* 11.13). Evil, having been proposed and rejected by the angels, is once and for all rejected.

[26] James Wetzel takes his speculation regarding Augustine's meaning in *ciu.* 11.13 in a different direction in "A Tangle of Two Cities," 13–16.

[27] Meconi rightly observes that Augustine gives "the metanarrative of evil a deifying stamp"; both the Devil's rebellion and his temptation of Adam and Eve are presented as the pursuit of a false deification. *The One Christ*, 66–67, cf. 69–70.

[28] Cf. *s.* 170.4 and *en. Ps.* 141.6–147.15.

words, from the perspective of its human members – he does think there is a kind of unspoken solidarity that binds these members together in a common project. This can be described as the mutual recognition of a shared commitment, albeit one based on personal goals that simply happen to coincide (*ciu.* 19.24). To participate in the earthly city is to be invested in upholding the myth of creaturely autonomy and, thereby, to approve of others' investment in the same myth insofar as it reinforces your own (*ciu.* 14.4).

In telling the story of the fallen angels, then, Augustine aims to show that what the earthly city calls freedom is in fact rebellion. While the vision that animates it is the promise of independence and happiness, its scriptural backstory vastly deflates its capacity to fulfill this promise. It tells of a kind of anticreation, a falling away from reality (*ciu.* 12.6). Here, we return to his exegesis of John's discussion of the fall of Satan. In reality, Augustine argues, the Devil did not enjoy felicity because he

> refused to be subject to his creator, and in his arrogance supposed that he wielded power as his own private possession and rejoiced in that power. And thus he was both deceived and deceiving because no one can escape the power of the Omnipotent. He has refused to accept reality and in his arrogant pride presumes to counterfeit an unreality. (*ciu.* 11.13)[29]

This unreality *is* the earthly city; the earthly city is the unreal city.[30]

Essentially, in making it clear that the Devil is not, and can never make himself into God's equal, Scripture undermines the first false claim of the earthly city. That is to say, the way of life it loves *cannot be* the legitimate alternative it wants to be because the earthly city is not the metaphysical equal of God's city. It is derivative: a counterfeit unreality. Even its independence is hollow. While the Devil gets what he wants through rebellion – the earthly city really is a realm under his dominion – on a deeper level, he is never beyond God's jurisdiction.[31] The Devil becomes sport for the angels because, as Augustine puts it, "no one can escape the power of the Omnipotent" (*ciu.* 11.13; cf. 11.33).

In other words, for Augustine, the rebellion of the Devil is, and can only ever be, a denial of the *meaning* of creation. Because all of reality exists in God, to exist at all is to continue to participate in God's world. For the

---

[29] Dodaro aptly calls Satan the original "spin doctor." Robert Dodaro, "Eloquent Lies, Just Wars and the Politics of Persuasion," *Augustinian Studies* 25 (1994): 90.

[30] Here I am referring to Eliot's "unreal city" from *The Wasteland*, which is itself an allusion to Dante's description of those shuffling toward hell in canto 3 of the *Inferno*.

[31] Cf. *trin.* 3.2.13.

Devil to sever himself entirely from God, he would have to destroy himself, and he would not want to do this even if he could (*ciu.* 12.3). Because he cannot but accept the gift of existence, all the Devil can do is deny *that* it is gift. Drawing boundaries around his usurped kingdom, the Devil refuses to let in God's love, which is to say that he refuses to recognize it. This self-insulation is what Augustine means when he says that the Devil and his followers "are deprived of his changing light which is shed upon all alike" (*ciu.* 11.1). *Where can I go, Lord, that you are not there?* His only refuge lies in illusion.[32]

Through his exegesis of the various scriptural passages on the Devil's rebellion, Augustine presents the whole motive principle of the earthly city as tragically unintelligible (*ciu.* 11.13–12.9). While we can enter into the Devil's motives, we can also see that his turn away from God is metaphysically perverse: "to defect from him who is the Supreme Existence, to something of less reality," only harms him (*ciu.* 12.7). It separates him from the source of his happiness and brings him closer to nothingness. The only explanation Augustine can give for this defection is pride (*superbia*): "the longing for a perverse kind of exaltation" which abandons "the basis on which the mind should be firmly fixed," in order to become "based on oneself" (*ciu.* 14.13). It is, as we have already seen, to become "too pleased" with oneself (*ciu.* 14.13). Thus, it is the Devil's pride that emboldens him to think he has a right to resignify reality (*ciu.* 12.6). While he cannot metaphysically upgrade himself, he can at least *call* himself something different. By revealing the logic behind the Devil's desire to "counterfeit an unreality" (*ciu.* 11.13), Augustine reveals *the* reason why the earthly city sets itself up over and against God (*ciu.* 11.16). Yet, he also reveals the absurdity of this choice. To live in illusion cannot yield happiness in reality.[33] Any time a creature seeks independence from God in order to claim happiness for itself, it severs itself from the source of its happiness.

Because of the exegetical work he has already done, Augustine is able to explain why pride seeks God's happiness by trying to take his place (*ciu.* 14.13). For Augustine, the Devil's rebellion reveals that pride (*superbia*) hates its own contingency. It is *invested* in forgetting that whatever it has it

---

[32] In this way, Matthew Puffer's observation that lying is the fundamental evil and the origin of all sin is entirely true. See Matthew Puffer, "Retracing Augustine's Ethics: Lying, Necessity and the Image of God," *Journal of Religious Ethics* 44, no. 4 (2016): 687.

[33] With an unforgettable image, Augustine makes a related point in book 4, exclaiming, "How can a man escape unhappiness, if he worships Felicity as divine and deserts God, the giver of felicity? Could a man escape starvation by licking the painted picture of a loaf, instead of begging real bread from someone who had it to give?" (*ciu.* 4.23).

has received as gift. This, of course, is problematic because the entire economy of creation is an economy of gift: every creature receives its existence as gift, and those capable of happiness are only capable of receiving it as a gift (*ciu.* 12.1). While God is the only Being "whose felicity springs from his own goodness" (*ciu.* 12.1), even God's happiness is intrinsically relational, since God is a Trinity. Accordingly, Augustine thinks, when the creature begins to think that becoming *like God* apart from God will make it happy, it misunderstands what becoming *like God* means.[34] It reduces God to his status and forgets that God's happiness is bound up with love. To covet God's status instead of desiring to share his life of love is to tragically misunderstand happiness.

Two books later, Augustine uses the same psychological reasoning to explain why autonomy looks like freedom from the perspective of the earthly city. While, he thinks, the will can truly be free only when it acts with God's help, in the Genesis story, Adam falls for a different idea of freedom. Loving himself with a love that hates being dependent, Augustine explains, Adam began to forget that God was the source of his Edenic peace. Instead, he imagines a life in which all of his faculties would be entirely under his command, but he a servant of no one. Acting upon his desire for this state, Adam found that he had overestimated the power of his own will, and that a life liberated from God's dominion actually left him "at odds with himself," his passions warring against his reason. Autonomy, therefore, was not the "freedom he so ardently desired" (ibid.). Instead, it landed him in "a harsh and pitiable slavery under him with whom he entered into agreement in his sinning" (*ciu.* 14.15).

Here, the story of our Fall intersects with the story of the Angelic Fall. According to Augustine, when the Devil fell "away from God to follow his own leading," he also began to covet humanity with "the proud disdain of a tyrant" (*ciu.* 14.11). Thus, when the Devil offers Adam and Eve the same autonomy he has taken for himself, he does not come as a liberator but a conqueror; he wants subjects (cf. *ciu.* 10.19). Ironically, even though the Devil sees his own autonomy as freedom, he knows that Adam and Eve's rebellion will bind them to him. He is content because he is at the top of the earthly city's totem pole.

Strangely, then, the idea of autonomy is an illusion that the earthly city's members buy into for themselves, but one they peddle to get what

---

[34] David Meconi's chapter "Made to Be Godly," in *The One Christ*, is particularly illuminating on this point. Meconi, *The One Christ: St. Augustine's Theology of Deification* (Washington, DC: Catholic University of America Press, 2018), 34–78.

they want from others. In Augustine's account the demons exert power by directing humanity's "thoughts and desires ... towards any facts which suit those thoughts and desires," and gain power over them by "appealing to the lowest elements in human frailty" (*ciu.* 10.32). In the economy of the earthly city, fallen desire is leverage (*ciu.* 11.16). The seduction of Adam and Eve reveals, then, that the earthly city is the original pyramid scheme. The fallen angels seduce humankind in order to gain power over us, and we end up doing the same to each other (*ciu.* 14.11; 4.32; 12.28).

Indeed, Augustine explains, the desire to dominate one's fellow creatures follows necessarily upon the giant chasm between the created and the uncreated will. God needs nothing from His creatures (*ciu.* 10.5). In creating us, God is not animated by a desire to have subjects, but by a Love that loves to share itself. This, Augustine believes, has been made abundantly clear by Scripture, and, above all, by its proclamation of the Son who went so far as to die on a cross to ensure this could happen (*ciu.* 14.28). Yet, pride cannot see this. Its hatred of being dependent blinds the rational creature and leads it to refashion God in its own image. This is why the Devil paints God as a rival Master. Loving his own power as *his*, the Devil forsakes his ability to see the point of God's kingdom. As the archetype representing every creature that hates its own dependence, the Devil reveals the cost of hating "a fellowship of equality under God" (*ciu.* 19.12)

In the end, Augustine's treatment of the Devil's rebellion might well be the most important gloss on the earthly city that we can find in *City of God*. Refusing to accept his inescapable creaturehood, he initiated a sham rebellion, luring other creatures into his sham kingdom to shore up his illusion. Stripping this power play of its glamor, Augustine reveals its emptiness and the emptiness of the earthly city's whole project. In the end, rebellion turns out to be mere rebellion: a refusal to participate in God's kingdom that gains nothing in the process. The earthly city might be the heavenly city's foil in character, but in reality, it is merely its shadow.

TRYING TO SEE DARKNESS

In books 12–14 of *City of God*, Augustine goes on to flesh out an ontology of the earthly city. Evil, he explains there, is nothing in itself.[35] Rather, it is the absence of what should be according to God's creative intention.

---

[35] For helpful treatments of Augustine's account of evil, see Donald A. Cress, "Augustine's Privation Account of Evil: A Defense," *Augustinian Studies* 20 (1989): 109–128; Donald X. Burt, "Courageous Optimism: Augustine on the Good of Creation," *Augustinian*

Moral evil, then, is a deficiency in the will: a refusal to participate in God's plan for us. If we attempt to render this choice intelligible, we can only do so invoking the premise that God is a threat to our happiness. And yet, Augustine explains, *that* we believe this premise in the first place is intelligible only in the way that we can "see" darkness or "hear" silence (*ciu.* 12.7). While we are familiar with both, we only apprehend them by noticing the absence of light or sound. Similarly, while the effects of the turn away from God ripple outward into every facet of reality, the turn itself is unintelligible. For Augustine, it amounts to a failure to find the most beautiful, good and lovable Being beautiful, good, or lovable.

While we might be tempted to attribute this failure to ignorance, Augustine thinks this would be to mistake the effect for the cause. It would imply that Adam's intellect had become darkened *so that*, rather than *because*, he turned toward himself. Yet, without this possibility, Augustine is left with no way to adequately explain why Adam would distance himself from God. All he can say is that Adam did, and did so voluntarily (*ciu.* 12.9). Connecting this fundamental incoherence with the incoherence at the core of the earthly city's project, Augustine roots the etymology of the earthly city's biblical name in the Hebrew word *balal*: to confuse (*ciu.* 16.4). The earthly city is called Babylon because, at bottom, its way of thinking is confused. Confusion defines the earthly city.[36]

Still, we might ask, what does all this really mean? How does Augustine's privation theory of evil shed light on his understanding of the earthly city? Certainly, the fact that the earthly city is evil does not imply that it does not exist. Neither, of course, can it imply that *amor sui* does not exist. And yet, on Augustine's account, something must fail to exist if the earthly city is evil: what is that? We have already seen a hint of Augustine's answer to these questions in his teaching about the devil; in choosing *amor sui*, he fell to a lower state of being, which is to say that he came to exist less fully than he would have otherwise. For Augustine, being, intelligibility, and love are to some degree transferrable qualities; where there is a lack of intelligibility, there is a lack of being, and a lack of love. In this way, *amor sui* plunges all of the members of the earthly city

---

Studies 21 (1990): 55–66; and Rowan Williams, "Insubstantial Evil," in *On Augustine* (London: Bloomsbury, 2016), 79–106.

[36] In addition, *confusio* has a strong connotation of shame, the same shame that strives to cover over its sin. It cannot bear to be naked. For a history of the connotations that Babylon evoked in the ancient and medieval world, see Andrew Scheil, *Babylon under Western Eyes: A Study of Allusion and Myth* (Toronto: University of Toronto Press, 2016).

into a lower state of being because they all lack the life-giving effects of the love they have collectively refused.

To put this another way, the earthly city's refusal of *amor Dei* has circumscribed its members to the realm of *amor sui*. While this refusal is not nothing – it is an actual choice made by free agents – it does lead to a kind of nothingness because it leads to an absence of *amor Dei* in the earthly city and, importantly, in the world.[37] In failing to participate in *amor Dei*, therefore, the earthly city undermines what could have been: first, what would have been, had the its members used their freedom well, and second, what the members of the earthly city would have been, had they used their freedom well. In other words, what fails to exist as a result of *evil* is the good that the members of the earthly city would have been and done, had they remained a part of God's city.

What the privation theory of evil implies, therefore, is that the earthly city only exists because its members have refused to participate in *amor Dei*. Of course, to say this is simply to repeat what we have already established: the earthly city only becomes a distinctive entity by falling away: by becoming a shadowy parody of the community to which its members once belonged. Perhaps a better way of understanding the existence of the earthly city, then, is to say that the earthly city exists because its members exist. Paradoxically, then, we can say that the earthly city remains in existence because of God's graciousness toward His creatures – even as it only remains in existence because these creatures refuse to recognize the graciousness of God. At bottom, God sustains the members of the earthly city in being because they are His creation. This is the mystery of God's generosity. And yet, importantly, God does not will the earthly city. The chain of causality that now flows from fallen wills is what makes the earthly city fall into existence (*ciu.* 12.28). Its members, who are sustained in being by God, sustain the earthly city in being apart from God.

In applying this aspect of Augustine's vision to our evaluation of the earthly city, it is helpful to return to an earlier section of *City of God* where Augustine challenges the antinomy between Divine providence and human freedom (*ciu.* 5.8–10).[38] We have seen that Augustine thinks that

---

[37] Rowan Williams helpfully distinguishes between the metaphysical status of evil and its empirical presence; evil as experienced, he writes, is "something that manifestly *impresses* itself upon the subject." "Insubstantial Evil," 87.

[38] For a thorough and persuasive account of the nature of freedom in Augustine's thought, see David C. Schindler, "Freedom beyond Our Own Choosing: Augustine on the Will and Its Objects," in *Augustine and Politics*, ed. John Doody, Kevin Hughes, and Kim Paffenroth (Lanham, MD: Lexington Books, 2005), 67–98.

the earthly city claims a higher status than it actually deserves. It remains to be seen how he works out what is actually due to the earthly city. In order to do this, Augustine has to distinguish what is independently due to the earthly city, what is due to the earthly city misusing the power given to it, and what the members of the earthly city do that remains in harmony with nature. Importantly, he is able to do this by distinguishing between primary and secondary causality. God, Augustine explains, is the primary cause of everything and sustains everything in existence. But God has also built voluntary causes into the very structure of reality; he has allowed certain creatures to have real agency in the world (*ciu.* 5.9). Because some creatures misuse this agency, Augustine tells us, God is the giver of all power, but not the giver of all wills (*ciu.* 5.10). God does not constrain the will of rational creatures; he invites them to act freely in *amor Dei.*[39]

In some instances, then, secondary causes can be properly called the first cause of a given act. Because God is not the giver of all wills, some things that creatures will are not in harmony with what God would have them will. This is why Augustine attributes actions that are not in harmony with God's will to the creature. In fact, Augustine thinks, Scripture often refers to actions in terms of the first cause that wills them. This, for example, is why Paul attributes sin to human beings (*ciu.* 14.3). The actions that he defines as living according to a human standard are those that are *only* according to a human standard (*ciu.* 14.4). They are the product of a human lie that stands in tension with God's truth.

In fact, we find that this way of speaking permeates Augustine's entire discourse. Where created intention is in harmony with God's intention, Augustine highlights God's causality. Where created intention is out of harmony with God's will, he highlights its human origin. Having surveyed his theory of primary and secondary causality, we can see that this is not an effort to diminish human agency. Augustine is adamant that rational creatures are freer agents when they act in *amor Dei*. Rather, it a way of

---

[39] This, of course, should not be interpreted as a Pelagian statement, but, instead, in light of a richer understanding of grace as the ground of free agency. See, e.g., *ep. Io.* 4.7: "See how he hasn't removed your free will. As he said, *he makes himself pure.* Who makes us pure if not God? But God doesn't make you pure if you are unwilling. Therefore, because you unite your will to God, you make yourself pure. You make yourself pure not of yourself but through him who came to dwell in you. Yet, because you do something there by your will, something has been bestowed upon you. But it has been bestowed upon you so that you may say, as in the psalm, *Be my helper; do not abandon me* (Ps 27:9). If you say, *Be my helper,* you are doing something. For, if you are doing nothing, how is he helping you?" Augustine, *Homilies on the First Epistle of John,* 71.

speaking that traces chains of causality back to the first cause with which they are in harmony. As we will see in our discussion of *consuetudo* in the fifth chapter, this way of speaking actually does work for Augustine: it allows him to criticize human custom (*consuetudo*) without implying that all mores and human traditions are corrupt. For Augustine, if human acts are in harmony with God's creative intention, they are cooperative acts, and if not, they are products of human will.[40] Because Augustine thinks that the difference between praiseworthy and blameworthy behavior always falls along the lines of participation, he prefers this way of speaking because it reliably distinguishes between the two.

For our purposes in this chapter, however, this use of language leads us back to the question of the earthly city's agency: what does Augustine think the earthly city is responsible for? What phenomena can actually be attributed to it? Ultimately, we must recall that the earthly city has no agency apart from that of its members. Insofar as these members act out of *amor sui*, however, they constitute the earthly city. Considered in this way, we can say that the earthly city is primarily responsible for its failure to effect God's plan in the world. Because God has built human agency into the economy of the created world, our failure to participate in its original economy of gift has real consequences. There is an inevitable chasm between the quality of action animated by *amor sui* and the quality of action that would have been, had it been undertaken in *amor Dei*. In this way, the earthly city's refusal to be a conduit of grace is like a cloud casting shadows on a world that should be bathed in light (*ciu.* 12.23). Thus, first and foremost, the earthly city is responsible for an absence of light in the world. In the end, this absence is the only thing for which the earthly city is independently responsible.

That said, in a secondary way, the earthly city is also responsible for the reshaped world it brings about. While *amor sui* is deficient in that it is all that remains of love when God's love is refused, it is still a powerful motive of action, which is to say that it still makes a real and irreversible mark on the world. More than this, it creates new economies in which we can participate – and, as we will see in Chapters 5 and 6 – these are economies that seem to stand as the primary mode of exchange and interaction in the world. Returning to Augustine's distinction between will and power, what we see is that the actions of the members of the earthly city *as* participants in the earthly city are wholly due to our misuse of powers we have been

---

[40] Augustine does use the language of cooperation in *City of God*; see, e.g., the preface of book 7.

given as gift.[41] The earthly city's patterns of behavior, institutionalized in various political and social forms are the effect of a misused, yet God-given power to shape social life. Insofar as we act according to *amor sui,* we participate in the earthly city and are responsible for the ways in which *amor sui* shapes history.

What the earthly city is not responsible for, however, is its very power to act. This was a gift and, Augustine reminds us, a good part of the rational creature's nature. And yet, this power is the chief source of the earthly city's pride. Accordingly, Augustine's work is to highlight that any greatness the earthly city can claim is only a result of abusing its gifts, and therefore a hollow boast. For Augustine, *any* greatness creatures achieve on their own is less real than the glory they would have gained in God. This is the irony of pride: the counterpoint to the paradox of humility. The earthly city cannot be truly glorious because it has forfeited the power that would have made it "soar above all the summits of the world, which sway in their temporal instability" (*ciu.* 1.*praef*). By deflating all of the earthly city's claims to have achieved anything better than it would have achieved in God's city, Augustine limits the earthly city's responsibility to evil.

Adding to the richness of Augustine's account of the ontology of the earthly city is his analysis of peace in book 19. Here, what comes to the fore is the parasitic quality of the earthly city's activity in the world. By highlighting the dependence of the fallen creature on its rational nature, Augustine again presents perversion as something that only restricts being. Evil, he has already told us, cannot exist on its own, but only in a good nature (*ciu.* 12.3). In book 19, Augustine extends this logic to show that every idea of peace animating the fallen will is necessarily related to, and derivative of true peace. The members of the earthly city, he tells us, are not in a state of peace in that they are not united to God who is the source of peace. And yet, "they have amongst them some tranquility of order, and therefore some peace" (*ciu.* 19.13). Because Augustine thinks it is impossible to be entirely outside the scope of the order of nature, even the members of the earthly city are still to some degree in harmony with this order – but not insofar as they are of the earthly city, but rather, insofar as they are creatures.

Here, then, we return to the idea of rewriting the reality of a world already endowed with meaning. For Augustine, the refusal of God's love

---

[41] As Williams puts it, "the more power, dignity and liberty adhere naturally to a created being, the more energy there will be for the pursuit of false or destructive goals." "Insubstantial Evil," 88.

necessarily reorganizes and reshapes the creature's interpretation of its own inclinations. And yet, the creature cannot dispense entirely with what has been given to it by nature; the will might become the arbiter of meaning, and the imagination the manufacturer of its visions and goals, but the imagination operates within certain parameters. As such, the creature's natural reactions to what it encounters in the world – the painful, the pleasurable, the frightening, the inspiring – feed into and inform its vision of peace. The variable, however, lies in the fact that the received meaning of all things is subject to review. The earthly city always reserves the right to edit reality. It never surrenders its capacity to "give permission" to God, which is another way of saying that it never gives itself over to God.

Ultimately, what this means for our understanding of the earthly city is that its members' wills might be severed from God's will as their foundation, but they will never act in a way that is entirely unrelated to God's will. Nature is the default and sin only distorts it. Its objectives are always derivative. As such, the patterns of behavior that define the earthly city are the product of a pursuit of a vision of peace that is related to true peace while rejecting its source. Treating a chosen part of peace as the whole, the earthly city pursues a counterfeit peace, but not an entirely unnatural one. Because dwellers of the city will choose to blot out different aspects of nature at different times, depending on what they find inconvenient, it is best to say that what binds the city together is its reservation of the *right* to edit reality.

SIN'S FALLOUT

A final piece of the puzzle to our understanding of the earthly city is Augustine's account of the Fall's repercussions. As we have already noted, Augustine thinks that all of humanity fell in Adam so that we are born into a state of alienation from God. We have also already seen that Adam's retreat from God did not win the freedom he foresaw; for Augustine, God was the first cause of the order Adam had found in himself, and the rejection of this cause had a natural consequence in Adam that he did not expect. What is worth examining now is how God interacts with the wills of his creatures in a way that effects either mercy or justice, depending on the response of the creature.

This theme actually appears early on in *City of God,* though in a disguised form. As we will see in the next chapter, book 1 addresses the most pressing questions arising in the aftermath of the sack of Rome: why do good things happen to bad people? Why do bad people get away with crimes, or even prosper? Why, in fact, "does the divine mercy extend even to the godless and ungrateful?" (*ciu.* 1.8) Discoursing on Matthew 5:45 – God "makes his sun rise on the good and on the bad, and sends his rain alike on the righteous and the unrighteous" – Augustine emphasizes that God continues to offer many temporal blessings to His creatures as an invitation to return to Him, in the same way that he allows many temporal sufferings as an invitation to return to Him. Ultimately, as Augustine sees it, God's providence is bound up with invitation: the "patience of God" is designed to invite us to return to Him.

In the same way, Augustine explains, God allows Adam to experience the natural consequence of sin as a punishment that also serves as an invitation: the soul that "rejoiced in its own freedom to act perversely had disdained to be God's servant ... [and] was deprived of the obedient service which its body had first rendered. At its own pleasure the soul deserted its superior and master; and so it no longer retained its inferior and servant obedient to its will" (*ciu.* 13.13). Because Adam's rebellion brought him out of alignment with God's order in a way that harmed him, his punishment serves a pedagogical function in highlighting its consequence. That is to say, it prepares Adam to seek mercy or, if he refuses this, remains in its own right as a just punishment.

In fact, we find, Augustine makes a similar observation about the function of pain in book 19. Because God did not take away our nature after the Fall, the pain sin causes our nature serves to remind us of what is lost and what can be regained: "For when a man grieves at the loss of the peace of his nature, his grief arises from some remnants of that peace, which ensure that his nature is still on friendly terms with itself" (*ciu.* 19.13). Because we are not deprived of our nature, then, we retain a desire for true peace and resist the counterfeit peace of the earthly city.

However, because pride hates its own dependence, the members of the earthly city *as* members of the proud city, hate this resistance. In fact, Augustine thinks, a fundamental aspect of the earthly city's mission is to obscure the fact of human frailty, or, rather to devise some rationalization of how the suffering intrinsic to the human condition is something from which its members deserve to be exempt.[42] It is the earthly city's manufacturing of such narratives, Augustine thinks, that allows us to distract ourselves from a reality that should dispose us to return to God.

---

[42] Again, because the earthly city is not a true community, but an association bound together by a shared idea of autonomy, it does not matter that this suggestion – that *I* am exempt – is private. *Amor sui* need not claim that everyone else is exempt as well.

CONCLUSION

Recalling the psychagogic purpose of *City of God*, it is clear that Augustine's exploration of the earthly city is designed to shed light on our own secret thoughts in order to expose their incompatibility with our most fundamental desires. By developing a psychology of the earthly city that we cannot but find in our own thoughts and behaviors, Augustine aims to implicate us in the repercussions of these thoughts and behaviors in a way we are inclined to resist. Normally, he thinks, we are disposed to associate evil with the other – with those who are our enemies, or those who perpetrate grievous crimes. By implicating us in the hidden and insidious workings of the earthly city, Augustine also shows us that we are not only culpable for the state of our world, but that we in fact perpetuate the earthly city in existence by our participation in the patterns of behavior that define and strengthen it. In this way, Augustine hopes to move us in the same way God hopes the punishment of the Fall would move us: toward genuine remorse.

What is more, Augustine's development of the ontology of the earthly city helps us see through its false promises. Through his scriptural exegesis, Augustine reveals the edited version of the earthly city's alluring vision to be an incoherent power play. In the end, he reveals, the earthly city is merely a shadow of the city of God. The former is entirely opposed to the latter, but is not the equal and opposing force of Manichean lore. The disjunction between appearance and reality permeating every aspect of the earthly city marks it as counterfeit. Chipping away at the reputed power and glory of the earthly city, Augustine leaves us with a truer vision: the earthly city is unoriginal, responsible only for its failure to participate in the renewal of Creation.

Having seen the vision of the earthly city that animates Augustine's way of writing *City of God*, we can now proceed to the next stage of our inquiry: the tracing out of his psychagogic strategy as it unfolds in the text. Given that *City of God* deconstructs before it reconstructs his readers' vision, in the next three chapters we will focus on the deconstructive arc of Augustine's argument, first getting our bearings by a close reading of book one, then stepping back to consider its whole trajectory, and finally, situating the political history of books 1–5 within it. After this, we will consider the *telos* of this psychagogic argument – the sacramental worldview – and the place of politics within it.

2

The Sack of *Roma Aeterna*

Pride, Custom, and the Possibility of Cultural Renewal in Book 1

In the close reading of book 1 that follows, I will argue that Augustine sets up *City of God* as a work designed to help his readers see the world in a radically new way: not as it appears from the imperial heights of Rome but as it appears from the graced heights of faith. Having explored Augustine's vision of the earthly city in the previous chapter, this may strike the reader as the wrong dichotomy; for Augustine, after all, the battle is between the two cities, earthly and heavenly. And yet, Augustine cannot begin by addressing the earthly city qua earthly city: no one identifies with such a city, just as no one imagines that they are in the wrong when they are incensed – and the readers whose charge Augustine is answering are incensed.

Augustine, recall, writes *City of God* in response to a very concrete set of circumstances: the sack of Rome and the ensuing attempt to cast blame upon the Christians. Thus, while it is proper to read the text as an attempt to divest readers of the logic of *amor sui* and to invite them into the sacramental worldview of *amor Dei*, it is also noteworthy that the text does not simply begin in this way: rather, it takes a complaint made on a certain set of terms and connects those terms to the logic of the earthly city. To put this another way, Augustine thinks that the Romans blame the Christians for the sack because they misunderstand the status of their own city; they have erected it as an eternal city – *Roma Aeterna*.[1] Using this misunderstanding as an entrance point, Augustine uncovers its assumptions and challenges the

[1] Catherine Conybeare helpfully relates the opening lines of *City of God* to sermons Augustine gives around the time of the sack in "The City of Augustine: On the Interpretation of *Civitas*," in *Being Christian in Late Antiquity: A Festschrift for Gillian*

worldview from which they make sense. He, in other words, uses the Roman indictment as an opportunity to embark on a much more ambitious project, namely, the total overhaul of his readers' worldview. Boldly announcing to his Roman readers that their worldview is all too imbued with the logic of *amor sui*, he begins the work of divesting it of its distortions and so transforming it into the sacramental worldview of the city of God.

Indeed, looking at the preface more closely, what we find is an opening designed to help his Roman accusers entertain the possibility that they have distorted vision. Thus, while his initial proclamation that the city of God is glorious may appear in the form of an imperial boast, as Fr. Allan Fitzgerald has persuasively argued, these words are actually designed to call the imperial worldview into question; that is to say, they set up a striking contrast between the way the Romans normally use the term *glory* and the way the city of God uses it.[2] Signaling to his readers that they may not have as good a grip on the nature of reality as they suspect, he writes,

I know how great is the effort needed to convince the proud of the power and excellence of humility, an excellence which makes it soar above all the summits of this world, which sway in their temporal instability, overtopping them all with an eminence not arrogated by human pride, but granted by divine grace. (*ciu.* 1.*praef*)

Gazing on the world from the vista of the world's summits, he suggests, his Roman readers have set their lot on a height destined to fall, and worse, they have failed to notice the power of humility. Indeed, from the imperial perspective, the claim Augustine makes seems farcical. Yet, he announces, "the King and Founder" of the city of God has come in the flesh to reveal the hidden power of humility – a power rooted in its ability to receive *amor Dei* as gift (ibid.).

Thus, rather than casting the city of God in the mold of an earthly empire, Augustine is actually suggesting that Rome is a *simulacrum* of a city that is totally beyond his readers' capacity to imagine. Provocatively, then, he presents his readers with a worldview that radically relativizes their own.

Clark, ed. Carol Harrison, Caroline Humfress, and Isabella Sandwell (Oxford: Oxford University Press, 2014), 142–145.

[2] Fr. Allan Fitzgerald notes that Augustine provocatively calls the city of God "most glorious" in a way designed to highlight the difference between the way the Romans would use the term and the way he is using it: "He thus distances himself from the glory of Rome to speak of a different sense of glory, now transformed into that which defines the heavenly city." Allan D. Fitzgerald, OSA, "Christ's Humility and Christian Humility in the *De Civitate Dei*," *Mayéutica* 40 (2014): 241.

Roma Aeterna, it turns out, is a city destined for destruction: a counterfeit imitation of the one city that is truly eternal and truly glorious.

Yet, more must be said if we are to clarify the precise way in which the glory that Augustine gives to the city of God differs from Roman glory. Though a full answer to the question requires the entire ensuing chapter, a tentative answer begins to emerge once we consider the true object of Augustine's praise: God. As the following examination of book 1 reveals, Augustine is praising the city of God as *God's* city, and it is glorious, not because of any independent achievement of her members, but because of God's activity in her. Indeed, this point is immensely important to recognize, as it is the only grounds for his claim that the sacramental vision captures something new – something beyond the vista of the imperial heights. Viewed in its light, the opening lines of *City of God* serve as a perplexing invitation into a mystery: the glimpse of a truth unattainable from the perspective of Rome, and indeed of *amor sui* more broadly. Viewed through the lens of the earthly city, however, they make an unremarkable statement, appearing as one more self-congratulatory boast that mimics the prerogative of the powerful. Ultimately, then, the success of Augustine's psychagogic project rests on his ability to show his readers that the distinction between *amor sui* and *amor Dei* is a distinction with a difference: he must convince them that there is a facet of reality beyond the imperial sights of Rome. Rather than another form of veiled self-praise, the text's opening lines are meant as an exclamation of praise rooted in gratitude: a participation in what Augustine will later describe as *latreia*, or the worship due to God alone. They are the beginning of his psychagogic rhetoric.

THE PLACE OF THE TWO CITIES IN THE PREFACE

I just have suggested that, in opening lines of the preface, Augustine praises the city of God as God's city and not as the Romans praise their own city. That is to say, Augustine distinguishes the praise that issues from *amor Dei* from the praise that issues from *amor sui*, arguing that the logic of the earthly city is incapable of grasping the difference, just as it is incapable of seeing the city of God as it really is. Even so, it must be said that the community purportedly infused by *amor Dei* can be difficult to see regardless of where one stands. Sin mars the witness of the pilgrim church, and pride makes it difficult to distinguish its witness where it does exist. In short, *amor sui* threatens to sweep away our belief in *amor Dei* and, indeed, our ability to conceive of a genuine difference between the two cities at all. If we expect the city of God on pilgrimage to prove its existence by acting rightly, the fact that sin mars the lives of believers and unbelievers alike makes it difficult to concur with Augustine on this most basic of his teachings. Nevertheless, the move to frame the difference between the two cities on the basis of moral behavior is not traceable to Augustine.[3] For him, the fundamental difference between the two cities is rooted in the quality of its loves, not the actions of its members. Though many have construed these as identical statements, in Augustine, the former is prior to the latter and is fundamentally constitutive of the distinction between the two cities.

To put this more plainly, for Augustine, the love that binds the city of God is, primarily, God's love for us, not our love for God.[4] The latter exists only insofar as it participates in the former. In his account, moreover, *amor Dei* literally undergirds the city of God's very existence; ontologically, it is what ties its members to their God and to each other. This infusion of God's own Love – the Holy Spirit – into the city of God as the glue that holds it together may well have moral implications, but they are entirely secondary.[5] Augustine never points to moral qualities as the *ground* of the city of God's glory but as its fruit. Moreover, he repeatedly characterizes the city of God on pilgrimage as a *corpus permixtum* – mixed not just in the sense of having good and bad members but also in the members themselves.[6] They are, to be sure, in the process of being

---

[3] As Chuck Mathewes puts it, "the church is not an elite club ... but a hospital." Charles Mathewes, "A Worldly Augustinianism," 399.

[4] In this way, I disagree that the city of God is best defined as the city of those who "love God rightly ... unified by their common love of God." Weithman, "Augustine's Political Philosophy," 236. Similarly, Ernest Fortin writes that the city of God is "made up entirely of godly men and its whole life may be described as one of pious acquiescence in the word of God." Fortin, "Political Thought of St. Augustine," 20. Against these moral interpretations of the city of God, I am arguing that the city of God is the community made up of those who let God love them and is unified by God's love for them, which they receive and return, growing in *amor Dei* by participating in it.

[5] Often, Augustine describes Charity or the Holy Spirit as the glue binding the city of God together. In *De Doctrina Christiana*, for example, Augustine writes that when we reach beatitude, it will be "with the Holy Spirit binding and so to say gluing us in there, so that we may abide forever in that supreme and unchangeable good." Augustine, *Teaching Christianity*, trans. Edmund Hill, ed. John Rotelle (Hyde Park, NY: New City Press, 1996), 123, 1.34.38. For an exploration of Augustine's use of *agglutinare* and his presentation of the Holy Spirit as the glue of the Church, see Joseph Lienhard, "The Glue Itself Is Charity: Ps. 62: 9 in Augustine's Thought," in *Collectanea Augustiniana: Presbyter Factus Sum*, ed. J. Lienhard, E. Mueller, and R. Teske (New York: Peter Lang, 1993), 375–384.

[6] Cf. *ciu.* 1.35, 18.49, and 20.9. As Michael McCarthy puts it, "the unfinished or unrealized quality of the Church always stands at the center of [Augustine's] reflection." McCarthy,

healed and transformed through grace, but it is a process that is perennially unfinished in the *saeculum*. Ultimately, for Augustine, the pilgrim city
is marked, not by its moral perfection, but by its devotion to God and its
willingness to return to him for healing and forgiveness whenever it strays.

With this having been said, we can move to the main theme of *City of
God*'s preface. If, as Augustine announces, the work is a defense of the
actual city of God, it will be no surprise that Augustine begins by presenting the *saeculum* as a battleground where the city of God and that city's
simulacrum fight for the title of "The Just City." Though not yet named as
such, this *simulacrum* is the earthly city we have already seen. Already, it
typifies pride by exemplifying the parodic overreaching that imitates that
to which it cannot, and will never be able to, attain. That is to say, it puffs
itself up. Though the prerogative to rule over the proud and humble alike,
Augustine states, is God's alone, "man's arrogant spirit in its swelling
pride has claimed it as its own" (ibid.). The city animated by this spirit
"aims at domination ... dominated by that very lust of domination [*ipsa ei
dominandi libido dominatur*]" (ibid.).[7] It justifies itself, certainly, but is
not, thereby, just.

While it remains to be seen whether Augustine thinks Rome *is* the
earthly city, it is at least noteworthy that Augustine uses Rome to introduce the character of the earthly city. Writing that "the King and
Founder" of the city of God "has revealed in the Scripture of his people
this statement of the divine Law, God resists the proud," but "gives grace
to the humble," Augustine immediately contrasts it with a passage from
Virgil's *Aeneid*, wherein Anchises reminds his son Aeneas of Rome's
destiny to rule the world (*ciu.* 1.*praef*).[8] Here, we have two kinds of
prophecy in contrast: one a revelation of divine law, the other a myth,
an invention of a poet. Rome's duty, the poetic prophecy proclaims, is "to

---

"Ecclesiology of Groaning," *Theological Studies* 66 (2005): 28. For other works treating
the unfinished quality of the Church in Augustine, see Cavadini, "Spousal Vision,"
141–148, esp. notes 49 and 50; and John Sehorn, "Monica as Synecdoche for the
Pilgrim Church in the *Confessiones*," *Augustinian Studies* 46, no. 2 (2015): 243–245.

[7] CCSL 47.1.

[8] Founder (*conditor*) is an important term for Augustine in *City of God*, because whenever
he uses it in reference to anyone else but the Father as Creator, or Christ, as Founder of the
city of God, he is indicating that they have broken off from him – so, he uses it for the
founders of heresies, like Manes and Pelagius, and self-seeking political founders, like
Romulus. These are all people who, he thinks, made themselves their own foundation.
Though Augustine uses Virgil disparagingly here, it is clear that he is also quite influenced
by him. For a careful treatment of Virgil's influence on Augustine, see
Sabine MacCormack, *The Shadows of Poetry: Vergil in the Mind of Augustine* (Berkeley:
University of California Press, 1998).

spare the humble and beat down the proud" (*parcere subjectis et debellare superbos*) (ibid.).[9] Though Rome had long celebrated its special mission by recalling this verse, once it is put next to the words of Scripture, a different read on Virgil's commissioned praise begins to emerge. Quite simply, saying that Rome spares the conquered and beats down the proud is not the same as saying that it resists the proud and gives grace to the humble. Rome has claimed God's prerogative only to distort it.

Read in light of our previous analysis of Augustine's earthly city, we can easily see that Augustine intends to portray Virgil's prophecy in a way that betrays Rome's neediness – her delight in hearing "this verse quoted in [her] own praise" is really delight in having others reflect her illusory superiority back to her (ibid.). The subtext of the verse, as Augustine presents it, is that Rome stands ready to subdue anyone who takes a stand against her because this reinforces the parodic glory in which she delights. Those who resist, by virtue of their resistance, are proud, and she delights in subduing them. Those who cower before her gratify her by their submissiveness, and so she spares them. In highlighting the parodic quality of Rome's boast in the opening pages of *City of God*, then, Augustine sets up a link between *Roma Aeterna* and the earthly city, rooted in their shared love of domination and preeminence and their concomitant willingness to boast about their own justice.[10] As we will see in the next few chapters, the first five books of Augustine's tome present Rome as ruthlessly hegemonic.[11] Augustine's Rome positions herself over her citizens and against her enemies because she is confident

---

[9] CCSL 47.1. Daniel Strand has recently argued that the *Aeneid* is "perhaps the exemplary text" of what he calls Roman sacral politics: the kind of politics that deifies the state by sacralizing civic life. Strand, "Augustine's *City of God* and Roman Sacral Politics," in *Augustine's Political Thought*, ed. Richard Dougherty (Rochester, NY: Rochester University Press, 2019), 227–228.

[10] Harrison, with Markus, argues the opposite, writing, "The Empire has no real place in Augustine's idea of the two cities: it is neither synonymous with the city of God, the predestined elect, as earlier Eusebian imperial theology might have held; nor can it be identified with the city of the world, the unrighteous damned, as Hippolytus held. It is, as Markus cogently demonstrated, theologically neutral. It is part of the context, the secular context, in which the life of man now takes place, in which the members of the city of God and the city of the world pursue their, at present, intertwined courses." Harrison, *Christian Truth and Fractured Humanity*, 203. Again, I do not think that the choice is between identification or equivocation. A sacramental reading of Augustine's prose yields a different relationship.

[11] That said, in one aspect at least, Rome does foreshadow the city of God: in its granting of asylum to anyone who sought it (*ciu.* 1.34). For an extended study of Augustine's treatment of this asylum and its comparison to a contemporary pagan treatment, see Philippe Bruggisser, "City of the Outcast and City of the Elect: The Romulean Asylum in

in her imperial prerogative – her right to spread civilization across the world.[12]

To be sure, Roman civilization was great, and the *Pax Romana* was certainly preferable to the increasing havoc of barbarian forces as they invaded the weaker parts of the empire.[13] In fact, Roman rule was arguably humane, especially in comparison to the great empires of the past: one need only think of the brutal tactics employed by the Assyrians and the Babylonians, melded into one in the biblical imagination.[14] At least in Rome, there were no forced exiles of whole populations, and, it seems, provincials benefited from a particularly Roman brand of law and order.[15] Though there are moments in *City of God* where Augustine's admiration and even gratitude for Rome shine through, the fact of the matter is that he, as a rule, chooses to highlight the gap between Rome and the truly Just City because this was the point that needed to be made. Thus, he begins by putting Rome's famous commission next to the words of Scripture, highlighting the distortions that undergird even Rome's manifest destiny. Whether he is worried about the effect of the sack of Rome on the faith of Christians or simply worried about the kind of patriotism that led Romans to reject Christianity, Augustine's immediate concern is clearly to draw his readers' ultimate allegiance beyond Rome to the city of God. In the first five books, he does this by deconstructing Rome's manifest destiny: unmasking the underlying *libido dominandi* that animates her pseudo-salvific activity.[16] By doing so, he also teaches his readers about the *ethos* of the earthly city – one element within the sacramental worldview that it is his ultimate purpose to convey.

Augustine's *City of God* and Servius's *Commentaries on Virgil*," *Augustinian Studies* 30, no. 2 (1999): 75–104.

[12] The historian Cochrane's grasp of the Greco-Roman *ethos* is helpful on this point: "The effort of Classicism was . . . an effort to rescue mankind from the life and mentality of the jungle, and to secure for him the possibility of a good life. That is to say it was envisaged as a struggle for civilization against barbarism and superstition." Charles Norris Cochrane, *Christianity and Classical Culture* (Indianapolis, IN: Liberty Fund, 2003), 174.

[13] See, e.g., *ciu.* 5.17.   [14] Cf. Scheil, *Babylon under Western Eyes*, 28–43.

[15] For a detailed account of Roman rule of the provinces and how it changed over time, see Jean-Michel Carrié, "Developments in Provincial and Local Administration," in *The Cambridge Ancient History*, vol. 12, ed. A. Bowman, A. Cameron, and P. Garnsey (Cambridge: Cambridge University Press, 2005), 269–312; J. Richardson, "Roman Law in the Provinces," in *The Cambridge Companion to Roman Law*, ed. D. Johnston (Cambridge: Cambridge University Press, 2015), 45–58.

[16] One gets a sense of the salvific aspect of the imperial cult in Ratzinger's discussion of Caesar Augustus in *Jesus of Nazareth: The Infancy Narratives* (New York: Image Press, 2012), 58–60, as well as in chapters 3 and 9 of Cochrane's *Christianity and Classical Culture*.

While Augustine's Rome stands poised to beat down the proud and only as an exception spares those who grovel before her, his God stands ready to give grace and only refrains from doing so in light of pride's incapacity to receive it. Because his fundamental stance is one of gift-giving, Christ speaks his words of counsel out of love. He wants to warn human beings about what pride will cost them. Thus, at the very least, Augustine's claim is that there is a radical distinction between Rome's self-exaltation and Christ's counsel. The former is motivated by *amor sui*, the latter by *amor Dei*. It is only if the distinction between these two loves is a distinction with a difference that Augustine can present the actual city of God as something beyond the script of the earthly city.

FRIENDS AND ENEMIES, RECONSIDERED

In the rest of book 1, Augustine uses the events of the sack in order to demonstrate that the difference between the two cities is, in fact, a distinction with a difference. In doing so, he draws heavily from Paul's letter to the Romans, chastening those who want to base righteousness in works, even as he exhorts his readers to good works. The themes worked out in this book – of why good things happen to bad people, of why bad things happen to good people, of the struggle to admit guilt and accept solidarity with those one views with contempt – all circle around the incongruity of the two cities' worldviews and, indeed, the difficulty of getting beyond the earthly city's viewpoint at all.

Reading book 1 closely, it becomes evident that Augustine uses the sack as a surprising teaching moment: to reveal the difference between the way God acts in the world and the way fallen human beings expect a god to act. Departing from the standard narrative in which victory was linked to divine favor, Augustine tells a story where God is present, not in conquest, but in sanctuary. In fact, as we will see, Augustine uses the juxtaposition between aggression and sanctuary for theological ends. If human beings, reading world events through the eyes of pride, are prone to misread the city of God in the earthly city's terms, it is for him to communicate the difference between the two cities throughout book 1 and, indeed, throughout the work as a whole. Secular history might be defined by the rise and fall of world powers, but, Augustine will argue, God enters the picture in the hidden workings of grace.

Thus, when Augustine discusses the enemies (*inimici*) of God's city in book 1, what is notable is not the way in which Augustine takes on the rhetoric of empire but the way in which he subverts it. While Rome strives to draw thick lines between its civilized members and its barbarian enemies, Christ extends friendship toward all. In choosing to note how many former enemies have corrected their errors *before* adding that many still remain enemies, Augustine emphasizes his agnosticism about who, in the end, will be a friend of God. This is an Augustine unwilling to give up on any, even his harshest critics. Famously, he writes,

> We have less right to despair ... when some predestined friends, as yet unknown even to themselves, are concealed among our most open enemies. In truth, those two cities are interwoven and intermixed in this age, and await separation at the last judgment. (*ciu.* 1.35)

Though Augustine uses the language of enemies here, it is evident that also he considers himself obligated to think of these enemies as the future friends they could be – those whom Christ loved first (Rom. 5:8).[17] Though this move does not destroy enmity, it does transform his response to these enemies. Equally significant is Augustine's understanding of the transition from being an enemy of Christ to being his friend. For Augustine, the human heart is not conquered by God in a military sense; if the term is at all applicable, it can only be in a spousal sense. That is, the human being can only be conquered by God in the sense of being won over by him: coming to discover God's favor and goodness, the human being responds in freedom and in love.[18] In Augustine's juxtaposition, set up as it is in the preface, the heavenly city's Founder does not strive to master his enemies only to lord it over them. Instead, he wishes for their friendship. Already, Augustine is setting up a vision of the city of God that resists imperial logic.[19]

---

[17] Strikingly, Jim Lee has argued that in his *Expositions on the Psalms*, Augustine actually portrays the earthly city as being transformed into the city of God over the course of time. James K. Lee, "Babylon Becomes Jerusalem: The Transformation of the Two Cities in Augustine's *Enarrationes in Psalmos*," *Augustinian Studies* 47, no. 2 (2016): 157–180. This is a compelling claim, especially in light of the vision put forth in *City of God*.

[18] The fact that Augustine thinks this depends on grace does not undermine the freedom involved in the response. Cf. *ep. Io.* 4.7, quoted above.

[19] As a provincial, Augustine is aware that conquered peoples, upon being incorporated into the empire, have no reason to expect elevation to the status of equals. Augustine refers to this in a discussion of the Roman mother of the gods designed to highlight the Roman (and human) mind-set in *ciu.* 3.12, writing, "But, whatever her birth, I do not imagine that those immigrant gods will have the insolence to despise, as low-born, a citizen goddess of Rome!" *Ciu.* 5.17 is an interesting passage on this topic – here, he is in the midst of showing that the Romans received the reward for their labors in the currency of power and glory. While he is, in general, favorable to the effect Roman rule had on the provinces, he complains that the Romans extorted money from conquered peoples in

THE EMPIRE AND THE REFUGE

After having proposed a new way of thinking about friends and enemies, Augustine spends a large portion of book 1 reflecting on and responding to the sack of Rome in its light. First, he focuses on the remarkable fact that the barbarians went above and beyond the customs of war to provide sanctuary for the conquered Romans. Thus, he tells us, the Romans "were kept safe and protected [wherever] his name stood between them and the enemy's violence" (*ciu.* 1.3):

They were spared for Christ's sake, pagans though they were; yet they scorn to acknowledge this. With the madness of sacrilegious perversity they use their tongues against the name of Christ: yet with those same tongues they dishonestly claimed that name in order to save their lives, or else, in places sacred to him, they held their tongues through fear. They were kept safe and protected there where his name stood between them and the enemy's violence. (ibid.)

While Augustine's discussion of this element of the sack makes a precise literal point – that those who blame Christianity for the sack should be grateful that this very Christianity prompted the barbarians to spare them – Augustine also uses it to convey a larger teaching about the character of the two cities and the relationship between them. Indeed, one might say, because Augustine is steeped in Scripture, its rhetorical layering of figurative on top of literal meanings seeps into his own work such that his treatment of the sack is decisively a work of art. In telling of the sack, I will argue, Augustine overturns the standard narrative of the victor, replacing it with a new narrative in which Christ is the unabashed protagonist. What is more, read figuratively, Augustine's account of the sack presents a vision that radically transforms the story about how God acts in human affairs. In inspiring the barbarians' act of mercy, Christ provides a way toward cultural renewal that had nothing to do with the imperial prerogative of a superior civilization.

Based on the themes we have already traced out, we can see why the image of refuge would provide Augustine with a fitting way to

---

order to pay for the sustenance of the Roman lower classes, writing, "It would have been better if the funds had been presented voluntarily through the agency of equitable administrators, after a peaceful compact instead of being taken by extortion form conquered peoples." He also suggests that it would have been better to grant citizenship to the provincials much earlier than they did. For a sense of the status of different groups in Augustine's own time, see Ralph W. Mathisen, "Peregrini, Barbari, and Cives Romani: Concepts of Citizenship and the Legal Identity of Barbarians in the Later Roman Empire," *The American Historical Review* 111, no. 4 (2006): 1011–1140.

communicate his vision of the city of God. In the first place, Augustine is writing to a world where the victor's prerogative is taken for granted. In a world where winner takes all, the conquered have no recourse to justice, only to mercy. As Xenophon's Cyrus put it upon conquering Babylon,

> it is an eternal law among all human beings that when a city is captured by those at war, both the bodies of those in the city and their valuables belong to those who take it. It will not be by injustice, then, that you will have whatever you may have, but it will be by benevolence that you refrain from taking something away, if you allow them to have anything.[20]

It is only by taking this reality seriously that Augustine's depiction of the city of God as refuge takes its full effect; in it, we have a divinely initiated extension of mercy that is not, by any measure, owed. But, it is needed, and this is the grounds upon which it is given. By taking the status quo as his starting point, Augustine is able to demonstrate the theological significance in the fact that the barbarians "showed mercy beyond the custom of war" (*ciu.* 1.1).

Nevertheless, it is strange that Augustine has no problem allegorizing an act of giving sanctuary which occurs amidst an act of aggression that he himself calls "bloodthirsty" and "monstrous" (*ciu.* 1.1). True, Augustine is presenting the power dynamics of the earthly city – its rules of invasion and victory – as the status quo in world affairs, but it is admittedly odd that he chooses the very enemy who has inflicted such sufferings on the Roman community to teach them such a lesson. Yet, when one thinks of the parable of the Good Samaritan or the story of Jonah, one is reminded that the notion of God's allegiances spreading farther than ours is a recurring theme in Scripture. In fact, this element of surprise achieves an important goal for Augustine. Because he knows that his contemporaries cannot forget the context within which sanctuary was given, he is able to use this awareness to problematize the entire imperial perspective, which, as we have seen, is the perspective of the earthly city. In other words, *that* the act of giving sanctuary occurs amidst great evil actually helps him signal that the city of God might not be what his readers expect it to be. It helps him resist an imperial gloss on the city of God.

Turning to his analysis of the sack itself, we find that Augustine begins by distinguishing between those grateful to the Christians' mercy for their

---

[20] Xenophon, *The Education of Cyrus*, trans. Wayne Ambler (Ithaca, NY: Cornell University Press, 2001), 229, 7.5.73. Cf. *ciu.* 1.5, where Augustine reminds his readers of what Sallust, "a historian renowned for his veracity," records as Cato reminding the senate of "the usual consequences when cities are sacked."

survival and those who blame Christianity for the sack, but attribute "their deliverance to their own destiny" (*ciu.* 1.1). While there are many things one can be said to achieve, being spared by another is hardly one of them. So too, no one can claim the right to be in God's city – as Augustine repeatedly stresses, everyone is born into the earthly city, and any conversion is due less to human goodness than to the graced recognition that it is good to cling to God. In fact, little that Augustine says in his discussion of the sack glorifies man. I have already alluded to the fact that Augustine begins his account of the sack by stressing that the barbarians spared many Romans "for Christ's sake," and that this ran against the grain of the normal practices of war (*ciu.* 1.1). Challenging his readers to look at Roman history, Augustine contends that the Romans never spared any of the defeated just because they took "refuge in the temples of their gods" (*ciu.* 1.7). It is surprising, then, that the uncouth barbarians not only respected the sanctuary of churches, but ushered the Romans into the largest churches they could find so "as to give mercy a wider range" (ibid.).

While one might expect Augustine to praise the barbarians for this, Augustine repeatedly refers his praise to Christ. Christ, he writes, is responsible for the benefits given "out of respect" for him (*propter Christi honorem facta sunt*) (*ciu.* 1.7).[21] It is easy to read this as a symbolic jab against Pelagianism – a subtle reminder that all good actions reveal the hidden workings of grace. On the surface, though, Christ deserves the praise quite simply because he displayed power over the barbarians. In invading Rome, the Visigoths bore the mark of the earthly city's *libido dominandi*. Yet, when the merciful (*miserantibus*) among them went to great lengths to save the Romans from "those who had no such pity (*qui similem misericordiam non habebant*),"[22] even the latter respected the sanctuary the churches gave (ibid.). As Augustine describes it, their thirst for blood was checked (*accipiebat limitem*) and "their lust for taking captives was subdued (*captiuandi cupiditas frangebatur*)" at the doors of the basilicas (ibid.). Quite simply, they were stopped short in their tracks.[23]

---

[21] CCSL 47.2.   [22] Ibid.

[23] Ibid. It is significant, I think, that these invaders were Arians. This is to say that even though they did not confess Christ as God, the level of reverence they did have for Him was enough to let Him have some efficacious power over them, a power that He used for good – for the salvation of others. In other words, I think their Arianism only highlights the mysterious power of God, showing that it is not primarily human effort that brings certain things about but a God who is bigger than us at work through us. Cf. *s.* 105.13.

Interestingly, then, Augustine holds that Christ's power "changed the whole aspect of the scene, even as he was adamant that the barbarians' behavior, by and large, remained decidedly earthly (*ciu.* 1.7). Writing that "all the devastation, the butchery, the plundering, the conflagrations, and all the anguish which accompanied the recent disaster at Rome were in accordance with the general practice of warfare," Augustine does not shy away from the fact that those who claim to be the servants of Christ were in some way also complicit in an act of military aggression (ibid.). Indeed, he highlights the unfinished quality of Christ's triumph over their hearts – something Augustine must include in the story if it is not to become mythical. Again, we see, Augustine's city of God is not simply the city of the altogether just, good, or perfect.

Resisting the idea that this new custom of mercy had something to do with the barbarians themselves, Augustine writes,

This [new custom] is to be attributed to the name of Christ and the influence of Christianity. . . . Let us hope that no one with any sense will ascribe the credit for this to the brutal nature of the barbarians. Their fierce and savage minds were terrified, restrained, and miraculously controlled by him who long ago said through his prophet, "I will visit their iniquities with a rod, and their sins with scourges; but I will not disperse my mercy from them." (ibid.)

Thus, while "the savagery of the barbarians took on such an aspect of gentleness that the largest basilicas were selected and set aside to be filled with people to be spared by the enemy," for Augustine, the barbarians' actions were not natural in origin but supernatural (*ciu.* 1.7). In making this point, Augustine maps his allegory onto the distinction, self-evident in the Roman mind, between the civilized and the barbarian.[24] In the Roman narrative, it was the Romans' "virile morality," that made their civilization great: they believed that Roman custom (*consuetudo*) was simply better at keeping "vices under restraint" than the customs of their neighboring foes (*ciu.* 1.31). Civilization was thus to be associated with law and

---

[24] For the connotations linked to the concept of "barbarian" in the Roman world, see, e.g., Benjamin Isaac, "The Barbarian in Greek and Latin Literature," in *Empire and Ideology in the Graeco-Roman World: Selected Papers* (Cambridge: Cambridge University Press, 2017), 197–220. Benjamin explains that in both Greek and Latin writings, barbarians were considered to be wild and uncivilized. The term, he writes, "Often indicates untutored savages, peoples barbarous in language and by descent. Generalizations are common: foreigners are naturally wicked; loyalty for them depends upon success; they are treacherous and impious. Their rites are immoral and bloody; they are ignorant and lack intellectual curiosity, discipline and inhibition. They are unnecessarily cruel" (220). See also "Barbarians and Ethnicity," in *Late Antiquity*, ed. Peter Brown, Glen Bowersock, and Andre Grabar (Cambridge, MA: Cambridge University Press, 1999), 106–129.

custom, which set restraints on human savagery and refashioned human-ity into its full *humanitas*. For this to occur, the Romans like the Greeks thought, human nature must be trained in virtues that could only be cultivated by a serious civilization. In the first five books, Augustine engages with the Roman idea of *consuetudo* as a cultural code of conduct capable of regulating citizen behavior, if only to show its limitations. It is, for Augustine, *the* solution the earthly city can offer to the problem of disordered desire: a system of self-regulation that takes advantage of the desire to be on the right side of things, or, at least to be considered as such.

We will come back to this theme in the latter part of this chapter, but for now, what is important is that Augustine is invoking the Roman idea of civilization, not to demolish it, but to imply that Christ is more effica-cious at restraining lusts than Rome has ever been. By referring the Romans back to their own history, Augustine shows that the Romans have behaved no better than the barbarians when it comes to war – at best they can point to the celebrated Marcus Marcellus who wept before sacking Syracuse. He, the poets say, was so filled with humanity that he had a mind to "preserve the honor of his enemies" so that "no violence should be done to the person of any free citizen" (*ciu.* 1.6). To be sure, Augustine thinks that this is a step in the right direction. Yet, as we will see, the *humanitas* of civilization takes Marcus Marcellus as far as it can go: it can draw his attention to the free, to the honorable, to those of status, but no further than that.

Contrasting the Greeks, the original claimants of civilization, with the barbarians, Augustine belabors his point, showing how the Greeks chose to go the temple of Juno to display their victory by loading it with booty, while the "uncouth" barbarians choose the largest basilicas as places of refuge for pagan and Christian alike (*ciu.* 1.4). By taking advantage of the cultural idea of the uncultivated barbarian Augustine is able to communi-cate another important lesson about the city of God: if the barbarians' mercy cannot be attributed to their nature or their culture, then the imperial framework has no resources to explain their behavior. Quite clearly, in Augustine's allegory, Christ works in the barbarians despite their barbarism. In this way, he makes it clear that their humanity, their pity is not to be attributed to anything the barbarians were *qua* barbarian. As such, their barbarianism stands as a convenient symbol of the fallen-ness of human nature. What is to be attributed to barbarianism is the fact that men rape, pillage, steal, torture. It is inhumanity, the absence of that self-restraint which civilization is designed to cultivate. The question Augustine will ask throughout the first five books is whether and to what extent culture can really cultivate *humanitas* without cultivating a kind of *inhumanitas* at the same time.

Thus, in the end, Augustine is quite happy painting a picture in which mercy appears in a muddy scene of destruction because he wants to resist the imperial narrative in which civilization saves the day. Not only does Augustine's Christ triumph by restraining and even transforming the hearts of men who, of their own fallen volition, are bent on conquering Rome, he does this, in a way that redounds to the good of those who might normally be considered political or religious "enemies." In the end, this is the plot twist. Unlike the pagan gods, who protect their own, Christ's mission spreads outward: it casts broad nets. Ultimately, it is by locating Christ's victory not in the conquering of Rome, but in his ability to create sanctuary that Augustine challenges the imperial story. The pilgrim city, we see, is not a society of the perfect, but simply a people willing to let God work through them in a way that redounds to the good of others.[25] With Christ as the chief protagonist in his story, Augustine presents the city of God as an *anti-imperial* presence in an imperial event.

MERCY AND JUSTICE

After having presented the city of God as a refuge that protects those whom one would normally call enemies, Augustine interrupts himself with a question from his readers – "Why does the Divine mercy extend even to the godless and the ungrateful?" (*ciu.* 1.8).[26] To Roman Catholics, the question was an obvious one – not only was Augustine asking them to identify with their barbarian invaders (who were Arians), he was asking them to be grateful that their current detractors had survived, while members of their own community had been tortured, raped, and killed. Does God not protect his own?

It is significant that Augustine countenances this question. Why *does* God bless the ungrateful? While, over the course of his answer, Augustine exposes the pride distorting the question, he is also uncharacteristically gentle with the one who asks it: is a question that must be articulated in order to be worked through. Stepping back and reading the question in an

---

[25] For a recent treatment of the formative function of pilgrimage in Augustine's thought, see Sarah Stewart-Kroeker, *Pilgrimage as Moral and Aesthetic Formation in Augustine's Thought* (Oxford: Oxford University Press, 2017).

[26] Augustine also countenances this question in a particularly poignant way in *s.* 296. See esp. sections 6–12.

Augustinian light, its subtext is easily grasped – we, it says, are faithful to God – *we* follow his laws, so why does God bless our enemies and allow us to suffer? Augustine's preliminary answer is clear, if not unsurprising: God's ways are not our ways. While we are caught in the webs of parsing out who deserves what, God makes the sun to shine on all, regardless of their gratitude. Augustine understands the indignation of his interlocutor who asks, how is this fair? But Augustine wants to turn the question around, saying that "God's patience still invites the wicked" (ibid.). God, in other words, does not give up on us even after we give up on each other. Every blessing given to another person is an invitation to gratitude and should be celebrated as such. To be struck by this is to experience, Augustine hopes, a paradigm shift, or at least the glimpse of its possibility.

There is, however, another way in: if Augustine is implying that there is a strain of presumption in the original question, the fact that God gives people good things despite their ingratitude also applies to those of us who ask it – God still gives us good things despite our ingratitude. Despite our presumption, he remains patient with us. For Augustine, our outrage at God's beneficence to the ungrateful does not condemn us, but reminds us that, insofar as we feel it, we remain to some degree bound by the same sinfulness we scorn in others. Thus, when Augustine concludes that "God's mercy embraces the good for their cherishing, just as his severity chastises the wicked for their punishment," it is not clear who the good and the bad are, or, indeed, whether they are different people at all (ibid.). Augustine will resolve the point in a letter a few years later:

In this life we cannot say that we are without all sin. Rather, we are good insofar as we are children of God and bad insofar as we are sinners. Jesus called the same people both good and bad, and even Seneca reminds us that we are all bad. (*ep.* 153)

As we saw with the recharacterization of friends and enemies, for Augustine, it is insofar as one accepts God's mercy that one is made good, and insofar as one refuses to use what is given as an occasion of mercy that it becomes a punishment. With this suggested, Augustine shifts the question – if it is the case that everyone's life is interwoven with joys and sorrows, the better question is, "what use is made of the things thought to be blessings and of the things reputed evil?" (*ciu.* 1.8). Here, the question is not "why do bad things happen to me, while good things happen to people who don't deserve them" but "how am I to endure what is before me?"

If Augustine's goal is to resist a facile sorting of the good from the bad wherever he finds it, then what we see here is Augustine reminding his Christian readers that their own transformation is far from complete. The experiences that they interpret as just punishment for the wicked are no different from the ones they also experience. This is why Augustine gives his readers a new question. Rather than trying to deduce why others receive what they do or do not deserve, he directs his readers' attention to the question of how they ought to meet their own sufferings. The good man, he reminds these readers, is tested and cleansed by suffering, which is to say, that he is not already perfect before he suffers. Rather, he is humbled, purified, and healed by suffering. In Augustine's account, then, the goodness open to humanity is very much a goodness in process – and a process very much in God's hands.

This having been said, Augustine is able to conclude that the sufferings that pervade this life are, in part, a result of everyone's hard-heartedness. In fact, he muses, "this seems to me a major reason why the good are chastised along with the evil . . . because both alike, though not in the same degree, [inordinately] love this temporal life" (*ciu.* 1.9). Going on, he explains to his fellow Christians what he means: though we strive to live differently, "we tend culpably to evade our responsibility" to those whose lives we judge when it is "irksome" to correct them or when we are "afraid" of offending them (ibid.). In other words, we do not truly love our neighbor in *amor Dei*. While Augustine reaffirms the boundaries that prudence lays out for fraternal correction, he is adamant that the faithful should not be "indulgent to the sins of others" when they actually are in a position to "reprehend and reprove" them (ibid.).[27]

Here, Augustine chooses his words carefully – to reprove is not to damn, but to act in *imitatio Christi*: to speak truth in love. Reaching beyond satisfaction with a life that merely "abhors the deeds of the wicked," Augustine actually calls his Christian readers to love the wicked (ibid.). Read in this light, it becomes clear that the Christians who refrained from prudent fraternal correction fell short because they should

---

[27] For a study of Augustine's own attempts to correct his flock through letter writing, see Jennifer Ebbeler, *Disciplining Christians: Correction and Community in Augustine's Letters* (Oxford: Oxford University Press, 2012). Essentially, Ebbeler argues that Augustine is very influenced by Paul and follows takes his rebuke of Peter as a model for loving fraternal correction. What is most interesting about her study is that it shows that Augustine hoped and expected fraternal correction to become a mark of Christian culture, such that it would be well-taken. This was not, however, always the case and Ebbeler explores why.

have desired the good of those whose deeds they despised. As he puts it, the Christians "ought to have despised [self-interest] so that the others might be reformed and corrected and aim at life eternal ... or, if they refused to be partners in this enterprise, so that they might be borne with, and loved as Christians should love their enemies" (ibid.). Here, Augustine offers a dramatic expansion of perspective. After Christ, what is expected of the good is not merely the disdain of the wicked, but an active pursuit of their friendship. The all-too-human habit of relegating others to the band of the wicked only obscures this responsibility and gives us an excuse for preferring comfort to love.

Indeed, Augustine believes, human beings have a terrible habit of locating their own good opinion of themselves in a self-selected arena of life – one that impresses, but is not fundamentally inconvenient – and, he warns, fraternal correction is often inconvenient. This being so, he highlights the hidden ways in which human beings can remain "constrained by self-interest" even as they live an ostensibly holy life (ibid.). The narrowing of focus to appearances, whereby the importance of difficult acts of love is occluded, is a danger not only for our "weaker brothers" (*non solum quippe inferiores*), but also, and perhaps especially, for those who "have a higher standard of life."[28] Even clerics can "delight in flattery and popularity" and "dread the judgment of the mob" (ibid.). Warning against the little concessions human beings are tempted to make for the sake of others' good opinion, Augustine engages in fraternal correction himself, rooting premature attempts to separate the wheat from the chaff in a lack of love and self-knowledge.

Ultimately, what Augustine is doing in the early parts of *City of God* is cautioning his readers against the idea that the city of God on pilgrimage is the moral city. Relocating the measure of goodness from externalities to *amor Dei*, Augustine again points to the radical generosity of Christ, encouraging his readers to cling to him so that they might experience and imitate his generosity in truth. By this point in book 1, it should be clear that Augustine has thoroughly muddied an easy division between the upright and the depraved, whatever form this takes. Instead, he gives us

---

[28] Even in this, Augustine is getting inside the perspective of a ladder of superiority – if his reader says, "Of course this is true of the weaker members of the Christian community who, marrying and living in the world, have not the heart to offend those who have power over their livelihood," he sets them up to be indicted for what they clearly see in those less ascetic than them. Much of this is laced with an anti-Pelagian bent, but for Augustine the Pelagian heresy is merely an articulation of the fallen human condition and so has broader implications.

a vision of humanity that is, across the board, limited by *amor sui*. And yet, Christ provides a way forward.

PRIDE'S POLITICAL FALLOUT

Next, Augustine turns his sights to those whom he thinks have especially borne the brunt of society's hard-heartedness: the sack's rape victims.[29] In the attention Augustine pays to these women, we see him mitigate the effects of what he sees as a distorted version of fraternal correction: the harsh judgment animated by pride. As we have already seen, Augustine associates *amor sui* with pride, and, especially in the early books, with the prerogative of empire. Here, Augustine takes up the idea of the Roman *simulacrum* and shows the limits of a culture that regulates behavior through praise and blame, but without love. Consciously modeling a form of fraternal correction that stands as an antidote to this phenomenon, Augustine strives to uncover the limitations of civilization. That is to say, he wants to show that civic virtue alone is not a sufficient guardian of a good community. As we will see, Augustine's alternative is a fraternal correction rooted in fellow-feeling; one fundamentally tied to his depiction of God's city as a *refuge*. As such, the first work of this fraternal correction is to "administer consolation" to the victims of the other kind – to bring them beyond the indictment of prying eyes (*ciu.* 1.16).

While Augustine is clear that he is defending the chastity, not only of the minds but even of the bodies of these women, in giving the related example of the young girl whose midwife destroys her maidenhood "whether by malice, or clumsiness or accident," he indicates that he is writing in a world where this innocence is too often called into question (*ciu.* 1.18). While Augustine appeals to the better nature of his readers, writing, "I do not suppose anyone would be stupid enough to imagine" that the midwife's action would affect this woman's virginity, the very fact that a midwife might do this through malice indicates the opposite (ibid.). Indeed, the fact that Augustine has to "firmly" establish that these women are not to blame for what has been done to them tells us that he is speaking to a community in which they have received blame (*ciu.* 1.16). Augustine is painfully aware of how the habit of sizing others up magnifies the trauma of an already horrifying ordeal, writing that even though the violence of another "does not destroy a person's purity," the reason that

---

[29] For a detailed discussion of this topic, see Melanie Webb, "On Lucretia Who Slew Herself," *Augustinian Studies* 44, no. 1 (2013): 37–58.

it engenders "a sense of shame" is that it "may be believed that [it] was accompanied also by a consent of the mind" (ibid.). Recognizing this, a community has a choice: it can magnify the natural fear of being judged by taking this fear as a sign of a guilty conscience, or, it can actively work to assuage this fear by words of consolation. Because pride is driven by the desire to be and to be known to be on the right side of things, and because this desire is intrinsically competitive, it gives no incentive to judge mercifully.

Not surprisingly, then, we hear that these women have been criticized no matter what they have done. Some, he writes, have killed themselves rather than submit to rape. Others, realizing that it was not right to "escape another's criminal act by a misdeed of their own," have refused to do so (*ciu.* 1.17). Though Augustine could not more strongly state his opposition to suicide, his take on the former group of women is telling: "surely any man of compassion would be ready to excuse the emotions which led them to do this (*quis humanus affectus eis nolit ignosci*)?" (*ciu.* 1.17).[30] These women, then, are not to be judged harshly: instead it is the Christian's obligation to stand ready to forgive them, recognizing the great strain under which they found themselves. Regarding the other group, those strong enough to endure these emotions, Augustine makes it clear that anyone who takes their refusal to kill themselves "as a charge against them will lay himself open to a charge of foolishness" (ibid.). Here, then, Augustine's line is firm: those who have committed suicide under such great pressures are to be forgiven, and those who have found it within themselves not to do so are to be consoled. In all cases, what is called for is human feeling – a feeling animated by Christ's compassion.

Next, Augustine entertains an objection: "But, it will be said, there is the fear of being polluted by another's lusts" (*ciu.* 1.18). This is nothing other than a calling into question of the victim's moral fiber: surely, it suggests, in experiencing sexual pleasure, these women might have been corrupted. Reading in the question a desire to pass judgment on the woman, he reflects it back on the reader, asking, "What sane man (*quis eadem sana mente*)[31] will suppose that he has lost his purity if his body is seized and forced and used for the satisfaction of a lust that is not his own?" (ibid.). Augustine's way of proceeding is telling; of course, no one thinks this of himself. Augustine goes on, "Now suppose some woman with her mind corrupted ... in the act of going her going to her seducer to be defiled. ... Do we say she is chaste in body while she is on her way?" (ibid.). Here, the

---

[30] CCSL 47.18.   [31] CCSL 47.19.

return to a female example is significant. It extends the measure by which Augustine expects his readers to have judged their own case and applies it to the women under scrutiny. As the reader sees well in his own case, in the woman's likewise, it is her preexisting disposition that reveals how she will respond. Here, Augustine's reader is compelled to conclude that "when a woman has been ravished without her consenting," she has no reason to punish herself, and, those who think differently are applying a very different measure to her then they would to themselves (ibid.).

Recalling that Augustine began the book by juxtaposing imperial conquest with the extension of sanctuary in order to distinguish between pride and humility, here we see Augustine return to his diagnosis of pride's neediness in order to point out its social ramifications. Because pride constantly seeks reassurance of its own superiority, it loves to pass judgment on others. Yet, doing so, it forgets its own limitations and falls prey to the illusion of its own justice. Left to its own devices, pride becomes harsh, drawing more and more of its "inferiors" under its microscopic lens. Inevitably, it will draw in the vulnerable, unable to resist its ability to lord over them.[32] Insofar as a culture falls prey to own pride, Augustine thinks, it can only separate the impure from the pure according to its own standard. In this way, pride cannot provide a motive for genuine mercy. The only response, Augustine thinks, is to foster a fraternal correction grounded in *amor Dei*, which, I have argued, is exactly what Augustine strives to model.[33] Thus, through fulfilling his pastoral duty to the rape victims of his community, Augustine reveals the social fallout of a way of thinking animated by the drive for superiority.

THE NATURE OF ROMAN CONSUETUDO AND ITS INTERNALIZATION

Of course, it is difficult to for Augustine to discuss the plight of Roman rape victims without dealing with the specter of Lucretia. Famously killing

---

[32] In short, for Augustine, *amor sui* moves those who live out of it in a way that expresses its hegemonic nature. Necessarily, this love works against and distorts the natural impetus of the human person, which is toward society. Because *amor sui* is essentially self-referential, it cannot resist the drive to subjugate insofar as it can. Insofar as this desire takes on a moral tinge – which it is bound to in some – *consuetudo* will take on the mission of making a people morally perfect. This, however, constitutes a denial of the fall, a denial of the limits of human perfectibility that entails violence.

[33] That is, he strives to act in the knowledge that Christ incorporates his city into Himself in order to renew her loves through His love.

herself after Tarquin the younger raped her, Lucretia had become a model of female virtue for the entire Roman world. On Livy's telling, nothing Tarquin could say would seduce Lucretia, and "not even the fear of death could bend her will," only yielding when he threatened to frame her by lying her dead body next to that of a slave, Lucretia was well aware of her own innocence (Livy, *Ab urbe cond.*, 1.58).[34] Though her father and husband affirmed it too, declaring that Tarquin "alone was guilty," and arguing, like Augustine, that the mind alone could sin and "without intention there could be no guilt," the story ends with a disturbing twist. Crying out, Livy's Lucretia exclaimed,

"I am innocent of fault, but I will take my punishment. Never shall Lucretia provide a precedent for unchaste women to escape what they deserve." And with these words she drew a knife from under her robe, drove it into her heart, and fell forward, dead.[35]

Though Lucretia knew her own innocence, she killed herself in order that others would not use her as an excuse to escape punishments that they rightly deserved. Or, so she said. As we will see below, Augustine also suspects that she wanted to have the final word about her reputation and died so as to preserve it against a culture that could be all too harsh.

It is partly for Lucretia's sake that Augustine sharpens his critique of Roman *consuetudo*, already latent in his early discussion of the limits of civilization. Though Augustine classifies *consuetudo* as an external mechanism, there is an important way in which it can become internal: a way in which it can seep into the soul. This is why Augustine displays such urgency in his efforts to console rape victims. He knows that they, like Lucretia, feel pressure to display their innocence.[36] The precise character of this critique becomes clearer at the end of the book through his treatment of Scipio's political wisdom, which provides a hermeneutic for reading the rest of book 1. Scipio, Augustine writes, was wise in counseling against the destruction

---

[34] Livy, *The Early History of Rome*, 101.   [35] Ibid.

[36] Rightly, I think, Dennis Trout argues that "re-textualizing Lucretia was ... an act of radical discourse: by effacing a public symbol still current more than four hundred years after it was canonized in Livy's momumental [sic] history of Rome, Augustine intended to confront contemporaries with the culturally subversive implications of a Christian understanding which discounted the values that symbol had so long denoted." Dennis Trout, "Re-textualizing Lucretia: Cultural Subversion in the *City of God*," *Journal of Early Christian Studies* 2, no. 1 (1994): 55. Cf. Louis Swift, "Pagan and Christian Heroes in Augustine's *City of God*," *Augustinianum* 27, no. 3 (1987): 516.

of Carthage because he knew that "the removal of a great and strong and wealthy enemy state" would lead to Rome's corruption:

His intention was that lust should be restrained by fear, and should not issue in debauchery, and that the check on debauchery should stop greed from running riot. With those vices kept under restraint, the morality which supports a country flourished and increased, and permanence was given to the liberty which goes hand in hand with such morality. (*ciu.* 1.31)

Here, Scipio is praised for understanding that fear can be used to check disordered desire. Fear, Augustine explains, "restrains" vices by making sure that lust is not acted on – it makes sure that it does not "issue in ... debauchery" (ibid.). This knowledge is what allowed the "virile morality of Rome" to flourish. It is what allowed the early Romans to be the kind of men who could form a republic and even an empire. And yet, Augustine suggests, in the people as a whole, it was never anything but an external and temporary solution to the problem of *libido dominandi* (*ciu.* 2.18). As soon as the external mechanism was lifted – that is, as soon as the Romans conquered Carthage – Rome had no resources for restraining the desires that spring from self-love. Fear, in the end, did not *correct* the disordered desires of Roman citizens. It merely bridled them from the outside, as if by a contrary force: an imperial force.

If *consuetudo* is an extension of Roman law, a way to get inside the Romans' heads and hearts, it is no accident that Augustine appeals to Roman law in his analysis of Lucretia's motives. Picking up on Livy's suggestion that Lucretia yielded at the threat of being dishonorably framed, Augustine writes that it was, similarly, because Lucretia "loved glory," the reward of living out Roman *consuetudo* nobly, that she was driven to suicide (*ciu.* 1.19). As Augustine construes it, Rome has such control over Lucretia through its *consuetudo* that she passes judgment on herself in its stead. In examining Lucretia's self-punishment, he appeals to "Roman law and Roman Judges":

To execute a criminal without trial was, according to you a punishable offense. If anyone was charged in your courts with having put to death a woman not merely uncondemned but chaste and innocent, and this charge had been proved, would you not have chastised the culprit with appropriate severity? (ibid.)

To put this another way, Augustine thinks that Lucretia judged herself too harshly, that she might be exonerated in the eyes of others. Lucretia wanted to avoid shame, but in order to demonstrate the vehemence of her hatred for the crime, felt compelled to turn against herself: "That highly extolled Lucretia ... did away with the innocent, chaste, outraged Lucretia" (ibid.).

Thus, while Rome's *consuetudo* of glory is extremely effective at regulating behavior, it does have a cost. It is infused with a kind of severity.[37]

This, of course, is why Augustine turns next to Cato; because Cato represented the greatness of spirit that Rome so esteemed, it is particularly important that Augustine challenge the praise usually given to him. Again, the issue is suicide. Like that of Lucretia, Cato's example set a standard for the whole Roman world. In refusing to bow to Julius Caesar, he, above all others, had the strength of mind to act honorably, choosing death over disgrace. Dismantling this depiction of Cato, Augustine represents his suicide as a "mark of weakness," casting it as an inability to "sustain adversity," rather than a noble self-possession (*ciu.* 1.23). In short, in Augustine's telling, Cato preferred to die because he was not able to endure the humiliation of receiving Caesar's pardon. By custom, he was trained to avoid humiliation, and avoid it he did, to his own destruction. Asking why Cato did not encourage his son to follow his example, Augustine highlights the unnaturalness of this internalized *consuetudo*: though Cato thought it weakness, it was the strength of Cato's natural love for his son that prevented him from willing his destruction as well. Cato, in Augustine's eyes, saw what was good more clearly in his son's case than his own. Repainting Cato's self-possession as a kind of avoidance tactic, Augustine highlights the weakness of pride, which cannot bear to endure the kind of humiliations that chip away the noble self-image *amor sui* wants to promote. Custom, *consuetudo*, cannot mitigate this problem: it can only exacerbate it.

Again, we see, Augustine is critiquing the limits of systems of praise and blame that seem to produce heroic acts, but draw on honor as a foundation.[38] For Augustine, the desire to have and to keep a good name provides no truly social motivation, but is instead always competitive. Now, as we approach the end of book 1, we see that it is a force that paradoxically results in self-hatred, even self-destruction.[39] However, this

---

[37] I thank my reviewer for pointing out that another issue at play is the way in which Lucretia must lie in order to communicate the truth. Sensitive to the need to overstate her case if she were to successfully emerge from the scenario as heroic, Lucretia descended into the incoherent position of condemning herself as if she were guilty in order to demonstrate her innocence. Here we see the difficulty of trying to speak the truth in a fallen political community, especially without the support that God gives to the good conscience (cf. *ciu.* 1.19).

[38] Cf. J. E. Lendon, *The Empire of Honour: The Art of Government in the Roman World* (Oxford: Oxford University Press, 2001).

[39] For a deeper study of the logic of self-harm in Augustine, see David Meconi, "Ravishing Ruin," *Augustinian Studies* 45, no. 2 (2014): 227–246.

turning against the self is not only to be attributed to the insidious effect of *consuetudo*; it is not merely the result of something that comes upon the person from the outside. Rather, it is the meeting of an external phenomenon with an inclination already present in the heart: pride's distaste for imperfection.

With regard to his Christian audience, this anxiety about imperfection comes to the fore through the voice of Christians who fear sin. Telling us that he writes "for the benefit of men and women who suppose that they ought to lay violent hands on themselves to prevent themselves and not others from sinning, for fear that their own lust might be excited by another's, and that they might consent," Augustine identifies the fear of sinning as a primary justification put forward for suicide (*ciu.* 1.25):

There remains one situation in which it is supposed to be advantageous to commit suicide ... when the motive is to avoid falling into sin either through the allurements of pleasure or through the menaces of pain. (*ciu.* 1.27)

Responding to this supposition, Augustine goes on:

If a person has a duty to kill himself to avoid succumbing to sin ... does he suppose that he has to go on living so as to endure the pressures of the actual world, which is full of temptations at all times. ... Has perverse silliness so warped our judgment and distracted us from facing the truth? For on this assumption, why do we spend time on those exhortations to the newly baptized ... [if] there is available an excellent shortcut which avoids any danger of sinning; if we can persuade them to rush to a self-inflicted death immediately upon receiving remission of sins. (ibid.)

Augustine considers this, however, to be "quite crazy"; suicide, he writes, is "monstrous [*nefas*]"[40] and not a solution for anything (ibid.). In fact, it is a form of escapism predicated upon despair at the impossibility of achieving perfection here and now. This escapism, however, is what imperial *consuetudo* fosters – this is why Augustine needs to resist the earthly city's vision of the just city as the city of the "good."

CONCLUSION

Augustine ends book 1 very much where he began it: with a recalibration of Christ's friends and enemies. To the most brazen of these so-called enemies, he writes that Rome is in ruins only because its morals are in ruins: "You refuse to be held responsible for the evil that you do, while

---

[40] CCSL 47.28.

you hold the Christian era responsible for the evil which you suffer. . . . You have not restrained your sensuality. You have learned no salutary lesson from calamity. . . . *And yet* it is thanks to God's grace that you are still alive. In sparing you he warns you to amend your ways" (*ciu.* 1.35). Again, Augustine emphasizes the patience of the God who remains benevolent despite our ingratitude. Turning to the Church, he gives the concomitant warning:

She must bear in mind that among those very enemies are hidden her future citizens; and when confronted with them she must not think it a fruitless task to bear with their hostility until she finds them confessing the faith. In the same way, while the City of God is on pilgrimage in this world, she has in her midst some who are united with her in participation in the sacraments but who will not join her in the eternal destiny of the saints. . . . But, such as they are, we have less right to despair of the reformation of some of them, when some predestined friends, as yet unknown even to themselves, are concealed among our most open enemies. In truth, those two cities are interwoven and intermixed in this era. (ibid.)

Thus, to conclude, book 1 ends with a condemnation of any vision that assumes the just city is the city of the perfectly just; it is, in its entirety, an indictment of any attempt to boast in superiority, whatever its ground. Calling its readers to endure this life in a way that is open to God's transformative work, Augustine closes off any escape routes that might falsely suggest this transformation is not necessary. In short, book 1 is a microcosm of the psychagogic argument that unfolds over the rest of the *City of God*. Now, it is for us to trace this unfolding.

3

Exposing the Worldly Worldviews of Empires, Patriots, and Philosophers

Augustine's Psychagogic Strategy

At the end of the first chapter, I suggested that Augustine pairs an exposé of the earthly city with an argument as to our shared responsibility for it. He does this in order to enliven our desire to break free from the delusions and contradictions of the earthly city. And yet, for Augustine, there are a number of pseudo-solutions to the problem of *amor sui* that only appear to get beyond the logic of the earthly city. He must, therefore, guard his readers against premature imitations of true liberation lest they inadvertently remain within the earthly city's confines. To put this another way, Augustine has to challenge humanity's misplaced hope.[1] If the earthly city loves the world in the way that Scripture suggests, then it hopes for ultimate peace in the world; this is precisely what makes false solutions to the problem of *amor sui* so appealing. What is more, because it is easy to see that the world is not as it ought to be, it is easy to become dissatisfied with *some* aspect of the chaos generated by the earthly city and to construe its resolution as the whole solution. Hoping to help his readers become attuned to the insufficiency of this approach, Augustine structures the first half of *City of God* as an indictment of all worldviews generated by the earthly city. In other words, he seeks to shed light on all the ways in which his readers' own viewpoints, supposedly a response to some evil other, remain "of" the earthly city. This intention forms the

---

[1] While acknowledging that the earthly city's hope is misplaced, Michael Lamb's look at Augustinian hope in a political context provides a worthy counterpoint to what I am emphasizing in this chapter. Michael Lamb, "Between Presumption and Despair: Augustine's Hope for the Commonwealth," *American Political Science Review* 112, no. 4 (2018): 1036–1049.

structure of his psychagogic argument, that is, his attempt to cure his readers of distorted vision.

Following Augustine's argument, I find that books 1–9 in particular are constituted by Augustine's attempt to undercut ever more compelling, but similarly premature solutions to the problems generated by *amor sui*. Starting out, as we have seen, with a response to those who blame the Christians, Augustine's argument quickly balloons to a challenge against any mind-set that would leave readers in the earthly city. His message throughout is as follows: despite the earthly city's efforts to mitigate the problems its own self-love generates, its solutions to the world's problems can only ever be *simulacra* – parodies of the true solution. These *simulacra* are the solutions offered by empire, by political philosophy, and by philosophy as a way of life. Beginning with the promises offered by civilization, I trace the challenges Augustine makes to Roman *consuetudo* (custom) and its ability to yield just politics. Turning to his treatment of the philosopher-statesmen, I show that these, too, are incapable of undoing the political damage done by the earthly city, willing as they are to endorse falsehoods for the sake of political stability. Turning finally to Augustine's treatment of the philosopher, I find that he stresses the inadequacy of any virtue rooted in self-sufficiency; insofar as it is rooted in the self, it remains proud. Ultimately, I argue, Augustine leaves his readers with no way to solve the problem of *amor sui* on their own. Sealing them in at all sides, Augustine points to one way out: through the Mediator.[2]

IMPERIAL PROMISES

The first *simulacrum* of the way out of the earthly city is the liberation promised by Rome itself. This is the first because it is the first to be known; Rome advertises its message everywhere. We have already seen that in a world that is caught up in barbarism, Rome presented itself as the shining light of civilization: the Just City. For Augustine, recall, Rome is the impostor city. The earthly city's crowning achievement, Rome has managed to imitate God in the most convincing way possible: it spares the humble and beats

---

[2] Dodaro has an exhaustive account of how Augustine conceives of the "just and justifying" Christ as the Mediator. Dodaro, *Christ and the Just Society*, 107. Compellingly, Dodaro argues that Christ stands at the center of Augustine's whole worldview, so that in him, humanity is offered a new path toward virtue "freed from the pretensions of moral self-reliance." Ibid., 71. In brief, Christ comes to cure our ignorance and weakness by teaching us to rely on him and helping us to rely on him.

down the proud. It brings civilization to a savage world. It calls its emperor *salvator mundi*.

It does not take long for Augustine to begin pointing out the many ways in which Rome fails to live up to its self-endowed reputation. Yet, what troubles Augustine is not just that Rome falls short of its self-image, but that it *pretends not to* – and, to a large degree, succeeds in this ruse. This drive to keep up appearances, Augustine thinks, is why the Romans needed to blame the sack of 410 on something un-Roman. To say that Rome fell to Alaric, not because of a corruption related to its imperial character, but because of an un-Roman religion is to keep Rome on a pedestal, unsullied by the less savory aspects of its history. The idea of a beautiful Rome lost to the past, but always on the cusp of being regained, might keep the Romans devoted to their city – it might even improve their city for a time – but it does not allow them to see Rome for what it is.[3] Unless Augustine drives home the message that Rome is not what she claims to be, his readers are at risk of falling for and, as a result, getting stuck in the imperial project placed before them. As Rowan Williams puts it, Augustine wants to save his readers from "the doomed project of organizing our own moral world and refusing to return to our true beginning, which is not in us."[4] The Roman *literati*'s myth of *Roma Aeterna* is but one iteration of this doomed project.

Augustine's ultimate concern with this kind of project follows upon his fears about the tyrannical bent of the earthly city. He is worried about convincing *simulacra* because they are designed to captivate us. Augustine's Rome, like Augustine's Devil, wants status and will squander its citizens' lives in order to maintain it (*ciu.* 5.18). Moreover, insofar as Roman citizens are animated by the imperial mission handed onto them, they will be willing to squander each others' lives for its sake as well, and the cycle of bloodshed will continue.[5] Thus, Augustine spends the first five

---

[3] As Oliver O'Donovan notes in his famous essay, "empire, because it unifies us, tempts us to think that the constraints [of the human condition] can be overcome; but in gaining ground for one of us at one point, it loses another. . . . The story of human progress which it [that is, empire] represented was illusory." O'Donovan, "Augustine's 'City of God' XIX and Western Political Thought," 109.

[4] Rowan Williams, "Insubstantial Evil," 104.

[5] I make this argument this more fully in "Augustine's Ciceronian Response to the Ciceronian Patriot," *Perspectives on Political Science Perspectives on Political Science* 45, no. 2 (2016): 113–124, reprinted in *Augustine's Political Thought*, 200–222. Thomas W. Smith makes a similar argument in "The Glory and Tragedy of Politics," in *Augustine and Politics*, ed. John Doody, Kevin Hughes, and Kim Paffenroth (Lanham, MD: Lexington Books, 2005), 187–216.

chapters deconstructing Rome's self-image in order to undercut the temptation it poses to its citizens. We will explore this in greater detail in the next chapter, but now it is enough to note that Augustine writes lest love of Rome be one more reason for its citizens to tarry in the earthly city. For Augustine, Rome presents itself as an escape, coaxing its subjects into seeking their personal fulfillment in the imperial system. Certainly, Augustine places a large amount of blame for this on the statesmen who arrange it, yet, in some ways the scheme is self-perpetuating. The bulk of those who perpetuate the Roman *simulacrum* do so on a subconscious level (*ciu.* 4.32). The induction of each successive generation into a world synonymous with Rome is rarely conspiratorial. Instead, it happens in the haze of custom.

In order to get a better sense of this, it is helpful to turn to Augustine's *Confessions*, where he talks about the force of Roman custom (*consuetudo*) in his own formation. Propelled into a world more interested in avoiding barbarisms than barbaric behavior (*conf.* 1.18.29), Augustine recalls how he grew more wary of committing a grammatical error than of succumbing to jealously of those who did not (*conf.* 1.19.30). Noting how carefully his teachers observed the linguistic conventions handed on to them, he reflects on how this conventional world, woven around him through the consent and participation of the adults in his life, served as a shroud, separating him from the natural world. Those who had the words to interpret reality interpreted it with one voice, saying "prestige matters."

Indeed, this is not surprising. As Augustine warns in *City of God*, it is easy for a human community to set up a social order that originates with a human lie precisely because it is a *human* lie: something that human beings would like to be true (*ciu.* 14.4). Yet, to rewrite the meaning of things according to shared perceived utility is to make that social order into its own foundation; it is to *replace* the natural order with *consuetudo*.[6]

---

[6] For a glimpse into how Augustine thinks of *consuetudo* in a broader sense, his discussion of the difference between superstitious and useful human institutions in book 2 of *De Doctrina Christiana* is particularly illuminating (II.19.29–II.40.60). Essentially, the question there is whether human institutions – the conventions that human beings have established rather than discovered – can be used, or whether they are intrinsically abusive. Can one *only* participate in them in a way that blocks the way to God, or can one refer one's participation in them *to* God – can one act in them of *amor Dei*? By acknowledging that some human institutions *could* be referred to God, he allows for a renewal (or use) of certain established practices, without indicating that they are ever practiced in a neutral manner. Conventions are human inventions justified by our choice to institute them. And yet, because the human community is a fallen community, *consuetudo* as we see it in the world is all too often shaped by *amor sui*. By indicating that our choice to perpetuate

Because the strength of any social order lies in its members' consensus about what is worth loving and doing, to the degree that a society is rooted in *amor sui,* it will promote the behaviors that lead to prestige and pay little attention to those that do not "pay off." It is this shared love of prestige, Augustine explains, that causes a society to value a rare jewel more than a slave who is a fellow human being (*ciu.* 11.6). To own such a jewel is to be set apart; to call a slave one's equal is to be brought back to earth. Thus, in *Confessions,* Augustine traces his parents' and teachers' praise of conventional virtues – persuasiveness, virility – back to the "same intoxication" that blotted God "out of this world's memory and led it to love the creature instead" (*conf.* 2.3.6).[7] Surrounded by adults drunk with this love, the young Augustine is ushered into the imperial bureaucracy, bidden to return with whatever prestige he can garner.

Though Augustine acknowledges the benevolence in their intentions – Augustine, recall, was a relatively poor provincial from the backwaters of the empire, so it makes sense that his parents saw his talents as a way out – he cannot help but think they were willing to sacrifice too much in the name of imperial prestige. One significant effect of his parents and teachers' love of prestige, Augustine reflects, is that it rendered them incapable of effectively uprooting the same desire in him (*conf.* 2.3.6). Instead, all they could do was to take note of its childish manifestations, striving to subdue them in the name of serious pursuits (*conf.* 1.9.15). Too taken with the empire's promise of a better life, Augustine's parents and teachers abandoned him to the *concupiscentiae* that were tearing him apart. Some even encouraged him in these desires, so long as their effects could be boasted in.[8]

---

something of these conventions, or even to create new customs, has the potential to become a choice made in harmony with God's will, he distinguishes between the refer-ability (if you will) of certain categories of human institutions *in se,* and the question of what they look like when practiced in *amor sui* or *amor Dei.* In *De Doctrina Christiana,* his concern is their refer-ability. Some customs, he tells his readers, are in themselves necessary and always have the potential to be practiced in harmony with God's will – such as grammar (III.29.40); some can be in harmony with God's will in a specific time and place – such as the patriarchs' practice of polygamy (III.20.28); but some are intrinsically abusive – such as the rites by which humans contract with demons (II.20.30). The line between the intrinsically abusive customs and those that can be referred, however, is different from the line between those that are referred and those that, in practice, are not. The question of how potentially useful customs are inhabited remains and depends on the shape that people's loves give them in the concrete world. *This* is the question fore-fronted in *City of God.*

[7] Augustine, *The Confessions,* 65.

[8] Here is where Augustine describes his mother, perhaps too harshly, as still lingering on the outskirts of Babylon; he faults her for putting off his marriage because she feared having

Thus, while Augustine sees the social nature of human beings as something fundamentally good, his reflections on childhood highlight the way in which he thinks human sociability can be turned to ill-use (cf. *doct. chr.* 7.*praef*). Augustine is not understated in his criticism of this phenomenon:

Woe, woe, woe to you, you flood of human custom! … Oh hellish river, human children clutching their fees are still pitched into you to learn about these exploits [that is, those of Jupiter the adulterer], and general interest is aroused when education is publically touted in the forum. … You clash your rocks and set up a great din: "This is the place to acquire literacy; here you will develop the eloquence essential to persuasion and argument." Really? (*conf.* 1.16.25–26)[9]

Thrown headlong into a world steeped in *consuetudo*, each generation is left to navigate it for itself. Worse, this navigation is an uphill battle; *consuetudo*, Augustine thinks, summons and enflames the *concupiscentiae* to which the human heart is already prone. As such, it is difficult to gain perspective on human custom. So, while Augustine sees vulnerability as an aspect of the human condition designed to bind humanity together, the way each generation behaves toward the next easily becomes the opposite of what it ought to be.

Thus, it is not surprising that Augustine sees this aspect of *consuetudo* as a grave problem. While, on one level, he does think that we participate in communities because we see something in them *for us*, he also thinks we are less autonomous than we would like to believe (*ciu.* 19.21). Because we are influenced by others before we even have a chance to evaluate this influence, Augustine sees human society as treacherous ground; many *simulacra* are on offer and many dead ends effectively disguise themselves as worthy pursuits.

Returning to *City of God*, we see Augustine is addressing the very same problem in his critique of empire. Empire, Augustine thinks, is frighteningly well equipped to gather workers into its project; it is the purveyor of prestige par excellence.[10] In order to undercut the absolutizing tendency of the Roman horizon (wherein everything points back to the glory of

---

a wife would hinder his academic success: "she warned me to live chastely, but did not extend her care to restraining within the bounds of conjugal love … this behavior of mine" (*conf.*, 2.3.8). Augustine, *The Confessions*, 66.

[9] Ibid., 55–56.

[10] Reflecting on the psychology undergirding Roman empire's system of honor, Lendon writes: "A rhetoric of concealment so elaborated invites investigation in its own right: permitting the efficient exercise of brute power under an unobjectionable veil, it allows proud men to obey without balking, orders to be given without inspiring hatred, sacks of gold to be accepted without shame by men who could not bear to be imagined other men's hirelings. First, then, honour is part of power because it acts as a cloak or a lubricant to other forms of power." Lendon, *The Empire of Honour*, 24–25.

Rome), Augustine exposes the futility of glory, showing the fame that the empire can offer to be a mere shadow of the immortal happiness that would actually be fulfilling (*ciu.* 5.10–18). He also exposes the motives fueling the imperial elite (*ciu.* 4.32). If his parents and teachers are the enchained captives staring at the cave wall, someone is projecting the shadows onto that wall.

At its core, Augustine explains, the imperial project is necessarily animated by pride.[11] Because pride seeks to imitate God by imposing its vision of peace on the world, the proud city, animated by proud citizens, puts all its energy into bringing *its* goals to bear on the world, and, subsequently, into preserving this state of affairs (*ciu.* 19.12). There is, Augustine thinks, a kind of twisted prerogative in the desire for mastery, as its very self-esteem poses in the proud mind as a qualification for leadership: peace, the proud say, cannot exist without *me* at the helm (*ciu.* 19.12). This belief is the source of the imperial prerogative; it justifies the audacity with which Rome divides the proud from the humble in order to crush them.

In 19.12, perhaps his most pessimistic assessment of fallen human nature, Augustine paints a picture that taps into the psychology of pride that we have already studied. Its warning for politics is as follows: insofar as a political community is weighed down by *amor sui*, its animating vision of peace will not yield a genuinely common good. Rather, it will only (in a truncated sense) benefit the powerful, which is to say that it will be shaped by their designs. If their plan does happen to benefit others, it only does so in a way that is convenient or necessary. As for getting the rest of the community on board with parts of the plan that are not to their benefit, this is a matter of violence or manipulation. There is little point in going out of one's way to appeal to those who cannot threaten the status quo. It is this kind of analysis that fuels the ancient protest that what masquerades as justice is often merely the will of the stronger. The awakening into the realization that the political world is a cave, a mere horizon cut off and controlled by invested opinion, is the birth of philosophy.

PHILOSOPHIC POLITICS

Augustine, of course, well understood that classical philosophy saw culture as a cave; ever since Plato penned his famous allegory, its very project

---

[11] Cavadini is helpful on this point, especially in "Ideology and Solidarity," in *Augustine's City of God: A Critical Guide*, ed. James Wetzel (Cambridge: Cambridge University Press, 2012), 93–110.

had been to get beyond this cave. Happiness, the philosophers taught, was more than prestige, power, or wealth; it had to do with the soul, with virtue, and with truth. Famously, in *Confessions,* Augustine describes how he was converted to philosophy by Cicero's *Hortensius*: a book, ironically enough, assigned in the schools of rhetoric without a thought to its content (*conf.* 3.4.7–8). Augustine describes how it was Cicero's message, and not just his style that touched his heart, awakening his longing for the true, the good, and the beautiful wherever he might find them. Once and for all, the young Augustine had come to see the world of convention as something to be transcended.

Because of this, however much he criticizes philosophy as a project of autonomous self-mastery, Augustine is respectful of philosophy as the journey toward the real. If the imperial answer to chaos, the imposition of a common peace and custom, is partial, the philosophical answer is, at the very least, less partial. By definition, it is open to a way out of the conventional. Still, for as much as Augustine sees the philosophic life as a significant step in the right direction, he is also wary of the ways in which it can seem like *the* escape route out of the earthly city. For Augustine, philosophy, especially in its Platonic form, is a forerunner, but *only* a forerunner to Christianity (*ciu.* 8.9). This is why he pushes for a philosophy willing to see itself as such: willing to accept revelation as a gift that recasts its old conclusions.[12] And so, it is with both respect and scrutiny that Augustine engages with the philosophic answer to the political problem.

In many ways, philosophy is the answer to the political problem. If political life is all too dominated by self-interested statesmen touting self-interested visions of justice, the conversion of these statesmen to philosophy would go far in reshaping society. They would enact good laws, which, in turn, would form good citizens, which, in turn, would preserve the political community. To reinstate this cycle in Rome is Cicero's purpose in writing works of political philosophy, and he is not alone. Many of the Roman *literati* hoped that if they could just cultivate public-spirited citizens, Rome would recover its health.

In fact, running throughout the political texts with which *City of God* 1–5 engages is the concern that myopic visions of the human good have led citizens to pursue private goods over and against the public good. To

---

[12] This is not always easy; as Pierre Manent has written, Christianity can seem "to weaken or blur what is most proper, most sharp, most 'interesting' " in the traditions it claims to fulfill. Manent, *Metamorphoses of the City*, 294.

Sallust and Cicero in particular, these private goods really are *privata* – lacking goodness. Obtained at the expense of the common good, those who pursue them lack not only a concern for the common good, but also the understanding that genuine personal goods align with the common good. This is why Sallust peppers his portrayal of the villain Catiline with hints as to Catiline's deficient sense of the good. It is also why Cicero lambasts Sulla for mistaking military advantage for happiness, and, by example, doing more to destroy Rome than anyone before or since (Cicero, *De Officiis*, 2.viii.27–29). Both Sallust and Cicero aim to repair the damage done to the republic by selfish visions of the good life.

It is to those who share this patriotic concern that Augustine appeals in the early books of *City of God*. By having Rome's complacent citizens confess that they have allowed those in power to do whatever they like so long as they could retain *their own* freedoms and pleasures (*ciu.* 2.20), Augustine's message to the patriotic reader is as follows: Rome was sacked for the very reason your own historians would have predicted. Too many Romans have preferred their own comfort over the demands of justice, and now Rome has paid the price (*ciu.* 5.12).[13] Here, Augustine trades on two ideas fundamental to classical political philosophy: the idea that a society needs to train its citizens into their sociability, and the idea that vice distorts a person's vision of justice while virtue sharpens it. By building these ideas into his political analysis, Augustine is able to pit Rome's most respectable voices against that of the mob. He is able to appropriate the most salient tenets of classical political philosophy to counter those seeking a scapegoat for the fallout of their own complacency.

THE PROBLEM OF CHAOS

And yet, for as much as Augustine accepts the idea that philosophy can enlarge statesmen's visions of the good life in a way that redounds to the common good, he is careful to point out that philosophy cannot actually bring about a just society. It cannot do this for the simple reason that it can never convince the whole citizen body to love justice for its own sake. While Augustine does not deny the effect a few good men can have in a given society, if they happen to attain power at the right time, he thinks they will always be swimming against the current (*ciu.* 5.12). Philosophy might cast itself as the cure of souls, but as soon as it turns its face toward

---

[13] Of course, it would not have occurred to the Romans that their city, destined for imperial greatness, might be just one empire in a long series that was about to be replaced.

politics, it has to deal with the problem of the many. Confronted with the fact that most people do not have access to philosophical ideas, or if they do, do not care to live a philosophic life, the philosopher-statesman must decide how he will go about directing the unphilosophical toward a justice to which they do not willingly tend. Ideally, the philosopher would avoid this problem by shaping the city from its founding. In this way, its citizens would be formed in just habits and opinions from the beginning.[14] But of course, it is unclear whether this has ever happened, and it certainly did not happen in Rome (*ciu.* 6.4). In Rome, the philosopher comes to the political scene *in media res*.

Augustine illustrates the frustration this fact causes for the patriotic philosopher by relaying and analyzing Varro's political philosophy. Here, above all, he highlights the tenuous relationship between political philosophy and *consuetudo*. Because the classical political philosophy with which Augustine is in dialogue is the progeny of the Greek civic republican tradition, it is deeply aware that a city's public practices and institutions are the predominant influence on most people's lives and beliefs (*ciu.* 2.7). Philosophy, almost by definition, is reserved for the few. Few have the opportunity to transcend the horizon communicated to them by the city, and even fewer have the desire. Because of this, the philosopher's assessment of the city has traditionally been twofold.

First, the philosopher sees that the customs of any given city have been either instituted or used by its statesmen to bind citizens together (*ciu.* 4.32). With the perennial threat of strife looming on the horizon, political leaders ask, how can we unite the members of our community to a common purpose, when they naturally tend toward divergent goals? A shared set of values and habits, the philosopher and the statesman understand, binds a community together. This unitive function of custom, both realize, is conducive to the city's prosperity because it provides much needed stability. That said, the second thing that the philosopher notes is that the content of this custom is all too often a product of and concession to vice. It is rarely in conformity with justice. In light of this analysis, the philosopher hopes to reshape these institutions, practices and opinions in light of true justice. Of course, in order to do so, he must have sizable social influence. This is where the dance between saying too little and too much comes into play. To say too much is to go the way of Socrates, but to

---

[14] Here, I am sketching the classical philosophical paradigm; an Augustinian political philosophy would undoubtedly highlight the insurmountable problem of sin hampering even the most rigorous attempt to educate citizens in virtue and right opinion.

say too little is to neglect one's duty to truth and justice. Where Varro comes down on this is not where Augustine would have him come down on it, but both agree that philosophy has its limits.

It is interesting that Augustine first introduces philosophy as a potential cultural influence midway through his argument as to why it would be a bad idea to reinstate the worship of Rome's traditional gods. Against those calling for a reinstatement of these rites in the wake of the recent disaster, Augustine argues on two fronts. After dealing with those who think angry gods must be appeased, Augustine turns to a more sophisticated audience: those who think the atrophy of the Roman cult signaled the loss of an important political institution. In response to these, Augustine highlights the disconnect between the *idea* of civil religion and its Roman reality. This is not an institution manufacturing good citizens.

The Roman gods, he is in the middle of telling this audience, were incapable of forming good citizens; they were not good role models and did not give sound moral advice (*ciu.* 2.22, inter alia). As such, to return to the Roman cult would be a step backward: the Christian God at least models and counsels virtue (*ciu.* 2.28).[15] It is at this point in the argument that philosophy enters the picture. Many of the philosophic schools, Augustine has an imaginary interlocutor interject, had robust teachings about the good life long before Christ came, and this was to Rome's benefit. Importantly, Augustine concedes the point. However, Augustine's question is whether philosophy is strong enough to counteract the negative social effects of *consuetudo*. Augustine thinks that it is not, and for two reasons: "these activities belong to Greece, not Rome, and even if they do belong to Rome – because Greece is a Roman province – they are not the commandments of the gods, but the findings of men" (*ciu.* 6.11).[16] By suggesting that philosophy only has a place in Rome because Rome has absorbed Greece into its empire, Augustine asserts that philosophy's place in Rome is *only ever* on the empire's terms. Human, it cannot touch the gods. The product of a conquered people, it cannot disturb the role of cultic worship in the imperial project.

---

[15] Fortin is good on this: Ernest Fortin, "Augustine and Roman Civil Religion: Some Critical Reflections," in *Classical Christianity and the Political Order*, ed. Brian J. Benestad (Lanham, MD: Rowman and Littlefield, 1996), 85–106.

[16] This is especially important given that Augustine's point in books 2 and 3 is to show that the demons masquerading as Roman gods have a role in encouraging the vices and passions dragging Roman mores into *consuetudo*; if *consuetudo* is not merely a human problem, but a problem related to false mediators, then it makes sense that Augustine is highlighting how the merely human philosophers cannot hope to overpower it.

Indeed, Augustine reminds his readers, from the perspective of the Roman establishment, philosophy was something of a threat. To communicate this, Augustine has Mucius Scaevola speak against the philosophers in the name of the Roman Cult. Augustine could not have chosen a better candidate; Scaevola was well known as a staunch supporter of Roman tradition and something of a martyr to the cause. As Augustine has already told us in book 3, he was the first Pontiff Maximus to be publicly murdered. Trying to protect the cult against Sulla's invading forces, he "threw his arms round the altar of Vesta, whose temple was regarded by the Romans as the most sacred sanctuary; but he was murdered there, and his blood all but extinguished that sacred flame which was kept alight by the ceaseless attendance of the Vestal Virgins" (*ciu.* 3.24). So much for Scaevola's attempt to stop the decay of Roman tradition.

Drawing out the implications of Scaevola's unwavering devotion to the Roman cult, Augustine focuses on his analysis of the different theological traditions informing Roman religion. Scaevola, Augustine tells us, identifies three; one coming from the poets, a second from the philosophers, and third from the statesmen. While Scaevola dismisses the poetic tradition as "trivial nonsense," its falsity is not of great concern to him (*ciu.* 4.27). This is the first red flag. What is of concern is the philosophic tradition. Philosophy, Scaevola thinks, has "no value for a commonwealth" because its teachings are at best irrelevant and at worst, harmful (ibid.).

Augustine points to two philosophical teachings that Scaevola found harmful: first, that Hercules, Aesculapius, Castor and Pollux were not gods, but dead men, and second, that the temples could not possibly have images of the true gods "because the true God has neither sex nor age" (*ciu.* 4.27). It is not difficult to see why these teachings were a threat to the Roman cult; if the Roman military heroes did not become gods because of their bravery, then the hope that one can emulate their bravery for a divine reward is undermined; if the temples do not have true images of the gods, then what are the people really worshiping?

What Augustine takes issue with here is what he has already criticized Varro for endorsing: the idea that it is politically expedient to deceive the many. Varro, he has already explained, believed that it was advantageous to the community that soldiers should think themselves of divine ancestry because the belief would make them "bolder" and "more energetic" in military endeavors (*ciu.* 3.4). That Varro endorses this belief "even if it is not true" suggests to Augustine that "many ostensibly religious rites" are actually the products of wisdom of this sort.[17] Varro might represent the wisdom of the sages, but, Augustine exclaims, "what a wide field" this wisdom "offers to falsehood" (*ciu.* 3.4).

Augustine goes on to trace the implications of this concession to falsehood for Varro's engagement with Roman culture, focusing in particular on the limits it places on Varro's capacity to work for cultural renewal. Varro, Augustine thinks, is remarkably candid about the degree to which he bows to a tradition out of harmony with what his philosophy would have it be (*ciu.* 3.4). While he "would have written on the principles dictated by nature, if he had been founding a new community," because he was born into "a community already ancient," he judged it necessary to conform to Roman tradition (*ciu.* 6.4). To Augustine, this is not surprising; if one message was sent by Rome to its citizens, it would be that Rome's institutions and traditions must be preserved at all costs.

Taking Varro as the representative of the Roman *literati* who wish to limit the effects of the vulgar on Roman culture, Augustine considers whether their approach – constrained as it is by Rome's imperial terms – is really capable of producing cultural renewal. He notes how Varro treats the civic, the poetic and the philosophical theological traditions. From Varro's perspective, the leeway the philosophers have in criticizing unnatural theologies is restricted to the poetic. The poets, Varro is not afraid to say, have created a mythology about the gods that is "false, degraded, and unworthy" of divine beings (*ciu.* 6.4).

Yet, Augustine points out, in saying this, Varro actually goes no further than Scaevola. While Augustine credits Varro for doing what he can to bring his brighter readers to philosophy, he is more interested

---

[17] In a striking reflection on this aspect of Roman society, Charles Norris Cochrane writes that in the elite Roman worldview shared by figures like Livy and Cicero, "religion resolves itself purely and simply into a matter of policy. In this respect the cults authorized by the college of pontiffs (*religions licitae*) correspond precisely to the demands of idealist thought. In origin and purpose, in the various techniques of propitiation and augury which they employ, in their ritual of purification and appeasement, their one and only object is to maintain the 'peace of the gods' (*pax deorum*). And for this literally anything will serve, so long as it is felt to be 'politically' expedient. ... But to say this is to suggest that the spirit of official religion was utterly pragmatic. Accordingly, it becomes purely irrelevant to inquire into its substantial truth or falsehood; 'formally' speaking, a question of this kind simply does not arise, though philosophers may well amuse themselves with such investigations, if they have the inclination to do so, provided that, in legal phraseology, they do nothing 'to upset the minds of the lightheaded ...' Against this they stood firmly on guard, ready, in case of necessity, to crush it with the full force of the state." Cochrane, *Christianity and Classical Culture*, 111–112.

in highlighting the degree to which the empire has defined the parameters of Varro's imagination. While Varro is genuinely more concerned about the poetic than Scaevola, somehow, Augustine wants to suggest, he cannot act on this concern. He cannot criticize the Roman cult because it would be tantamount to an attack on the very foundation of civic life. In short, Augustine's Varro is constrained by his civic piety.

Beginning to unravel Varro's contradiction, Augustine presents Varro's approach to civic theology as an esoteric attempt to exercise what little freedom he has.[18] The way Varro separates civic theology from natural theology, Augustine writes, is "surely tantamount to an admission that civil theology itself is false" (*ciu.* 6.4). Thus, looking closely at Varro's argument, he notes how Varro sought to bypass the limits placed upon him by political opinion through esotericism. "Marcus Varro," he exclaims, "you are the shrewdest of men, and without a shadow of a doubt, the most erudite" (*ciu.* 6.6). By treating human affairs before divine affairs, Augustine explains, Varro shows that what Rome *calls* divine affairs have actually been made up. Furthermore, by criticizing fabulous theology for qualities civil theology also possesses, he manages to indict civil theology without offending its powerful supporters. Taking Varro's analysis seriously, Augustine thinks that the careful reader can only come to one conclusion: Varro genuinely wants to help his readers worship the natural gods, rather than the gods of the city.

And yet, for Varro, natural theology can never really have a place in the city. Because Varro realizes that it is actually the poets' stories that draw people to the temples – they are what capture the people's imaginations (*ciu.* 6.6) – the best he thinks he can hope for is a civic theology that takes what it can of natural theology and makes it enticing by mixing it with poetic theology. While a philosophic statesman like himself ought to cultivate philosophic theology more than poetic theology, he cannot dispense with the latter entirely, simply because most people are "more inclined to believe the poets than the 'naturalists'" (ibid.). This cannot be helped. Philosophy, it seems, can only help the philosophical.

---

[18] For treatments of Augustine's criticisms of esotericism, see Fortin, "Augustine," 178, and "Augustine and the Problem of Christian Rhetoric," *Augustinian Studies* 5 (1974): 85–100; Thomas Harmon, "The Few, the Many, and the Universal Way of Salvation Augustine's Point of Engagement with Platonic Political Thought," in *Augustine's Political Thought*, ed. Richard Dougherty (Rochester, NY: Rochester University Press, 2019), 146n5; and Douglas Kries, "Augustine against Political Critics of Christianity," *American Catholic Philosophical Quarterly* 74, no. 1 (2000), 90.

For Augustine, Varro's writings reveal that pre-Christian Rome was held together by a fellowship of falsehood (*consortio falsitatis*)[19] between the poets and the priests. There was no real separation between the two orders – they each had a role in the imperial mission. One sowed vice, the other reaped it: "the theology of the theatre proclaims the degradation of the people, the theology of the city makes that degradation into an amenity" (*ciu.* 6.6). By taking advantage of the people's love of scandal, glory and prestige instead of doing what it could to foster virtue in them, Rome neglected its responsibility to its citizens and overturned the natural order in which the political is meant to serve the personal. Philosophy should have objected to this; Socrates did.

Both Varro and Augustine understand that poetic civil religion has a leg up in the city because it speaks to a people's shared desires. Furthermore, it grants a divine legitimacy to behaviors that philosophic men will not countenance. Still, Augustine maintains, the philosophers are more complicit in their pragmatism than they would admit.[20] To be sure, the philosophers do their best to contain the excesses this poetic culture creates, but this does not amount to much. They criticize the vulgarity of Roman myths and reinterpret the more unsavory ones as allegories for natural truths (*ciu.* 7.19). Just as Varro hopes that reading his books will convert others to natural philosophy, but has little way to speak to the culture at large, these philosophers' reinterpretation of the myths bear little fruit; they might interpret the myth of Saturn's cannibalism as an allegory for the changing seasons, but this reinterpretation will not alter the reason why most people enjoy plays about Saturn or worship at his temple (*ciu.* 6.8). In the end, philosophy can only reassure the *literati* themselves; it cannot change the broader culture.

Thus, while Varro aims to take a moderate position, Augustine thinks he concedes too much. There is, Augustine thinks, a line between idealism and realism, but it is not where Varro draws it. Like Varro, Augustine thinks it would be unrealistic to hope that people would flock to the temple of Plato instead of the temples where "the Galli are mutilated, eunuchs are consecrated, madmen gash themselves" (*ciu.* 2.7). Both Augustine and Varro recognize that the pull of these rites is rooted in vice (*ciu.* 6.6).[21] Still, it is one thing to see the limits of philosophy and

---

[19] CCSL 47.173.

[20] Cf. Ryan K. Balot, "Truth, Lies, Deception and Esotericism: The Case of St. Augustine," in *Augustine's Political Thought*, ed. Richard Dougherty (Rochester, NY: Rochester University Press, 2019), 173–199.

[21] Alluding to what is perhaps his favorite example of this – one that, importantly, also appears in the passages on *consuetudo* we have been studying from the *Confessions* – he

another to actively take advantage of – and thereby foster – the vices of the unphilosophical. By choosing to leverage the people's ignorance and vice, Varro participates in the habits that pull Rome's public project farther and farther away from the common good.

Augustine's goal in giving this rather incisive critique is to emphasize the power Roman *consuetudo* had over the minds of even its most brilliant citizens.[22] Varro could criticize poetic theology, but he was still bound to praise cultic worship. Likewise, Cicero could laugh at auguries, but he was still an augur (*ciu.* 4.30). Even Seneca, who did manage to write against Roman civil religion, was compelled to endorse participation in its public ceremonies and rituals, though he taught that the Wise Man was to have no religious attachment to them (*ciu.* 6.10). He, like Varro, thought that it was un-patriot to disturb the Roman cult.

Returning to Augustine's analysis of Cicero's civic piety, we see that he begins to look beneath the patriot's claim. Cicero, he argues, could only criticize superstition as long as he praised the religion of his forefathers at the same time. Augustine goes on to explain that this was difficult in that the religion of Cicero's forefathers was, in many ways, superstitious. That he felt compelled to try, however, was due to the immense shadow Rome cast in Cicero's mind. For Augustine, what Cicero experienced as the will of Rome was in some way the institutionally enshrined voice of the Romans.[23] Like Hermes Trismegistus's ensouled wooden idols, Rome seemed to have acquired a *persona* of its own through some kind of divinization process (cf. *ciu.* 8.24). Yet, because Roman *traditio* is inevitably of human origin, Rome ends up speaking as a mouthpiece for the custom-bound majority. As such, Augustine thinks, it is not clear where filial piety ends and the fear of the majority begins. What Cicero was free to say in his books, Augustine

quotes a play written by the poet Terence. In it, a young boy encounters a depiction of Jupiter as a golden shower. Delighting in Jupiter's adultery because it gives him an "authoritative precedent" to imitate, he exclaims: "And should I, a lowly mortal, shrink to do the like? Nay, thus I did, and with a right good will!" (*ciu.* 2.7).

[22] John Milbank makes a similar observation in *Theology and Social Theory*, noting that while the philosophers had "intimations of an idea of goodness" beyond that of the imperial, they could never "fully escape" Rome's assumptions about the good because these ideas were "inscribed at the level of myth and ritual." From this, Milbank concludes, I think rightly, that changes at the level of ritual are the only way to "really alter public belief and practice"; they are the only thing that can make "a genuinely non-polytheistic ontology possible." Millbank, *Theology and Social Theory*, 393.

[23] As I will later argue, the only way in Augustine thinks about institutions is as practices or things made by human beings. Often, the link between *instituta* and idolatry – the making of false idols – is implicit. For example, he often uses the term *institutum* to describe the institution of pagan rituals.

remarks, "he would not have dared even to mutter, in a popular assembly" (*ciu.* 4.30). Later, Augustine attributes this same fear to Varro (*ciu.* 6.10); for as brilliant and gifted as Varro was, and for as much as he wanted to worship the gods of nature, in the end he was "compelled to worship the gods of the City" because the majority would not have had it otherwise (*ciu.* 6.6). The liberation promised by philosophy seems to have its limits.

We have already spoken about Augustine's desire to emancipate his readers from a world circumscribed by Rome. Yet, from within this world, Seneca's position makes perfect sense. It is, Seneca would argue, imprudent to undermine the institutions that bind the community together, regardless of their legitimacy. Unavoidably, in response to the problem of making a community out of an aggregate, the city has made itself its own foundation; because it cannot count on virtue from its citizens for the right reason, it feigns the outcome of virtue by taking advantage of the citizens' vices. Cicero's promotion of the love of glory also amounts to this; by enflaming his readers' ambition for glory, he compels them to do the public-spirited thing for a private reason (*ciu.* 5.13).[24] For the Roman philosopher, whether Varro, Seneca, or Cicero, these kinds of practices were a necessary evil in an unphilosophical city.

Yet, Augustine thinks, this strategy is of a piece with the earthly city's usual political strategy (*ciu.* 6.7). Rather than address the fundamental cause of disunity, which is self-love, wise politicians have traditionally sought to mitigate its effects in ways that actually aggravate the cause. This might not be such a problem, were it not that *amor sui* has implications beyond the political sphere; because human beings have a destiny beyond political peace, it is unfair for those invested in political peace to form citizens in a way that makes their transcendent destiny even harder to reach (cf. *ciu.* 17.22).[25] All this leads Augustine to conclude that it is humanly impossible to escape the

[24] In his essay on rhetoric, Fortin also contrasts Cicero's willingness to say what is necessary to bring about a positive effect, and Augustine's unwillingness to do so. Ernest Fortin, "Augustine and the Problem of Christian Rhetoric." Cf. Fortin, "Augustine," 179–180; Harrison, *Christian Truth and Fractured Humanity*, 73; Veronica Roberts, "Augustine's Response to the Ciceronian Patriot," *Perspectives on Political Science* 45, no. 2 (2016): 119.

[25] Augustine makes a similar point with regard to Jeroboam, the king of Israel. Jeroboam, he writes, "established idolatry in his kingdom, and led God's people astray ... so that with him the people were addicted to the worship of images" (*ciu.* 17.22). Augustine explains that he did this because he was afraid that if he allowed the people to go down to Jerusalem to worship in the temple, "they would be seduced from his allegiance" to that of Rehoboam, the king of Judah. Yet, for Augustine, this political consideration was a failure in his duty to his people – he encouraged them in a religious practice that was not only addictive but that drew them away from God.

clutches of the earthly city on one's own; if this is true for the philosophers, it is true a fortiori for the rest of us. This, at bottom, is why *consuetudo* is such an insurmountable problem. As an all-encompassing web of meaning that encourages human beings in their baser desires, it keeps people enslaved to harmful habits and opinions. It is the earthly city's manipulative way of handling dissension among the ranks.

For Augustine, civil religion is a particularly insidious institutionalization of *consuetudo* because it takes advantage of the natural authority of the divine. For those not seduced by its other strategies, the "divine" authority of the cultic empire provides a veneer of legitimacy to what, otherwise, would be raw displays of power. Augustine gives a chilling analysis of this aspect of Roman religion when it comes to the marriage bed. Asking why the bridal chamber is filled with so many gods, he dismisses the pious idea that it might be to preserve decency:

Not at all. It is to ensure that with their cooperation, there shall be no difficulty in ravishing the virginity of a girl who feels the weakness of her sex and is terrified by the strangeness of her situation. For here are the goddess Virginensis, and Father Subigus (to subdue, *subigere*) and Mother Prema (to press – *premere*) and the goddess Pertunda (to pierce – *pertundere*) as well as Venus and Priapus. What does all this mean? . . . Do you mean to tell me that Venus alone would not be adequate? She is, they say so called (among other reason) because "not without violence" (*vi non sine*) can a woman be robbed of her virginity. (*ciu.* 6.9)

The ominous tone of Augustine's analysis here is unmistakable, and has been noted before.[26] Indeed, it is of a piece with his overarching suspicion of the glamor of greatness, most memorably captured in the encounter between Alexander the Great and the pirate:

The King asked the fellow, "What is your idea, in infesting the sea?" And the pirate answered, with uninhibited insolence, "The same as yours, in infesting the earth! But because I do it with a tiny craft, I'm called a pirate: because you have a mighty navy, you're called an emperor." (*ciu.* 4.4)

Insofar as civil religion co-opts the divine, it adds to this glamor, exacerbating the problem of a legitimacy acquired apart from justice.

Returning to Augustine's treatment of Seneca, we see that Augustine's primary concern is to ask how Seneca's policy can hope to break into what appears to be a self-enclosed system invested in being untouchable.[27] Philosophy may have liberated Seneca from Roman ideas about the

[26] Cf. Cavadini, "Feeling Right," *Augustinian Studies* 36, no. 1 (2005): 208.
[27] Describing the Roman gods in books 6 and 7, he paints a picture of the Roman pantheon that is not just anthropomorphic, but Romano-centric. As in Rome, there are the few

gods, but this was not a liberty he could in turn extend to the many. Here, Augustine clearly has the Apostles in mind; their liberation *did* extend outward. Like Cicero and Varro, Seneca wrote for the educated classes: those of "livelier and superior intelligences" (*ciu.* 6.10; *ciu.* 7.*praef*). The rest only saw what he did in public. Because he was so well respected, he lent his credibility to Roman rituals by participating publicly in them. This, Augustine thinks was worse because "he acted this insincere part in such a way as to lead people to believe him sincere" (*ciu.* 6.10). Playing on the ease with which the philosophers lambasted the theology of the theater, Augustine paints Seneca as worse than an actor; he was someone the people admired and therefore imitated.

We have already seen how, from Seneca's perspective, his policy makes sense. What Augustine thinks Seneca cannot see is that the public good is not a genuine common good – it does not take the real *summum bonum* of its individual members into account and simply assumes that most people will not be able to live the good life. The problem, Augustine thinks, is that Seneca cannot imagine a world where "the many" have access to truth.[28] They always have been and always will be stuck in the realm of opinion. For Augustine, this is a failure of the imagination, but it does not surprise him that Seneca takes this view. And this is the point: *no one*, not even the most gifted thinkers, can cast off the chains of *consuetudo* completely. No one can achieve perspective on the earthly city by himself.

Here, Augustine melds the two subjects of this chapter into a single point. While he warns against the degree to which we underestimate the force of custom such that we think we can escape the snares of the earthly city, he also warns against the degree to which pride feeds into this miscalculation. For Augustine, pride narrows the scope of our imagination. Though he does not say that Seneca consciously delights

---

figures of great fame, the select gods who are at once the most renowned and the most slandered by the poets. Then there are the rest, the "mob of deities," sheltered from scrutiny "by their very obscurity" (*ciu.* 7.4). These are each assigned small tasks "like the sub-collectors of taxes, or like craftsmen in Silver Street, where one small piece of place passes through many hands to achieve the final result, although it could be finished by one thoroughly competent craftsman." Calling these gods "fantasies of the human imagination (*figmentis humanarum opinionum*)," it is clear that they are products of an imagination patterned by Rome. Cf. Cavadini, "Ideology and Solidarity," 130.

[28] As Pierre Manent has written, "Christianity's point of impact is the separation between the few and the many. What Christianity attacks is not social or political inequality, but the pertinence of the distinction between the few and the many, the philosopher and the non-philosopher, with regard to the capacity to attain or receive the truth." Manent, *Metamorphoses of the City*, 272.

in his superiority, Augustine seems to think that his pride prevents him from imagining that the people's liberation from custom is possible. The many are vulgar, and in the classical world, there did not yet exist a widespread belief that they could be rescued from this. The Christian teaching that all are capable of being liberated was new.[29] It was not, Augustine thinks, something that could come from the world. Thus, after all that philosophy promises, in the end Augustine does not think it has the tools to effect real cultural renewal. Because it is human in origin and, on top of that, taken in on the empire's terms, it cannot fully root out the lies that are so central to pre-Christian Roman *consuetudo*.

In the end, Augustine's point is that what philosophy could not do, Christianity has done – it has toppled the Roman cult and allowed true religion into the city. While philosophy was only ever for a few, Christianity is announced to all by fishermen and women (*ciu.* 10.29). In the Christianization of the empire, Augustine thinks a significant weapon of the earthly city, civil religion, has been destroyed. While he is no Eusebius – he is well aware that the earthly city remains a significant power in the world – the introduction of what Fortin calls a transpolitical religion, is nothing less than revolutionary.[30] It announces that political customs are beholden to a standard beyond the city and clears a significant obstacle to cultural renewal.

INTERNAL CHAOS

We began this chapter by noting Augustine's concern with false solutions to the problem of the earthly city: methods of trying to escape its effects that do not address their cause. First, we explored Augustine's indictment

---

[29] On this topic, the preface to book 7 is particularly salient: "I am using my most earnest endeavours to destroy and eradicate the baneful and long-held notions which are the enemies of true religion, and which have been fixed in the darkened minds of mankind through centuries of error, putting out deep and tenacious roots. I am co-operating (*cooperantem*), in my small measure, with the grace of the true God, relying on the help of him who alone can accomplish this design. No doubt the argument of my previous books is more than sufficient to achieve this object for livelier and superior intelligences; but they will have to possess themselves in patience; and I ask them, for the sake of others, not to think superfluous what for themselves they feel to be unnecessary. The task before us is a matter of supreme importance to establish that the true and truly holy Divinity is to be sought and worshipped not with a view to this mortal life, which passes away like smoke (although we do receive from the Divinity the help needed for our present frailty), but for the sake of the life of blessedness, which must needs be the life of eternity" (*ciu.* 7. *praef*).

[30] Fortin, "The Political Thought of St. Augustine," 27.

of *consuetudo*. *Consuetudo*, we learned, shapes our interpretation of our world and, thereby, directs our desires and pursuits in a way more suited to maintaining our shared illusions than attaining actual happiness. *Consuetudo* is also inherently bound up with power and prestige, and its sway reaches its zenith through the imperial structure. Thus, while Rome might be the capital of the earthly city in Augustine's world, it is also its most visible *simulacrum* of the heavenly city. As empire, it can advertise its justice everywhere. Its promise is this: Rome can raise its most deserving citizens out of a life of barbarism and obscurity, giving them a share of its own glory. But, to deserve this, its citizens need to be entirely invested in the imperial project.

Through the Roman case, then, we saw that societies, and most especially powerful empires, can establish a horizon of meaning that is difficult to transcend on our own. Considered in this light, philosophy becomes a viable alternative as it promises a way out of custom's cave. Yet, in indicating that Rome managed to constrain the thought of even its greatest minds, Augustine casts doubt on philosophy's power to make a public difference. It cannot make Rome into the just city and it cannot lessen the hold that *consuetudo* has on the minds of most Romans. Indeed, it cannot even give its followers a clear vision of the empire's constraints on their minds. Philosophy might be allowed to maintain a small realm of independence, but at the edges, it folds in the face of power. When it comes to the question of cultural renewal, philosophy falls short where it matters the most.

Still, philosophy has always presented another option; if the city cannot be made just, at least the soul can. Augustine well understood the attraction of the retreat into contemplation, and even lived such an existence for a time at Cassiciacum. In Augustine's world, philosophy represented the opportunity to conform oneself to the true, the good, and the beautiful. Indeed, its promise to be the cure of souls made it, at once, the easiest and the hardest *simulacrum* to expose.[31] It very nearly provides a way out of the earthly city. For the Augustine of *City of God*, philosophy is the easiest *simulacrum* to expose insofar as it gives Augustine the most shared premises to work with, especially in its Platonic form (*ciu.* 8.9). It is the hardest, however, in that it gives its followers the least reason to admit defeat. The idea that philosophy is the soul's self-administered cure does a far better job of reinforcing the myth of autonomy than *consuetudo*

---

[31] For Augustine's reception of this aspect of the platonic tradition, see Paul R. Kolbet, *Augustine and the Cure of Souls Revising a Classical Ideal*, Christianity and Judaism in Antiquity 17 (Notre Dame, IN: University of Notre Dame Press, 2010).

does. *Consuetudo* is always flirting with chaos; in its dalliance with the people's passions, it can never wholly conceal the chaos under its surface. The ordered *apatheia* of the Wise Man's soul, however, is something else (*ciu.* 14.9). One can almost believe that he has found peace.

Here again, we see that Augustine's main concern is the problem of false hope. For Augustine, false hope keeps us in the earthly city, but the falsity of our hope provides a potential pathway out of it. Augustine's job is to bring evidence of this falsity to our attention, so as to interrupt the stories we tell to bolster our hopes. As we saw briefly in the first chapter, one of these interruptions, woven into the fabric of our experience and highlighted by the Genesis story, is the very interruption of our freedom by our conflicting passions and desires. This was the state won by Adam through his rebellion. Reading the human condition through Scripture, we saw, Augustine understands the slavery we experience in this life to be the effect, rather than the cause, of the Fall.

As such, Augustine finds any attempt to get around this effect *without* addressing its cause not only futile but harmful; it prevents us from seeking the true cure for our condition.[32] It is in this particular respect – and not in principle – that Augustine approaches philosophy critically in *City of God*. In fact, his approach to politics is much the same – not by criticizing political life in principle but insofar as the earthly city has distorted it. With regard to the philosophers' project, his conviction is as follows: to the degree to which philosophy operates outside the premise that the mind's natural rule over the emotions depends on its subordination to God, it promises something human beings cannot achieve by their own efforts.[33] It comes too close to Adam's original aspiration. It is in bringing philosophy back in line with this insight that the distortions in its teachings will be repaired; in criticizing philosophy, Augustine aims to make it more truly itself. Our task is to follow the line of criticism that pushes against the possibility of the philosophers' autonomous expedition out of the earthly city.

---

[32] As Augustine comments, with regard to Peter after his betrayal of Christ, he was "better off in being displeased with himself when he wept than he was in being pleased with himself when he was overconfident. And the holy Psalm says, 'Fill their faces with shame, so that they may seek your name, O Lord' (Ps 83:16) – that is, so that those who were pleased with themselves when they were seeking their own name might be pleased with you when they seek your name" (*ciu.* 14.13).

[33] Recently, Sarah Stewart-Kroeker has done significant work on the redemption of the emotions in Augustine's thought. See, in particular, Sarah Stewart-Kroeker, "A Wordless Cry of Jubilation: Joy and the Ordering of the Emotions," *Augustinian Studies* 50, no. 1 (2019): 65–86, and "World-Weariness and Augustine's Eschatological Ordering of Emotions in *enarratio in Psalmum 36*," *Augustinian Studies* 47, no. 2 (2016): 201–226.

This line of criticism reaches its zenith in book 19 of *City of God*. There, Augustine lays out the teachings of the rival philosophic schools in order to highlight the implications of the very parameters in which they debate about the human good.[34] Happiness, they argue, is either the good of the soul, or the body, or both (*ciu.* 19.1–3). Regardless, it is something that the human agent can achieve or acquire – something he can grasp or hold in himself. As such, Augustine concludes, wherever they come down in this debate, "they have wished, with amazing folly, to be happy here on earth and to achieve bliss by their own efforts" (*ciu.* 19.4). Because of this wish, they have (to various degrees and in different ways) structured their inquiry after a pattern that obscures the intrinsic dependence of the creature and that denies the unavoidability of suffering in the *saeculum*.

That the philosophers' anthropology is tinged with a desire for self-sufficiency, Augustine thinks, is most clear in their depictions of the Wise Man. Though Augustine is aware of the disputes among the schools, his goal is to bring out a certain underlying disposition that manifests itself in diverse ways across the schools. Dipping in and out of the various schools' dogmas to weave his case, his argument is thus less technical than symbolic.[35] Since he is of the conviction that all the schools aspire to the

---

[34] Cf. Veronica Roberts Ogle, "Sheathing the Sword: Augustine and the Good Judge," *Journal of Religious Ethics* 46, no. 4 (2018): 722–233; John Cavadini, "Trinity and Apologetics in the Theology of St. Augustine," *Modern Theology* 29, no. 1 (2013): 48–82. He writes that the Platonic spirituality allows one to "begin to see God, one who is enough like the real God to justify arrogating to oneself, for one's philosophical achievement, the title 'wise,' but a 'god' who does not relate to sacrifice at all, but to achievement and its reward, glory. This is a God who must remain distant, whose distorted vision is an image of the distortion in the philosopher's own soul ... so the spirituality of attainment is written right into the Godhead. It is a convenient distortion of the real Trinity" (65).

[35] John Cavadini rightly argues that in *City of God*, the Stoics "appear in the *City of God* not really 'as themselves,' as they say in movie credits, but in a way as the exact analogue, in the world of pride, to Christ." Cavadini, "Feeling Right," 212. Because Augustine is so fluid with his usage of philosophic doctrines, there has been much debate over whether he truly understood Stoic doctrine, with Richard Sorabji arguing for strong reasons that he, in the end, did not, and Sarah Byers making a compelling counter argument that he did. Both delve deeply into the technicality of the Stoic system of thought. For this debate, see Richard Sorabji, *Emotion and Peace of Mind: From Stoic Agitation to Christian Temptation* (Oxford: Oxford University Press, 2000), and Sarah Byers, *Perception, Sensibility, and Moral Motivation in Augustine: A Stoic-Platonic Synthesis* (New York: Cambridge University Press, 2013), and "The Psychology of Compassion: Stoicism in City of God," in *Augustine's City of God: A Critical Guide*, ed. James Wetzel (Cambridge: Cambridge University Press, 2012), 130–148. Cf. James Wetzel, *Augustine and the Limits of Virtue* (Cambridge: Cambridge University Press, 1992), 117–121.

life of the Wise Man, it is sufficient for him to show that their shared aspiration is shaped by a wish for self-sufficient happiness.[36]

Asserting that this wish is at loggerheads with the reality of the human condition in the *saeculum*, Augustine highlights the points at which the myth of the Wise Man breaks down. Unsurprisingly, these are the points at which suffering comes to the fore (*ciu.* 19.4). In focusing on the teaching of the Stoics, the most radical of the moral philosophies, Augustine argues that their unwillingness to admit the evil of suffering is an attempt to safeguard the happiness of the Wise Man, but that even they are compelled to say that the Wise Man should escape this life when suffering becomes too much. While this confession should imply that their Wise Man is not happy when he suffers, the Stoics will not admit this. Even the more moderate schools who admit that physical suffering is an evil maintain that the Wise Man is always happy in his virtue.

This, Augustine explains, is because the philosophers portray virtue as a quality that protects those in whom it resides against suffering (*ciu.* 19.4). Prudence, fortitude, temperance and justice, they teach, are guards against a loss of perspective that might cause the weak to think they should do whatever it takes to escape pain (*ciu.* 9.4). As such, the Wise Man is the one who remembers that these virtues are far more important than any other goods one can hope to attain. They alone keep the soul in order; they are what allow the Wise Man to retain complete control over his actions and reactions (*ciu.* 14.8). For the philosophers, what follows from this is that the Wise Man is untouchable: because he knows his goodness is in himself and cannot be lost, he can look at whatever trials come his way and be glad (*ciu.* 14.8). Regardless of the semantic differences between the Stoics, the Peripatetics and the Platonists, Augustine classifies them all as invested in the idea that the Wise Man is happy (*ciu.* 9.4).

And yet, Augustine thinks, when the virtues promise that they are sufficient for happiness, they promise too much (*ciu.* 19.4). Or, rather, they ask the philosopher to settle for too little. Mental exercises that cast sufferings as inconsequential, Augustine thinks, constitute a denial of the human condition. Even the virtuous person will only be happy "when he reaches that state where he is wholly exempt from death, deception, and distress, and has the assurance that he will forever be exempt" (*ciu.* 14.25). This alone, he stresses, is the state that "our nature craves," and

---

[36] I make this argument in greater detail in "Therapeutic Deception: Cicero and Augustine on the Myth of Philosophic Happiness," *Augustinian Studies* 50, no. 1 (2019): 13–42.

anyone who reduces it to a craving for virtue is, essentially, ordering himself "not to wish for what is beyond his power" (ibid.). To say that virtue is either the only good or, at least, so much more important than the other goods that it is sufficient for happiness, Augustine concludes, is wishful thinking. It is a story orchestrated by "mortal men in their endeavour to create happiness for themselves amidst the unhappiness of this life" (*ciu.* 19.1).

Moreover, insofar as the philosophers' arguments constitute a denial of the human condition, Augustine thinks, they underestimate the problem of vice in the soul. This comes to the fore in their analysis of the Wise Man's soul. Though Augustine does not deny that there is a natural hierarchy ordering the parts of the soul, he challenges the way in which the philosophic schools (collectively and despite nuances in their respective teachings) portray the proper relationship between reason and the passions (*ciu.* 9.4–5). Across the board, he observes, the philosophers celebrate a mind that dominates the passions with imperial prerogative. The passions, they say, cannot be reasoned with; to achieve the Wise Man's "reign of virtue," one must control, suppress, or, deny consent to them (*ciu.* 9.4). In this account, the mind is not merely superior, but the source of *all* that is good in the human being (*ciu.* 14.8). The movements of the lower parts of the soul are merely disturbances that impede the mind.

Even the best philosophers, Augustine explains, justify this attitude toward the passions by teaching that they come from the body (*ciu.* 14.5). As such, it is philosophy's job to purify the mind of their influence and work toward the liberation of the soul from its bodily prison (*ciu.* 13.16). For Augustine, however, this account is not quite right. While the passions are afflictions that only belong to this life, this does not mean that they are the sole or even the primary cause of sin (*ciu.* 14.9). To make this mistake, he thinks, is to read the human condition through the lens of pride.

In arguing this, Augustine taps into his larger exposé of the psychology of pride. He believes there is a hierarchy of being in creation, but his is not a metaphysic in which the higher says to the lower, "I have all the perfections you have, and more"; this would be the attitude of the demons (*ciu.* 11.16). Instead, Augustine's ontology is best encapsulated in the participatory relationship between creation and its Creator. Even if material beings exist in a lesser degree or are ontologically less perfect than spiritual beings, they are still good: the products of God's creative intention. Viewed in this way, all creatures, by virtue of their createdness, contribute to the fabric of the world in a positive and even unique way; they have a role to play in the larger economy.

Analyzing the different parts of the human soul in this light, Augustine parts ways with the philosophers, even as he agrees that the mind is higher than the emotions (*affectiones*). Augustine's is a hierarchy of harmony; to say that the emotions should be properly subordinated to the mind is not to say that the mind contains all the good of human nature while the emotions only limit that goodness. Rather, it is to say that the emotions should play their role in a way that supports love of God and neighbor (*ciu.* 14.9). By making the passions the cause of vice, the philosophers not only fail to tell the whole story, they also distort it.

Unsurprisingly, Augustine is not at a loss to account for this partial tale. Again, it is a question of pride. For Augustine, the human condition is such that, no matter how intelligent we are, we simply cannot get over the blindness of our fallen condition by ourselves. What is worse, the more intelligent we are, the more we are prone to thinking we can, and the less open we are to help (*ciu.* 10.29). Thus, Augustine thinks, the philosophers' hope in their own virtue is fundamentally responsible for the distortion in their anthropology. They are invested in the idea that the passions are the source of vice because, in their experience, the passions are what limit their agency. If they could only control these forces, they reason, they would be entirely in control of themselves and thus would be at peace (*ciu.* 19.4)

And yet, as we have already seen, Augustine thinks that sin is much closer to us than this narrative would suggest; the disobedience of the body, recall, is the effect, not the cause of original sin (*ciu.* 13.13). Interpreting the philosophers' wishes through the Genesis story, Augustine reads the tendency to scapegoat the body as an attempt to shift the blame to something other, something with which the philosophers do not identify (*ciu.* 14.5).[37] For Augustine, however, our sin is radically ours, and no good comes from trying to escape this fact. In imagining a happy Wise Man, the philosophers hide this fact from themselves. They leave no room for a Mediator.

Viewed in this way, then, philosophy attempts to get around the chaos of the fallen condition as much as empire or political philosophy do. It is also equally unsuccessful. The philosophers who try to imitate the Wise

---

[37] It was, after all, the rational soul with which the philosophers truly identified themselves. For the Platonists in particular, the body was a mere prison, while the soul was the true locus of personhood. Cavadini fleshes out this theme in many of his articles, especially in "Feeling Right" and "Ideology and Solidarity," cited above. I am indebted to him for my understanding of this point.

Man, Augustine thinks, only end up imitating his insensitivity. Targeting Stoicism again, Augustine challenges Stoic *apatheia*, reading it as a *simulacrum* of true peace that is entirely unfitting in the world as it stands (*ciu.* 14.9; 19.4–7).[38] Moreover, he argues, anyone who seems to have created order in his soul by himself, has, in fact done it in the wrong way and for the wrong reasons (*ciu.* 19.25). The virtues that are "related only to themselves and are sought for no other end" are products of the drive to be the self-sufficient person we wish we were. Thus, while the *amor sui* of the earthly city tends to foster strife and chaos, it also produces men and women who are "so charmed" by their own self-control that they find the wherewithal to make it more and more complete (*ciu.* 14.9). Yet, Augustine stresses, "hardness does not necessarily imply rectitude, and insensibility is not a guarantee of health" (ibid.).

Because Augustine approaches these teachings from the perspective provided by Christian revelation, he considers the Stoic model of the Wise Man to be out of joint with the model Christ reveals in Himself. As John Cavadini explains, "The Stoics are present in the *City of God* in a way as the enantiomer of Christ, the mirror image of Christ's emotional life only formatted according to pride instead of love."[39] For Augustine, the Incarnate Christ's acceptance of emotions, imitated by Paul and the other Apostles poses a serious challenge to the idea that we can, or should be, unaffected by suffering, especially in the face of sin and death (*ciu.* 14.9). In Christ's light, it becomes clear, the Stoic Wise Man who denies consent to his passions does so at the cost of also repressing his human feelings – feelings designed to move him to greater mercy (*ciu.* 14.8). This, for Augustine, is especially true when it comes to grief. The Stoic judge who cannot grieve, and, on top of that, denies that a good man would be harmed by physical suffering, has no reason to restrain his use of torture if it is "deserved" (*ciu.* 19.6); the Stoic general has no reason to restrain his use of force if the war is "just" (*ciu.* 19.7).[40] Christ's deep vulnerability – his ability to be affected by the actions of others – exposes any *apatheia* actually achieved in this world as

---

[38] Ogle, "Therapeutic Deception," 33–39.

[39] Cavadini, "Feeling Right," 211. He later adds, "They substitute perfect self-control for what Christ can offer, which we have characterized as self-possession, and so the Stoics serve as a kind of a clamp on the imagination, a dead end which blocks the imagination even more firmly than lust did, because they present the prospect not of a healed humanity but of the complete renunciation of humanity. At least lust, because of the potential for shame, left a doorway to repentance." Ibid., 212.

[40] Cf. Ogle, "Sheathing the Sword," 729–732.

a pseudo-tranquility bought by suppressing one's emotions and keeping others at a distance (*ciu.* 14.9).

Though much more could be said about this topic, and in much greater detail, for our purposes in this chapter it is enough to point out that Augustine thinks the philosophical solution to the problem of the disordered soul veers off-course in both its diagnosis of the human condition and its cure. While Augustine hardly denies that the virtues are the qualities of soul that bring order to the soul, he asserts that true virtues cannot be motivated by the desire for self-sufficiency. Insofar as they are, they will be permeated with the desire to be unmoved – to escape vulnerability. The desire to be an independent agent, one that is never acted upon against one's will, Augustine thinks, has a cost. It requires a closing-off or a hardening of oneself that is antithetical to the disposition required for love. In this way he exposes the notion of the self-sufficient Wise Man as ultimately contradictory.

CONCLUSION

In this chapter, we have looked at three false solutions to the problem of the earthly city: the promise of empire, the promise of philosophic politics, and the promise of philosophy as a way of life. In analyzing why he thinks these solutions are premature and what they tell us about the difference between the two cities, we have begun to glimpse how radical a shift in perspective Augustine is suggesting. In grasping why Augustine spends time attacking what look like respectable ways out of an unsatisfactory world, we see that his concerns are not quite what we expect. In discovering Augustine's concerns we see that he wants to effect a complete Copernican turn in us, moving us from the perspective limited by *amor sui* to a perspective inspired by *amor Dei*. In order to persuade the proud of the power of humility, he has to show us that we do not see well by ourselves (*ciu.* 1.*praef*). In this way, he hopes he can convince us to seek what we do not see (*ciu.* 19.18).

4

Roman History Retold

Situating Augustine's Political Pessimism within His Psychagogic Argument

In the second chapter, I suggested that Augustine's main goal in *City of God* is to persuade the proud of the *virtus* (power or excellence) of humility. Humility, he claims in the work's preface, is powerful because it is the quality that allows us to "soar above all the summits of this world, which sway in their temporal instability" (*ciu.* 1.*praef*). And yet, we have already remarked, to call this a power of humility is entirely counterintuitive; it pushes against the obvious truth that power and success are intimately intertwined in this world. That divine power that bears up the humble, Augustine suggests, remains hidden to us, either because we stand at the base of the summits and are overshadowed by their might, or because we stand at their crest and fail to look up.[1] Boldly proclaiming the power of humility, Augustine sets a challenge for himself: he must convince us that our ability to see the world *as it is* is always limited, regardless of where we stand in the world.

And yet, as we have already seen, Augustine cannot give his apology *ex nihilo*. Rather, he has to begin by addressing the myths of an already narrated *saeculum*: a world whose meaning has become Rome. Indeed, not only have we seen Augustine accuse Rome of parading as the just city and the *salvator mundi*, we have also seen him suggest that even her greatest lights struggled to liberate themselves from her imperial ideology. This being so, it is no great surprise that Augustine thought it necessary to disentangle the meaning of life in the *saeculum* from Rome's interpretation

---

[1] Augustine inverts this imagery in his first homily on the Gospel of John, likening John to a high mountain that received wisdom on behalf of the people (*Io Ev. tr.* 1.2–6). Augustine, *Homilies on the Gospel of John 1–40*, trans. Edmund Hill, OP, ed. Allan Fitzgerald, OSA (Hyde Park, NY: New City Press, 2009), 40–43.

of that meaning if he was to succeed in his project of liberating his readers from the earthly city.

In this chapter, I argue that most of this work takes place in the first five books of *City of God*, and is bound up with his reinterpretation of Roman history. This is significant because these five chapters are frequently cited as evidence that the political community is the realm of sin. As we will see, there are good reasons for this. However, recalling our plan to read *City of God* through Augustine's psychagogic intention, it is important to situate Augustine's discussion of Roman history within its proper rhetorical context. By focusing on how Augustine's recalibration of Roman history is designed to undo the distortions contained within Rome's own self-understanding, we notice that its pessimism is something akin to the application of contraries, designed to detach his Roman readers from an idolatrous attachment to their earthly *patria*, so that they might embrace a heavenly one.

To Augustine, the fact that many attributed the recent sack of Rome to the Christianization of the empire was evidence that, for many, the meaning of life was too shaped by Rome. This concerned him, of course, because it posed an obstacle to their belief in Christianity and motivated them to attack Christianity, thereby threatening the faith of others. We have already seen his response in Chapter 2. Pinpointing belief in an eternal Rome as the source of the issue, Augustine begins by demoting this *Roma Aeterna* to the status of parody and proceeds to highlight the stagnation into which Roman civilization had fallen, while contrasting it with the renewal that Christ offered.

Lamenting the effects of the sack, Augustine also points out that the Roman gods – Troy's vanquished gods – were never much good at protecting those who served them anyway (*ciu.* 1.2–1.3, inter alia), and that these gods, by their example and requests, actually encouraged the Romans in the habits that were the *real* cause of Rome's decline, namely, its moral corruption (*ciu.* 2.2). Yet, he writes, the "well-educated who are fond of history," already know this (*ciu.* 2.3). This being the case, he asks, why do the learned keep this knowledge from the many who rail against the Christians? We have already seen Augustine indict certain Romans for propagating useful falsehoods in the name of political stability. Now, we see him return to the same theme: in failing to correcting those who interpret the sack in light of an idealized Roman history, he argues, the pagan elites have allowed the many to make false accusations against Christianity for their own ends – namely, for the sake of restoring old modes and orders.[2] It is likely that Augustine has

---

[2] Though focusing less on his evangelical purpose, Andrew Murphy makes a similar argument about Augustine's resituation of the Roman decline narrative, drawing

someone like Symmachus in mind here, someone convinced that Christianity was bad for Rome.

Christianity, the argument went, threatened political cohesiveness by drawing citizens' allegiance beyond Rome; without the ritualized worship binding citizens to the *patria*, what would keep the citizen body together? Though Augustine does what he can to allay these fears, showing instead how salutary Christianity is for politics, he also zeroes in on Roman history itself, arguing that its decline vastly predates the arrival of Christianity. Reminding his readers of the arguments of their own literary heroes, Augustine embarks on a telling of Roman history that, in many ways, is taken from Sallust and Livy. Yet, it also does more than this: it shows how these historians were swept up into Rome's collective project of falsifying the past. As we will see, this is precisely the thread that ties his treatment of Roman history together.

It is important to note that, in addressing Roman history, Augustine is not responding to a precise argument made consistently and rigorously across a certain set of books. Rather, he is attacking a cultural conviction represented by these books: a conviction about Rome's special destiny and character. Its message, as we have seen, was that Rome is a noble *patria*, brave, just, and resilient. It "spares the humble and beats down the proud" (Virgil, *Aen.*, 6.853). Quoting Cicero's complaint that his generation had "received the commonwealth like a magnificent picture, ... faded with age," and had failed to maintain it, Augustine famously suggests that the Roman commonwealth had been a figment of the Romans' imagination all along: a tapestry woven together by the words of its poets and orators, nebulous in its relationship to Rome's actual history (*ciu.* 2.21). In this chapter, we will take a closer look at this vision and Augustine's response to it. Ultimately, we will see, Augustine's retelling of Roman history tells us something significant about Rome and the earthly city: both exhibit a social life mired in strife, and driven by a frantic scramble to cover it up. What remains to be seen is how Augustine undermines and corrects the falsehoods that follow from the excessive patriotism of the Roman *literati*.

UNMASKING THE NARRATOR

In books 1–5 Augustine makes it his goal to call the idea of Rome's golden age into question – to distinguish early Rome from the Just City with

contemporary parallels. Andrew R. Murphy, "Augustine and the Rhetoric of Roman Decline," *History of Political Thought* 26, no. 4 (2005): 586–606.

which its apologists have conflated it. Aware that depicting Rome as a city worthy of total devotion was a preferred strategy of the patriotic *literati* who sought to reverse Rome's decline, Augustine has much to tell their followers about the limits of this vision. In the previous chapter, we saw that these *literati* believed that if they could only inspire their fellow Romans to love Rome as *patria*, they could convince them to dedicate themselves to the public good – in other words, they could cultivate good citizens.[3] Addressing this narrative at face value, Augustine asks when Rome was really the city that Livy, Sallust and Cicero claim her to be: "when was it, exactly, that 'justice and morality prevailed among them [the Romans] as much by nature as by laws?'" (*ciu.* 2.17–18). Illustrating his knowledge of Livy and Sallust, he asks, "was it in the age of Romulus, when the Romans stole wives for themselves, waging war on the fathers who sought their return [*ciu.* 2.17], or in the time before the Punic Wars, when fear of Carthage kept the Romans' greed in check? [*ciu.* 2.18]." To be sure, Augustine admits, Rome was once governed by better leaders, but this is as far as their narrative of decline has traction (*ciu.* 2.21). Taken further, it becomes a tool of Roman propaganda: for Augustine, the myth of Rome's golden age is what allows the Romans to look at their city, with all its real problems, and still call it *Roma Aeterna*. It is what allows them to see Rome as a city who has simply forgotten who she is.

But, Augustine wants to ask, what is Rome, really? In what way has she really been set apart for greatness? Indeed, in what way is she even a "she," a *persona*, at all? For Augustine, Rome's personality is entirely man-made because Rome is entirely man-made; it is nothing more than a group of people bound together by some kind of compact (*ciu.* 15.8). Moreover, from whose lips has Rome's great destiny been proclaimed? In reality, Augustine argues, these prophecies were put in the mouths of the gods by Rome's own poets, and, on top of that, retrospectively (*ciu.* 5.12).[4] Interestingly, Sallust admits something similar on behalf of the historians. The job of the historian, he writes, is not so different from that of the poet: his writings *make* a city great just as the deeds of the heroes did (Salllust, *Cat.*, 8).[5] Rome, in the end, is both made and narrated by its members. It is, to quote the Psalm, "the work of human hands" (Ps. 115, inter alia).

---

[3] For more on this, see my article "Augustine's Ciceronian Response to the Ciceronian Patriot," in *Perspectives on Political Science* 45, no. 2 (2016): 113–124.

[4] In developing this line of argument, Augustine continues the long tradition of philosophical distrust of the poets and historians.

[5] Sallust, *Cataline's War, the Jugurthine War, Histories*, trans. A. J. Woodman (New York: Penguin Classics, 2007), 8.

Engaging with the writings of Livy, Sallust, and Virgil, what concerns Augustine is that, by his time, their writings have been co-opted into Rome's imperial project by supplying its sacred literature (*ciu.* 1.24, 3.17).[6] Quoting Horace's dictum that "new vessels will for long retain the taste of what is first poured into them," Augustine explains how Virgil's poetry has been systematically poured into the "unformed minds" of young Romans for centuries, that they might have truly Roman imaginations (*ciu.* 1.3, cf. *Conf.* 1.13.22).[7] Thus, while those who write of Rome's golden age aim to make Rome better by enflaming their readers with public-spiritedness, Augustine associates the myth of a golden age with the same sickness that those who promoted it thought they were combating. The fundamental problem, Augustine argues, is not just the exaltation of the private over the public, it is also the exaltation of falsehood over truth.[8] By resorting to myth-making, these citizens inadvertently strengthened the hold of the earthly city on Rome. They participated in its tendency to cover over historical realities with self-justifying narratives.

Augustine illustrates the prevalence of this tendency in Rome's self-understanding in the way he recounts well-known Roman stories.[9] Importantly, Augustine treats these stories not merely as the work of

---

[6] To this point, Gillian Clark writes, "Latin-speaking school-boys were brought up on classical texts, from more than four centuries earlier, in which Rome meant the empire as well as the city. The *Aeneid* of Vergil was a core text of the late antique curriculum, so every educated person knew how Jupiter, king of the gods, declared that he gave Rome empire without end, without boundaries of space or time: *imperium sine fine dedi.*" "*Imperium* and the City of God: Augustine on Church and Empire," *Studies in Church History* 54 (2018): 54.

[7] Perhaps unwittingly, Augustine alludes here to the distinction made in the allegory of the cave between philosophic and sophistic education – while sophistic education treats the human mind as a vessel to fill, philosophic education seeks to turn the soul toward the Good. Plato, *Republic*, 518b–d. At the very least, he is channeling the Platonic insight that the city has a stake in keeping its citizens in the cave. Roman education, in other words, is best described as sophistic. Cf. Cochrane, *Christianity and Classical Culture*, 313–314. As Peter Brown has helpfully pointed out to me in an email, Livy's authority as a representative of Roman "volksgeist" is not merely a result of his collecting "Roman folk-wisdom," but the role his books had in the formation of the Roman imagination: this, Brown explains, was a "volksgeist made at school, not around the ancestral camp-fire." Carol Harrison gives an overview of Roman education in Harrison, *Christian Truth and Fractured Humanity*, 46–48.

[8] This is closely related to Augustine's theory of the imagination, which Hans Urs von Balthasar insightfully analyzes in *The Glory of the Lord II*, 123–127.

[9] For a close study of Augustine's reception of classical texts in the first half of the *City of God*, see S. Angus, *The Sources of the First Ten Books of Augustine's City of God* (Princeton, NJ: Princeton University Press, 1906).

patriotic individuals – though he does acknowledge this (*ciu.* 1.6) – but primarily as an expression of the Roman people. Augustine is able to do this because these stories were first seen as products of oral tradition. Casting the historian as the mouthpiece of the Roman people, Augustine proceeds to show, concretely, how the world in his own time came to mean Rome, and how history has been recast in order to justify the Roman project. This is where we begin to see Augustine expounding a crucial lesson about the earthly city: the relationship between distorted love and the promotion of distorted vision.

To Augustine, what the Roman storyteller emphasizes or fails to emphasize in his storytelling is a window into Roman priorities. Thus, when Augustine writes that "Marcus Marcellus, who captured the splendid city of Syracuse is said to have wept over its coming downfall and to have shed his own tears before shedding Syracusan blood," his readers would know that Livy attributes Marcus Marcellus's tears only partly to grief (*ciu.* 1.6). According to his report, Marcus Marcellus "is said to have wept, partly for joy in the accomplishment of so great an enterprise, and partly in grief for the city's ancient glory" (Livy, *Ab urbe cond.*, 25.24).[10] In other words, even Marcellus's grief is not oriented toward the persons under siege, but to the great city of the past. As Livy explains,

he remembered the sinking, long ago, of the Athenian fleets, the two great armies wiped out with their two famous commanders, and the perils she had passed through in all her wars with Carthage. He saw again in fancy her rich tyrants and kings, Hiero above all, still vivid in men's thoughts. . . . As all these memories thronged into his mind, and the thought came that within an hour everything he saw might be in flames and reduced to ashes, he determined on a last effort to save the city. (ibid.)

With this passage, it becomes clear that Marcellus's effort to save the city is rooted less in fellow-feeling and more in love of glory: he misses what would be visible to the eyes of compassion.[11] While, to be sure, "he

---

[10] Livy, *The War with Hannibal: The History of Rome from Its Foundation*, books XXI–XXX, ed. Betty Radice, trans. Aubrey du Selincourt (London: Penguin Classics, 1965), 329.

[11] Reflecting on the synergy between the way the stories were told and the motives of the Roman heroes themselves, Lendon writes, "The historical actors were, for the most part, educated in the same assumptions as the authors. . . . The old stories were part of the political as well as the literary culture, guiding lines of action as well as lines of text, and influencing bloody reality." Lendon, *The Empire of Honour*, 29. In other words, the literary culture that had immortalized Syracuse of old influenced the very men who undertook this siege and were, thereby, immortalized. Love of glory imbued both the stories and the hearts of their characters.

preserved the honour of his enemies," and is celebrated for having done so, for Augustine, it is significant that it does not occur to the Romans remembering him that Marcus Marcellus could have gone a step further: he could have refused to overthrow the city for the sake of its inhabitants' well-being (*ciu.* 1.6). Yet, this, Augustine thinks, cannot occur to them; they needed to subdue Syracuse for their own glory. From the perspective of *amor Dei*, there is a kind of poverty in celebrating a man whose tears missed the actual tragedy in front of him – tears that could never have stopped the shedding of all innocent blood.

Over the course of the next few books, Augustine continues to develop this line of argument, which reaches its apex in the middle of book 3. Here, Augustine focuses on two stories from Livy's early histories: the kidnapping of the Sabine women and the war with Alba.[12] Augustine focuses on these stories to make the point that their original telling failed to embody the humane reaction it should have elicited; there is a disconnect, in other words, between tone and content. In both cases, Augustine suggests that the storyteller, namely, Livy – but again, a Livy who, more than anything, represents the tradition poured into young minds at school – fails to give due consideration to the human cost of Rome's victories.[13]

While Livy focuses, for example, on the Romans' need for wives and their neighbors' unfair refusal to entrust their daughters to them, Augustine questions Livy's reading of the Sabine women's reactions to their forced marriages. While Livy seems to think that the Sabine women adjusted quickly to their new circumstances, Augustine wonders if this impression was not a result of necessity: "The wives," he writes, "dared not weep for slaughtered fathers, for fear of offending victorious husbands" (*ciu.* 3.13).[14] It is, Augustine implies, only because the early Romans did not pick up on their wives' real feelings that they were not incorporated into the story. Indeed, considering how driven Livy's Romans were by military glory, this is not surprising. In the end, it is Augustine who must do the work of recalibrating the story, highlighting

---

[12] In my reading of these passages on Roman women, I am indebted to Mary Keys and Ashleen Menchaca-Bagnulo, in whose company I first encountered them. Together, we were struck by Augustine's attitude toward women, which has been largely underappreciated in the literature. I would of course point to Melanie Webb's work as an exception; cf. Melanie Webb, "On Lucretia Who Slew Herself."

[13] For a discussion of how Livy "places himself and his narrative in the context that his narrative perpetuates," see Gary B. Miles, "History and Memory in Livy's Narrative," in *Livy: Reconstructing Early Rome* (Ithaca, NY: Cornell University Press, 1997), 73.

[14] Cf. Livy, *Ab urbe cond.*, 1.9–11.

what the original at once implies and fails to notice – that, because of their husbands' eagerness for war, these women were put in the tragic position of not knowing "for whom they should offer their prayers" – a fact obscured by the emphasis of the original story – and a fact that should have curbed the Romans' zeal for combat (ibid.).

Questioning the celebratory tone of the original story, Augustine goes on, "True, the Romans were victorious in this encounter with their neighbours. But how much suffering, on both sides, how many deaths of such near relations and neighbours, paid the price of victory!" (*ciu.* 3.13). Bringing the victory over the Sabines under scrutiny, it becomes clear the Romans' cause was, in many ways, dubious. The Romans were rejoicing in a victory over relations whom they had originally wronged.[15] This, Augustine thinks, was unfitting. As he has already put it, "Even if the Sabines were unfair to refuse to give their daughters on request it was surely much more unfair to take them by force after their refusal" (*ciu.* 2.17). It might have been, he goes on, according to *some* construal of the laws of war, just for the Romans to contest the decision of their potential fathers-in-law, but it was "contrary to every law of peace that he seized those who had been denied him and then waged unjust war with their indignant parents" (ibid.). In giving his readers perspective on the victors' perspective, both on their failure to consider the toll their actions had on their wives, and on their failure to recall the original injustice they themselves had perpetrated, Augustine highlights how Roman memory involves a kind of forgetting – a willful partiality shaped by an attitude of *Roma contra mundum*.[16]

Augustine makes this point even more forcefully in the next chapter. Here, he focuses on Rome's defeat of Alba, a neighboring city and, according to Augustine, a city more truly her mother than Troy (*ciu.* 3.14). Again, Augustine uses the story to highlight the partiality of Roman vision: Rome prefers to call the famous Troy her mother city and is more than willing to treat Alba like a conquest.[17] Augustine sees this as willful obfuscation. While Rome fails to grieve the destruction of her mother city, or even recognize her as such, Alba's status as mother city is a reality: the Romans came from Alba and continue to maintain

---

[15] Ibid.

[16] John Milbank has astutely pointed out that the Romans "only had the vaguest intimations of a justice and peace that were not fundamentally the exercise of a *dominium*" and that they, "like all pagans, think that there can only *be* virtue where there is something to be defeated." Milbank, *Theology and Social Theory*, 393.

[17] Livy, *Ab urbe cond.*, 1.25.

concrete ties to her citizens. In contrast to the link with Troy, which glorifies Rome without putting any responsibilities on her, the link with Alba is too real: it comes with inconvenient duties. It puts a damper on Rome's imperial ambitions.

While the blood ties between the two cities do play a central role in the traditional telling of the Alban-Roman conflict, what troubles Augustine is this traditional telling's inadequate reaction to them. As Livy tells it, when these two cities decide to resolve their stalemate by a to-the-death competition of three-on-three, the sister of the Roman triplets is betrothed to one of the Alban brothers. While the Albans start the competition out strong, killing two of the Romans, the remaining brother manages to kill all three Albans in a rush of adrenaline. Coming home a hero to throngs of cheering Romans, he sees his sister weeping for her lost betrothed. Enraged by her unpatriotic tears, he kills her, to the shock of the Roman people. While, in Livy, this is an inconvenient detail that puts a damper on the Romans' celebrations, Augustine shifts the focus to the sister who dies.[18] Like the Sabine women, this woman is caught between two loves that should not be in conflict. She is caught between her love for her brothers and her people, and her love for her betrothed: who can she root for without loss? She alone recognizes that there was more to grieve than to celebrate: both communities had suffered a "wholesale massacre" of their armies and a "shrinkage" of their populations (*ciu.* 3.14). For Augustine, the tragic female bystander whom the feuding men do not notice represents what is real – the presence of humanity in a world caught up in the pursuit of glory.

Perhaps these women are set apart because of the concreteness of their natural ties, or, perhaps they are set apart because Rome is less invested in reeducating them into its imperial project. Regardless, Augustine depicts these women as uniquely preserved in their capacity to feel grief at their current situation. They alone see clearly. They alone bear witness to the

---

[18] Livy, *Ab urbe cond.*, 1.26. While Livy admits that the deed was horrific, writing that "there were none who did not feel the horror of this deed," and subsequently reports that Horatius was brought to trial, two facts remain that indict the Roman people. Livy, *The Early History of Rome*, trans. Aubrey de Selincourt (New York: Penguin Classics, 1960), 61. First, Livy, knowing the eventual death of the sister, does not refrain from recounting the competition in a blow-by-blow account that draws the reader into the excitement – this indicates that the main recollection of the fight was bound up with the glory at stake – and second, Livy reports without remorse that Horatius was eventually acquitted due to his father's claim that his daughter deserved to die for her tears. Ultimately, the fight itself takes up much more room in the story-telling than the murder of Horatia. Augustine changes this emphasis.

natural sociability that Rome has sacrificed in its pursuit of imperial glory. And yet, this is precisely what Rome cannot see – it cannot, in other words, see the real protagonists in its own stories. In Livy's Sabine story, it is Jupiter to whom Rome's reversal of fortune is attributed, and in his Alban story, it is the victorious brother who, despite his murder of his sister, saves Rome.[19]

In Augustine's retelling of the former, however, it is *only* the Sabine women – hair flying and tears streaming – whose intercessions mark a turning point worth highlighting. While Augustine follows Livy in recounting how, when the Romans were losing, Romulus called upon Jupiter to keep his army from fleeing, such that "Jupiter was given the title of Stator," and he immediately goes on: "There would have been no end to the scene of horror, had not the ravished brides rushed out, tearing their hair, and throwing themselves at their parents' feet, assuaged their righteous indignation not by victorious arms but by dutiful supplication" (*ciu.* 3.13). By refusing to comment on Jupiter's efficacy beyond the fact that Rome had *given* him the name Stator, Augustine redirects his readers' attention to what he considers to be the true marvel – the women's ability to change the whole scene from war to peace. Jupiter may have inspired the Romans to keep fighting, but it was the women who achieved peace.

Similarly, in retelling the Alban story, Augustine highlights the sister's grief at meaningless bloodshed instead of highlighting the exciting twist of fate that gave the Romans their victory. In shifting emphasis in this way, Augustine directs the Romans back to the fact that their victory implied the destruction of another. While Livy artfully communicates the anxiety and the elation of the Roman people through his blow-by-blow account, Augustine is more interested in emphasizing their failure to translate this anxiety into compassion for those who faced defeat in their stead – those *they* had goaded into war (*ciu.* 3.14). In reality, it is only thanks to the sister "who had more human feeling than the whole Roman population" that the deficiency of fellow-feeling in the Roman people is made visible (*ciu.* 3.14). This is why her brother has to silence her.[20] For the Romans, it is a tragic accident that her brother was enraged at her grief. For Augustine, it is part and parcel of his character. The thumotic rage he tapped into in order to win the competition was the same rage that led him

---

[19] Livy, *Ab urbe cond.*, 1.10.
[20] Here, of course, Augustine cannot but read the event as an echoing of the fratricide upon which Rome was founded.

to kill his sister. *This* is the real face of the power that gave Rome its victory.

All this said, in recalibrating Roman history, Augustine highlights the problem of trying to locate the marks of the earthly city in an already narrated *saeculum*. While Augustine wants to embark on a history of Rome laid bare (*nuda*), he can only do this after engaging with its veneer (*ciu.* 3.14). In showing how the loves of a people shape their storytelling, Augustine highlights a central aspect of the earthly city's way of being in the world. Self-justifying rhetoric, it turns out, is one of its fundamental habits. The earthly city is not just strife, it is strife attempting to conceal itself.

THE BIRTH OF REPUBLICANISM RETOLD

Having engaged with how Roman stories are told, Augustine begins again, promising to "strip off the deceptive veils, remove the whitewash of illusion (*fallacia ... tegmina et deceptoriae dealbationes auferantur*)," and to "subject the facts" of Roman history "to a strict inspection" (*ciu.* 3.14).[21] In doing so, what he gives us is a history governed by power dynamics: it is a story of the powerful successfully maintaining the status quo through force and manipulation. That is, until they don't – until those who do not benefit from the status quo finally rebel against it. Through his history, Augustine shows that the dynamic of *amor sui* hinders Roman political life in all of its phases.

Starting at the beginning, Augustine tells us how the same brother who won his founding title by fratricide was later "torn to pieces" by angry senators (*ciu.* 3.15). These, in turn, only stayed the people's ire by claiming he had been assumed into heaven. The stories of the kings are no better: daughters plotting their fathers' murder with their husbands, and sons avenging their fathers' murder by murder – all with a view to gaining the throne. It is no wonder that the Romans developed such a violent allergy to monarchy. And yet, this is not where Augustine goes with the story, and, it is where Augustine departs from the standard Roman narrative that reveals his agenda. Though he does highlight the horror of the monarchic era, in the way he recounts republican history Augustine implies that there has not been as much of a break with the past as the Roman *literati* would have us think. While Livy frames the birth of a republic as the birth of Rome's mature liberty, Augustine presents it as

---

[21] CCSL 47.77.

the start of more of the same: more proof of the corrosive effect *amor sui* has on social life.[22]

This is particularly true of the republic's founding act: the ousting of Tarquin. Examined closely, this event is not the noble objection to injustice it first appears to be. While Tarquin committed many injustices that could elicit righteous anger, Lucretia's rape was not one of them; as we have already seen, it was his son who raped Lucretia and, Augustine points out, Tarquin was not even in Rome at the time. Instead, he was out "attacking Ardea ... on behalf of the Roman people" (*ciu.* 3.16).[23] For Augustine, the fact that the Romans did not wait to find out "what he would have done if his son's outrage had been brought to his notice" indicates that the Romans did not want to find out what he would have done (ibid.). They had already made up their minds that they wanted rid of him.

What is most interesting about Augustine's analysis here is the light in which it puts the Roman people. This is not a story about a virtuous citizenry refusing to stand for injustice. This is a people who had tolerated Tarquin for a long time. What changed? Reading Augustine's analysis in light of the details in Livy, the answer is clear: Tarquin asked them to perform menial labor. The Romans did not mind Tarquin when he made other nations subservient, but they did not want to be made subservient themselves – and Tarquin's recent public projects had made them so. Building the great sewage system was not prestigious, as earlier public projects had been (and as Livy implies, glory helped soothe the pain of arduous work).[24] Eventually, the resentment of having to perform undignified work outweighed pride in Tarquin's victories. This resentment is why the Romans' anger at Lucretia's rape was so easily channeled toward revolution.

Essentially, Augustine thinks, if the Romans had really loved justice, they would never have consented to Tarquin's rule in the first place. Tarquin murdered one of Rome's best kings, Servius Tullius. Yet, Augustine writes, the Romans "thought so lightly of his murder of his father-in-law, the best of their kings, that they made him king" (*ciu.* 3.16). Perhaps this is an unfair reading of the situation, given that Livy expressly says that Tarquin ruled by fear.[25] Nevertheless, it is the position Augustine takes. Rather than picking up on this detail of Livy's narrative, he instead focuses on the fact that Tarquin was a military genius.[26] In his

---

[22] Livy, *Ab urbe cond.*, 2.1.   [23] Cf. ibid., 1.57.   [24] Ibid., 1.56.   [25] Ibid., 1.49.
[26] Ibid., 1.52.

mind, the Roman people welcomed Tarquin when they realized the implications of his military prowess and deposed him when his demands
became too much for them.[27] As proof that the Romans were proud,
not just, Augustine zeroes in on the title they gave him, which was not
"Tarquin the Cruel" or "the Criminal" but "Tarquin the Proud" – in
other words, his pride rubbed up against their own (*ciu.* 3.16). While the
Romans were not troubled by the subjugation of other peoples or by the
murder of their best king, they were tired of sewage works. Here is the real
birth of Roman republicanism.

That said, in being driven by an outrage that constituted an excuse, the
Roman people were not, to Augustine's mind, quite responsible for the
birth of their republic. Ultimately, Augustine agrees with what Livy
already implies: the expulsion of the kings was achieved by one man –
Brutus. Brutus was able to enflame the Romans' private outrage and to
channel it toward political change because he was clever. In this way, too,
Rome reveals an important trait of the earthly city: the political manipu-
lation of the many by the savvy. Behind the outburst of popular anger,
Augustine thinks, is always a figure instigating it for his own ends. While
Brutus might have been patriotic, later figures were not quite so noble.

And yet, however patriotic Brutus might have been, he is, for
Augustine, a tragic figure. There is a tremendous cost to trying to create
a free order in a less than virtuous community. It is like trying to contain
chaos. To those who want to cultivate new Bruti, Augustine asks whether
the level of devotion this demands of Roman citizens is salutary. In asking
for leaders who can manipulate an unvirtuous citizenry to contain the
chaos *amor sui* causes, Rome, as a collective, puts all the onus on its
leaders. This, Augustine reflects, is not quite fair, as it allows the Roman
collective to avoid addressing the root cause of its antisocial behavior *and*
it asks its leaders to sacrifice too much. Indeed, in order to protect the
fledgling republic, Brutus was compelled to indulge the people's fear and
to exile his co-consul, even though Collatinus was a loyal servant of the
republic. Worse, when he discovered that his own sons had participated in
the conspiracy to restore Tarquin, he was compelled to execute them (*ciu.*
3.16). Even Virgil feels sorry for Brutus (*ciu.* 3.16; 5.18).

Still, even after everything Brutus sacrificed to protect the republic, it
was never the strong *res publica* the Roman *literati* depicted it as being.
From the beginning, Augustine tells us, the republic suffered a great deal
of internal strife (*ciu.* 3.17). Quoting Sallust, he reminds his readers that

[27] Cf. ibid., 1.52–55.

almost as soon as the Romans divested themselves of a king, the Patricians "reduced the plebeians to the condition of slavery," disposing of their lives and persons "in the manner of kings" (*ciu.* 2.18). In reality, the only way the people gained their celebrated rights and representation was by taking up arms and retreating to the hills.

It should, at this point, be noted that the counterhistory Augustine gives in book 3 relies heavily on his earlier engagement with Cicero. In *De Republica*, Augustine has already reported, Cicero argues for a commonsense connection between *societas* and *iustitia* over and against the sophistic idea that injustice is necessary for political prosperity. A republic, he teaches, can only be truly public – truly shared – if it is bound together by justice (*ciu.* 2.21). This, he adds, is what his contemporaries have forgotten and, this is why their so-called republic is *no longer* a *res publica* (literally, a public thing). Writing book 3 with this claim in the background, Augustine implies that the way things went in republican times was never how they ought to have gone: Rome, he wants them to conclude, was never fully social.[28] The just republic for which the *literati* were nostalgic never fully existed.

In a real *societas*, Cicero argues, and Augustine agrees, citizens would be motivated by a sense of justice. In a real *societas*, those who instigate unjust policies would be moved by good will to correct them once their injustice was brought to light. In other words, if a community were really concerned with protecting and fostering social bonds, the rectification of unjust circumstances would not require power plays on the part of the victim. And yet, in Rome, there was never any "give" on the part of the powerful. Changes came about, not by change of heart, but by rebellion. *This is the story of the earthly city.*

ROME *QUA* EARTHLY CITY

Ultimately, then, Augustine's reading of Roman history reveals how it has been shaped by *amor sui* from the start. For Augustine, *amor sui* has consistently impeded the Roman citizens' desire to correct the injustices from which they benefit such that they have tended to pile up (*ciu.* 2.20). While this does not necessarily mean that Augustine thinks Roman social life has been entirely defined by *amor sui*, it does at least mean that *amor*

---

[28] Yet, as we saw in Chapter 1, it is impossible for Rome to be wholly antisocial. Instead, it merely fails to be fully social, aping a truly just community with its parodic version of *ius*. I will return to this point in Chapter 6.

sui is the fundamental cause of Rome's decline. Thus, with regard to our present inquiry into the earthly city, Augustine's counterhistory help us understand that its animating principle, *amor sui*, fosters a very particular set of behaviors in a political community. Because Rome *qua* earthly city is decidedly trapped in these patterns of behavior, its decline shows us what they are. Through the lens of Rome, we see that the story of the earthly city within politics is a story of strife: tides of power pushed this way and that. There is no peace in Rome *qua* earthly city.

What is more, Augustine tells us, the only reason that there was any semblance of domestic peace in the era in which justice and morality purportedly prevailed among them is that the Patricians and the Plebians were united against Carthage. While superficially efficacious, this peace never required the Romans to think in a way beyond factionalism. As such, it could not heal their divisions. It could only distract them as long as a common enemy remained. Indeed, the kinds of leaders the Romans endorsed after the destruction of Carthage showed as much; these were powerful, ambitious men, who won favor either by promising to protect or destroy the "the existing state of things" (*ciu.* 3.17). They were leaders who advanced the power of a faction.

Looking closely at Rome *qua* earthly city, it becomes clear that the only thing that changes when political actors are animated by *amor sui* is that those who do not want to be dominated gradually take on the characteristics of those who dominate them. Augustine illustrates this in his analysis of the Gracchi. Though the Gracchi "wished" to return the lands that the Patricians "wrongly possessed" to the people, in hindsight, Augustine reflects, "the eradication of a long-standing injustice" was "a hazard of the greatest peril" and "fraught with utter ruin" (*ciu.* 3.24). Not only were both brothers killed and an immense number of Roman citizens slaughtered, but the event sparked the series of civil wars that eventually destroyed the republic.

In saying this, Augustine appears to concede the historians' claim that the Gracchi's attempts at reform instigated the chain of events that ended the republic, but actually, in Augustine's story, the Gracchi come midstream (cf. *ciu.* 2.21).[29] In other words, Augustine has set up his

---

[29] I do think there is something to be said for the idea that the Gracchi attacked the Roman checks and balances in the name of a social good and, in this way, unleashed a kind of progressivist spirit toward the Roman constitution. Because Augustine is weak on institutions, he does not focus on this perhaps legitimate critique of their not playing by the rules.

renarration of Roman history to highlight how the Gracchi's attempts at reforms are not whims coming out of the blue, but responses to long-standing injustices. Augustine, recall, has already pointed out that the kings' *libido dominandi* passed as quickly to the Patricians as their power did. While the Gracchi were traditionally maligned for undercutting the way things were done in Rome – for disturbing the procedural republic-anism that the Roman *literati* celebrated – Augustine implies that these procedures had already failed to realize the common good (*ciu.* 2.22). Something had broken in the Roman system, or, perhaps it had never quite gotten up and running. With this in mind, Augustine appreciates that the Gracchi were moved to challenge the status quo on behalf of the Plebeians. This speaks of their *humanitas*. The problem, however, is that, in a world dominated by the earthly city, these movements do not yield what they should. They are, rather, met with resistance. In the case of the Gracchi, their attempted reforms sparked a backlash that ended up harm-ing those for whom the change was originally entertained.

The story is an old one – from the perspective of the senatorial class, the land reforms proposed by the Gracchi were a threat to stability. As such, it was expedient for them to die. In murdering the Gracchi, the Senators hoped that that they would quash the people's rumblings and protect the status quo. Having already displayed the younger Gracchus's head on the Rostra as a similar warning, they even built the Temple of Concord as an implicit warning not to try again (*ciu.* 3.35). However, this did not have the desired effect and the leaders of the popular faction retaliated, each clamoring to exceed the other in radicalizing the Gracchi's proposals (*ciu.* 3.36). From one point of view, one could say that the Plebeians had finally begun to catch on; the tactics that had once brought them into line were beginning to lose their force. And yet, for Augustine, there is an element of tragedy in this shift.

By reinterpreting the reforms of the Gracchi as a response to long-standing injustices, Augustine recasts the way in which they were a turning point in Roman history. While he clearly feels the weight of the Gracchi's cause, he also feels the weight of the resentment that was unleashed by their example. While it was not *fair* that their attempts at reform were met with resistance, in the end, Augustine cannot but analyze the Gracchi's efforts in terms of their human cost, which was immense (cf. *ciu.* 3.26). Thus, while Augustine seems to understand why the people rebelled, he is caught between grief at the injustice of the Roman elite and grief at the people's own embrace of the *libido dominandi*. Indeed, Augustine does not find it surprising that the people thought it necessary to embrace the methods of the earthly city. From his perspective, the political horizon had become so narrowed that it would have been virtually impossible for them to imagine another way forward; human beings are imitators. Insofar as our imagination is darkened and our role models debased, we will have no recourse to alternative patterns of behavior. Put in political terms, Augustine's point is the following: if the dynamic of the earthly city is allowed to reign long enough, it is only a matter of time before the oppressed will respond by imitating the methods of their oppressors – this is what they see; it is "the way of the world."

Next, Augustine turns to the civil wars in an effort to link it up with his overarching account of Rome's self-destructive spiral. For the Roman *literati*, the wars between Marius and Sulla, the latter a Patrician, the former a Plebeian, represented the terrible face of factionalism that followed on the heels of the Gracchi. For Augustine, these were the fruit of the same self-love that had been dictating political choices since the Founding. For both, they showed the cost of countering injustice with the harsh justice of vengeance. Augustine recounts the horrors of these wars in great detail, emphasizing how each confrontation couched itself as a justified response to injustice. For what it was worth, Augustine admits, Marius started it. Yet, this being so, Sulla's revenge, "surpassed all bounds, and followed on too far in chase of the disease" (*ciu.* 3.27, quoting Lucan). The same was true of Marius's subsequent revenge, and each one that followed on it, all the way down to Caesar Augustus. While Cicero had hoped Caesar Augustus would be the one to "restore the 'liberty of the republic'" (*ciu.* 3.30), Augustine wonders how he could draw this conclusion; there was no more *res publica* to hold together. By Cicero's time and by Cicero's own admission, the social bonds that constituted the republic had been entirely rotted out (*ciu.* 2.21). All that could hold Rome's domestic life together was the power of a man who stood above both the Patricians and the Plebeians.

The story on the foreign front is no better. This is the story of an addiction used as a crutch. Because ambition for glory was something the Romans could ostensibly share without fighting among themselves (though the competition between Marius and Sulla for military honors that started the civil wars suggests that this was not a foolproof strategy), it did seem to stay Rome's internal collapse. The pursuit of glory bound the Romans together in a common enterprise, but in reality, even this outwardly directed agonism cost Roman lives (*ciu.* 3.18–19). To drive this point home, Augustine recounts a story from a particularly bloody defeat during the second Punic War. In it, Hannibal displayed his triumph by the number of baskets he managed to fill with the rings of dead Roman cavalrymen: "from this evidence the carnage of the rest of the army – a crowd of slain who lay there without gold rings – can be estimated by conjecture" (*ciu.* 3.19).

Unsurprisingly, Augustine tells us, after that the Romans experienced such a shortage of soldiers that they pardoned criminals, and freed slaves to fill the ranks. It is not clear that these men graduated to a better fate as a result. When, Augustine goes on, the Romans had no more public funds to arm these men, "individuals offered anything they had, their rings, their lockets, the pitiable emblems of rank, and even the senators had no gold left for their own use, still less the members of the other orders" (*ciu.* 3.19). While Livy tells this story to highlight the early Romans' patriotism, Augustine recasts it as a tragedy. Rome collectively chose to squander what it should have been protecting. While the Romans may have agreed to sacrifice their lives and goods for glory, the fact of the matter is that its pursuit only brought destruction. Glory may have been a public value, but it was not a common *good*.

In the end, Augustine's verdict on republican Rome is that it suffered from an inability to foster genuine community both at home and abroad. In committing itself to *amor sui*, it foreclosed this possibility, preferring to ground its sense of community in its *contra mundum* attitude, which did not ask citizens to restrain their *amor sui*, but merely to channel it into a shared project of seeking glory. For Augustine, the patterns of behavior in which Rome was trapped could only really have been reversed by its members' willingness to give up their desire for preeminence. And yet, bound to its love of dominance, it could only accommodate this love by distracting its members' ambition outward. It could only cement a sense of community in light of what they were *against*. By turning itself over to the ways of the earthly city, Rome rendered itself unable to correct the injustices within its community without generating worse ones, and as empire, these injustices bled out onto the world stage.

CONTEXTUALIZING AUGUSTINE'S HISTORY OF ROME

In presenting the dynamic of the earthly city as a cancer on Rome's social life from its very beginning, Augustine effectively guts the myth of Rome's golden age. Augustine's version of Roman history is one in which *amor sui* gains traction through the spread of the *libido dominandi*. It is no longer a story in which arch-villains like Sulla or Catiline bear responsibility for Rome's decline. Now, everyone is implicated. Even the guardians of

Rome's celebrated traditions and institutions are charged with protecting private interests in the name of procedural piety. And yet, Augustine's revisionist history is not a mere rejection of the traditional Roman story; there are still patriots capable of great sacrifice. The problem is that these cannot sustain a *ciuitas* rooted in *amor sui*. The glory and benefits designed to motivate a less than virtuous population only pull Rome further into decline. They spread the patterns of behavior already strangling its *societas*. In the end, self-love cannot yield authentic community.

Using the early books of the *City of God* to undermine the narrative that allowed the Romans to believe in a golden age and to scapegoat Christianity for the sack, Augustine's history of Rome hits the notes he thinks the Roman patriots need to hear. Showing his readers, first, that the earthly city masks itself as the just city, and second, that the strife it attempts to conceal is degenerative, Augustine provides a new kind of political education. Instead of teaching that Republican virtues once broadly existed, but were extinguished by luxury, Augustine teaches that fallen human nature marred the Roman project from the beginning. Instead of teaching that an unquestioning love of country was the greatest protector of the Roman project, Augustine teaches that this kind of love is disordered. Instead of teaching that civic virtue could be rekindled by patriotic stories, pagan rituals, and the promise of glory, Augustine teaches that virtues rooted in falsehood and ambition cannot sustain themselves. To flourish, the Roman virtues must be transplanted into new soil.

Accordingly, as pessimistic as Augustine's retelling of Roman history may be, it has a very specific purpose, which qualifies its ability to stand as his diagnosis of political life *tout court*. In brief, Augustine considers his readers' attachment to Rome to be a serious stumbling block to their conversion. We have already seen the great influence Rome has in shaping the imaginations of its inhabitants, which justifies this concern. As such, it is clear that the deconstruction of the mythology surrounding *Roma Aeterna* is vital to *City of God*'s purpose. By placing Rome squarely within the territory occupied by the earthly city, Augustine bars the way back to a just city on earth and reorients his readers' nostalgia for Rome's golden age toward eschatological hope. After presenting the Church as the place where "the commandments of the true God are made known, his marvelous works are related, thanks are offered for his gifts, and prayers are sent up for his favors," he addresses his patriotic readers directly (*ciu.* 2.28):

All this should be the object of your chief desire, you people of Rome, with all your fine natural qualities, your descendants of men like Regulus, Scaevola, the Scipios and Fabricius. ... The admirable and excellent qualities which nature has bestowed on you can only come to purity and perfection through true godliness; ungodliness will bring them to ruin and punishment. Choose now which course to follow. (*ciu.* 2.29)

By presenting Christianity as a better religion for the *ciuitas* than Roman civil religion, Augustine suggests that the patriot need not abandon his concern for Rome in order to join the city of God. Instead, it provides a foundation for all the virtues that benefit the political community.

Nevertheless, this is only half of Augustine's strategy. He does not want his patriotic readers to embrace Christianity merely because it is politically useful: he wants them to embrace it because it is true. Accordingly, Augustine must also present the city of God as a better object of devotion than Rome is. It is easy to see how his renarration of Roman history fits into this plan, but Augustine must also drive the point home by juxtaposing the benevolence of the two *patriae*. This is arguably the primary objective of book 5. There, Augustine examines "why God was willing that the Roman empire should extend so widely and last so long" (*ciu.* 5. *praef*). In reading about the feats of Brutus, Torquatus, Curtius, and Porsenna, one quickly concludes that it was due to the greatness of its heroes. These Romans were willing, not only to die for their *patria*, but also to kill their unpatriotic sons, to thrust their hand into fire in order to intimidate their enemies, to hurl themselves off a cliff to fulfill an oracle and to offer themselves as a holocaust "so that the anger of the gods might be appeased" (*ciu.* 5.18). Through "voluntary self-inflicted sacrifice" these Romans served their *patria*.[30]

Yet, by devoting themselves entirely to their earthly *patria*, Augustine goes on to show, these Roman heroes squandered their lives:

Those Roman heroes belonged to an earthly city, and the aim set before them, in all their acts of duty for her, was the safety of their country, and a kingdom not in heaven, but on earth; not in life eternal, but in the process where the dying pass away and are succeeded by those who will die in their turn. What else was there for them to love save glory? For though glory, they desired to have a kind of life after death on the lips of those who praised them. (*ciu.* 5.14)

Because their "sole motive" was the "hope of receiving glory from their fellow men," he goes on, Christ's words apply to them: "I tell you in truth,

---

[30] For a helpful contrast between Augustine's read on Roman heroes and his own understanding of heroism, see Robert Dodaro, "Augustine's Revision of the Heroic Ideal," *Augustinian Studies* 36, no. 1 (2005): 141–157. Cf. Swift, "Pagan and Christian Heroes in Augustine's *City of God*."

they have received their reward in full." (*ciu.* 5.15). This, of course, would not seem so tragic were it not pitted against the reward of the saints immediately afterward. In serving the city of God, Augustine argues, these patriots find not a shadowy parody of life after death, but eternal happiness. Thus, while Rome lures its citizens to their own destruction for a glory that is more glitter than gold, the city of God draws its citizens to their salvation. By presenting the disjunct between the two *patriae* in this light, Augustine does his best to argue that only the latter is a *patria* worth absolute devotion.

CONCLUSION

Recalling the psychagogic structure of *City of God*, we now see that his retelling of Roman history is part of Augustine's project of liberation. Viewing his patriotic readers as imprisoned by a parodic *patria*, Augustine considers himself obliged to remind them that their earthly home is less than perfect. By rendering them dissatisfied with the city in which they live, Augustine calls them forth to a life of pilgrimage. By calling on their patriotic impulses, he proposes a life of service that will reap true felicity as its reward. Yet, in detaching his readers from an excessive love of Rome, Augustine does not suggest that Roman patriots abandon their earthly *patria* to its own destruction. Instead, he argues that it would be better served by a religion that is not designed to cater to its earthly ambitions.[31] In this way, the Romans are free to embrace it, without detriment to the city that they love. Indeed, given that all these sentiments are echoed in Augustine's famous letter to the Roman Patriot Nectarius, it is fitting to conclude with a passage from it. He writes,

I am not surprised that, even though your limbs grow cold with age, your heart is warm with love for your fatherland, and I praise you for this. I am not unwilling, but even happy to hear that you not only hold it in memory, but also show by your life and conduct that for good men there is no limit or end in caring for the fatherland. For this reason we would like to have you yourself as such a citizen of a certain heavenly fatherland, in the love for which we face danger in accord

---

[31] In reading these passages, Fortin goes so far as to argue that, for Augustine, "Christianity does not destroy patriotism but reinforces it by making of it a religious duty." Fortin, "The Political Thought of St. Augustine," 24. I do not think, however, that this is true to the extent that Augustine thinks the Christian patriot can hold "twin citizenship." Ibid., 20. Instead, as I argue in the final chapter, there will always be a tension between the *ethoi* of the two cities, such that patriotism in Christianity becomes transfigured into something that a secular patriot would not recognize as such.

with our limitations and are at labor among those whom we help to attain it. If you were a citizen of it, you would judge that there ought to be no limit or end in caring for some small portion of it, even while you are journeying away from it on this earth. And you would become better to the extent that the city is better to which you offer the services you owe her, for you will find no end of rejoicing in her eternal peace, if you set for yourself in the present time no end for your labors. (*ep.* 91.1)[32]

In the end, then, Augustine's political warning to the patriotic Romans is this: insofar as your story is *only* the story of the earthly city, insofar as the imaginations of political actors are captured by the promises of the earthly city's methods, politics will close in on itself. It will cut itself off from the possibility of generating constructive responses to conflict. It will degenerate more and more into factionalism. If you want to effect genuine cultural renewal in your *patria*, you must embrace the heavenly *patria* as your true home, for it alone has the resources to heal the divisions caused by *amor sui.* Exhorting his patriotic readers to "take possession" of the heavenly *patria,* and to add themselves "to the number of our citizens," Augustine reveals the real impetus behind his retelling of Roman history (ibid.).

---

[32] Augustine, *Letters 1–99*, trans. Roland Teske, ed. John E. Rotelle (Hyde Park, NY: New City Press, 2001), 366. This letter has been much studied. See, inter alia, Gerard O'Daly, "Thinking through History: Augustine's Method in the *City of God* and Its Ciceronian Dimension," *Augustinian Studies* 30, no. 2 (1999): 47–49; Fortin, "The Political Thought of St. Augustine," 24; Robert Dodaro, "Augustine's Secular City," in *Augustine and His Critics,* ed. Robert Dodaro and George Lawless (New York: Routledge, 2000), 231–232, and Dodaro, *Christ and the Just Society,* 7; Peter Iver Kaufman, "Patience and/or Politics: Augustine and the Crisis at Calama, 408–409," *Vigiliae Christianae* 57, no. 1 (2003): 22–35; Erika Hermanowicz, "Catholic Bishops and Appeals to the Imperial Court: A Legal Study of the Calama Riots in 408," *Journal of Early Christian Studies,* 12, no. 4 (2004): 481–521.

5

The Sacramental Worldview and Its Antisacramental Distortion

Exploring Augustine's Theory of Signs and Its Implications for the Two Cities Doctrine

In the previous chapter, we looked at Roman history unmasked: stripped of the rhetoric designed to bind its citizens to their *patria*. We saw that, without a consideration of Augustine's rhetorical aim, this account of Roman history seems to suggest that politics is always and everywhere mired in sin, which, in turn, seems to concede politics to the earthly city. However, as Augustine's appeal to the Roman patriot makes plain, his pessimistic focus on Roman history is designed for a specific purpose: to divest readers of an unhealthy patriotism so that they may enter the city of God (cf. *ciu.* 2.29). What is more, Augustine also makes it plain that this history was never meant to stand as an exhaustive treatment of political life; writing in book 2 that he will return to the question of the just republic when the parameters of his argument permit him, Augustine lets his readers know early on that there is more to be said about politics than books 2–5 allow (cf. *ciu.* 2.21). For this reason, I would argue, it is fitting to read their treatment of Rome with book 19's re-presentation of politics as its *telos*. Having not yet explored this presentation, we have not seen Augustine's last word on the status of politics.

Of course, this is not to imply that we will find a rosy view of political life once we do: it is well known that book 19 is laden with a pessimistic streak of its own.[1] Instead, what makes book 19's treatment of politics distinctive is its placement within the text, or, the approach that its placement frees Augustine to take. As I have already suggested, the arc

---

[1] Though I do not focus on the rhetoric of book 19 in detail here, I do unpack the logic behind its pessimistic tone in "Sheathing the Sword," 722–732, and "Therapeutic Deception," 34–37.

of Augustine's argument can be divided into two basic movements. First, Augustine seeks to attune his readers to the ways in which their worldview is permeated with the logic of *amor sui*. Then, having demolished a variety of "worldly" worldviews, he presents the world anew, as it appears through the eyes of faith. Thus, the last twelve books differ from the previous in that they present their argument on terms set out by the city of God. To put this another way, rather than arguing against a series of views imbued with the logic of the earthly city, the second half of *City of God* argues for a vision of reality as it is revealed by the Christian God. This frame allows the last twelve books to remain more holistic in emphasis, even as they include arguments against the earthly city. Accordingly, when Augustine finally returns to the theme of politics in book 19, he is free to focus on what he sees as the central point: earthly peace is not the *telos* of human life even though the earthly city thinks it is and even though it is a true good. This conviction, I argue, provides the foundation for the rest of his political commentary.

Yet, even recognizing this, a significant difficulty remains for our project of gleaning the status of politics from *City of God*; Augustine never explicitly unpacks his understanding of the relationship between politics and the earthly city. Moreover, he wavers between using *ciuitas terrena* to mean the archetypal community of self-love and using it to mean this or that political community. Given the way in which this ambiguity aggravates the problem of interpreting Augustine's pessimistic tone, what we need, and indeed, what we have already begun developing, is a way of reading *City of God*'s political passages that brings out their intrinsic rationale. With this in hand, we will be able to interpret them holistically: in a way that is true to Augustine's overarching vision.

I am, of course, arguing that the intrinsic rationale of these passages, and of *City of God* as a whole, is sacramental.[2] As Robert Markus has noted in his excellent work on Augustinian semiotics, sacramentality – the quality of acting as a sign that points to God – is at the center of Augustine's whole worldview.[3] E. J. Cutrone also makes this point, arguing that Augustine views the material world as "revelatory of the divine mystery," pointing beyond itself toward a "deeper, inner reality."[4] Here,

---

[2] In this way, I am not focusing on Augustine's use of the term *sacramentum* per se. For a helpful situation of his use of it in his theological debates with other sects, see Dodaro, *Christ and the Just Society*, 147–159.

[3] Markus, "St. Augustine on Signs," 60.

[4] E. J. Cutrone, "Sacraments," in *Augustine through the Ages: An Encyclopedia*, 741.

I would like to argue that this is precisely the message about the world that *City of God* seeks to communicate. Because the whole text is ordered toward the establishment of sacramental vision in its readers, it also seeks to situate political life within the sacramental worldview; this means that the sacramental horizon, the horizon that *ought* to point beyond itself, is precisely one in which Augustine's vision of politics makes sense.

For this reason, our goal in the present chapter is to grasp the sacramental worldview that undergirds Augustine's way of writing about politics. From what we have seen so far, it should at least be clear that Augustine uses symbolic shorthand throughout *City of God* to convey his sacramental worldview. We can, for example, already say that Augustine speaks of the earthly city as earthly because of its terrestrial orientation; it seeks to conquer the world, and so receives its name from the world. This is but the tip of the iceberg; *City of God* is shot through with a sacramental grammar, and book 19 is no different. It is, therefore, imperative that we become attuned to the cues that Augustine is giving us in the text. It is imperative that we learn to read his sacramental grammar.

Fortunately, Augustine has left us with a well-developed semiotic theory that unpacks the logic behind this grammar. Beginning the chapter with an exploration of this theory as it is laid out in *De Doctrina Christiana*, I find that Augustine considers the reality of created things to be endowed with a given meaning that points to their Creator: this is a meaning that the earthly city replaces with its own antisacramental meaning. Returning to *City of God* in the latter half, I find the battle between the sacramental and the antisacramental worldview to be at the root of the psychagogic strategy we have been exploring; looking at key passages from the second half of the work, I argue that the *telos* of the text is a sacramental vision in which we can see two opposing economies at work in the world, one a parody of the other; ultimately, *City of God* is designed to help us see through the false claims of the earthly city so that we might resist them.

Accordingly, the present chapter makes two interrelated claims. The first is that *De Doctrina*'s semiotic theory is the sacramental worldview animating his symbolic shorthand in *City of God*, only viewed from another angle.[5] The second is that this sacramental worldview points to

---

[5] Though the bulk of this work is dated to much earlier than *City of God*, it still is the best work to study in order to access Augustine's semiotic views. For evidence that Augustine's theory remains largely the same, see *s.* 73.2, written between 426 and 430. Cf. Markus,

a very specific relationship between politics and the earthly city; namely, it undermines the credibility of the earthly city's claim on the political sphere and about the political sphere. In other words, Augustine's theory of signs, which distinguishes between sacramental signs and their antisacramental distortion, is an extremely helpful avenue for clarifying Augustine's stance toward politics. In short, if the logic of the earthly city is not the definitive ethos of politics, then it follows that a truer way of participating in political life lies beneath. Unfolding what this means for Augustine's understanding of politics will be the task of the final chapter. First, we must familiarize ourselves with his sacramental worldview and the theory of signs that pervades it.

AUGUSTINE'S SEMIOTIC THEORY

As I have just suggested, the most appropriate starting point for our present inquiry is Augustine's *De Doctrina Christiana*. While Augustine theorizes about *signa* in multiple works, *De Doctrina*'s explanation of the tripartite relationship between the sign, what it brings to mind, and the interpreter provides the foundation for his theory's ability to explain how and why the two cities interpret the world so differently.[6] In this way, it sheds new light on the sacramental vision put forth in *City of God* and the place of politics within it. The central questions that *De Doctrina* helps us explore are the following: how is it that a person comes to read empirically given experiences as evidence for a particular worldview? Does the interpreter actively choose this interpretation, or, does she passively receive that meaning? Is it possible to misinterpret signs? In this last question, another factor comes into focus: the sign-maker.

Lingering in the background of *De Doctrina Christiana* is the central tenet of Augustine's ontology: Scripture's revelation that the world was created in the Word and as an expression of the Word. Accordingly, while *De Doctrina* focuses on human beings as interpreters of signs, it presents human interpretation as irrevocably set against the backdrop of an already spoken Word: a Word yielding a world with an already intended meaning. For Augustine, the speaker of this Word is God, and the central problem we

---

"St. Augustine on Signs," "Augustine on Magic: A Neglected Semiotic Theory," and "Signs, Communication and Communities in Augustine's *De Doctrina Christiana*"; Ando "Signs, Idols and the Incarnation in Augustinian Metaphysics" and "Augustine on Language."

[6] Markus, "St. Augustine on Signs," 72.

face is our collective inability to read creation as the sign God intended it to be. And yet, as *De Doctrina* also shows, our interpretative difficulties are exacerbated by an alternative discourse: the cacophony of the earthly city. Ultimately, by choosing the Word as the starting point of his semiotic theory, Augustine gives the rubric in which the world's sacramentality – its pointing function – endows the world with an original meaning.

In Augustine's semiotic theory, the fundamental relationship is between signs (*signa*) and things (*res*). Augustine's sign theory, one might say, relates *signa* and *res* much in the same way that Aristotelian metaphysics relates matter and form: what counts, in the end, is the fact that the *signa-res* pairing expresses a particular type of relationship whenever it is used. As such, many things can be called *res* without being *res per se*, just as wood can be said to be the matter of chair even though it is not matter *per se*. Thus, signs are merely things considered insofar as they point to other things. Or, as Augustine puts it in book 2, a sign "is a thing, which besides the impression it conveys to the senses, also has the effect of making something else come to mind" (*doct. chr.* 2.1.1).[7] The word *agnus,* for example, brings the idea of a lamb to mind as well as impressing the ears with the sounds represented by the signs *ag-nus*. And yet, the lamb it indicates is not merely a thing, but itself can signify Christ.

In a way, the lamb is a special case, in that its Christological signification is given by Scripture. Yet in another way, it is paradigmatic; Augustine reads all created things as signs by nature, in that they all point to God as their cause. There is, therefore, "one supreme thing" that, for Augustine, is always *res* and never *signa*: God (*doct. chr.* 1.5.5). The world's creation in the Word, in other words, is the central case of *signa-res* around which his entire semiotic theory is built. It cannot be separated from his belief in creation *ex nihilo*. Teaching that we only read created things properly when we read them as things that point to – and point us back to – the Word in which they were created, Augustine presents a cosmos that is designed to orient creatures toward the creator.

In other words, *De Doctrina Christiana* treats both signs and things in terms of an original communication. This is why Augustine begins *De Doctrina* by warning against interpreting (and loving) created things as ultimate.[8] What motivates his oft-critiqued excursus into the use (*uti*) and

---

[7] Augustine, *Teaching Christianity*, trans. Edmund Hill (Hyde Park, NY: New City Press, 1996), 129.

[8] While this interpretation of created things strikes the fallen mind as a constraint on how we love them – and, perhaps the way Augustine counsels use of them aggravates this reaction – the

enjoyment (*frui*) of created things is his starting point of creation as communication; when we enjoy created things as ends in themselves, Augustine thinks, we fail to read them as the signs they really are.[9] In doing so, we turn them into signs of our own volition. Seeking a corrective to this vision, Augustine uses book 1 of *De Doctrina* as a re-presentation of created things in light of their original meaning, given in the Word and recovered through the Word (cf. Jn 1:3; Col 1:16; 1 Cor 8:6; Rom 11:36, inter alia). Book 1 is a depiction of a world of things borne out of an eternal speech act – out of a Word that has a divine meaning.

In book 2, Augustine reflects on the place of signs in this world. While he considers every created thing to be, ultimately, a divine sign, books 2 and 3 focus on the signs that human beings give in order to "transfer" what they have in mind "to someone else's mind" (*doct. chr.* 2.2.3).[10] These signs are of two sorts: those intended (*signa data*) and those unintended (*signa natura*). Some things we communicate on purpose; others we communicate unintentionally, as when we try to hold back tears without success. Here again, we see that Augustine's primary concern is communication, and, in this case, human communication. The relationship of this phenomenon to God's prior communication is as yet unclear; what we say to each other could be in harmony with or in opposition to it. Either way, what we communicate to each other matters because human beings can either illuminate or obscure the world's original meaning for each other. And so we find that we have returned to the problem of *consuetudo* by a different path.[11]

---

sense that Augustine is imposing foreign considerations onto our love of good things, is, from an Augustinian perspective, mostly because we have become used to defining the meaning of the things we love for ourselves, and our demands on them are often invisible to us.

[9] Much has been written recently in defense of the *uti frui* distinction, which to the modern mind suggests a violation of Kant's categorical imperative. See, e.g., Eric Gregory, *Politics and the Order of Love*, 323–350, and Sarah Stewart-Kroeker, "Resisting Idolatry and Instrumentalisation in Loving the Neighbour: The Significance of the Pilgrimage Motif for Augustine's *Usus–Fruitio* Distinction," *Studies in Christian Ethics* 27, no. 2 (2014): 202–221.

[10] Augustine, *Teaching Christianity*, 129. This, Augustine clarifies, does include the Scriptures because "even the signs given [therein] by God ... have been indicated to us through the human beings who wrote them down" (ibid.).

[11] To say that we only ever learn about things through signs is just another way of saying that we only ever live in an interpreted world. Signs impose themselves on us from without, suggesting meaning to us before we ask them to. And yet, the difficulty is that some signs speak to us while others do not. Indeed, as we have already seen, Augustine considers our ability to "hear creation speak" to be muffled by a cacophony of alternative interpretations of the world. What is more, insofar as we are not disposed to believe the

That said, Augustine does think that the things of the world can properly bear a multiplicity of proximate meanings. This is where the neutral meaning of the term *consuetudo* comes into Augustine's picture. While God makes signs by bringing things into existence, human beings can only ever be subcreators, taking what already exists and fashioning new signs out of it. The things of the world, then, come to us quite naturally as matter to be imbued with symbolic meaning.[12] For Augustine, it is only insofar as these imbued meanings imply an ultimate worldview that their signification takes on a moral quality. It is only insofar as they obscure the divine meaning that our signs are pejoratively "of" man.

Therefore, while Augustine so often condemns the words and ideas that are merely "from us," he does consider the creative project of making signs to communicate ideas to be an authentic exercise of human ingenuity (*doct. chr.* 2.25.38). To be sure, he does think that much of what we communicate is the fruit of what we have discovered in the fabric of creation or else builds on it.[13] Nevertheless, it is not Augustine's position that everything we communicate through signs has to be "inscribed in the permanent and divinely instituted rationality of the universe" in order to be true (*doct. chr.* 2.32.50).[14] Sometimes the truth of an idea is rooted in human agreement. Above all, what he has in mind here is the phenomenon of language. Greek might have a relatively set vocabulary but, he thinks, there is no reason it had to be this set of words (*doct. chr.* 2.24.37). Particular people, it is true, might have reasons for the words they pick

---

original meaning of the world over these other interpretations, creation will not convey its original meaning to us. In the end, creation only speaks with a clear voice in *amor Dei*.

[12] Here, I think Jacques Ellul's reflection on images is particularly apt: "the image contains within itself a deep contradiction. It is not ambiguous: it is coherent, reliable, and inclusive; but it is insignificant. It can have innumerable meanings, depending on culture, learning, or the intervention of some other dimension. For this reason I must learn to see before looking at the image. After seeing it, I must learn to interpret it. ... I call these images 'vision' because they are connected with the other images I am accustomed to. I would be tempted to say in this case that the order is reversed. The visual image exists, and then I attribute a meaning to it; but the vision appears only as the illustration of a previously established meaning." *The Humiliation of the Word*, trans. Joyce Main Hanks (Grand Rapids, MI: Eerdmans, 1985), 8.

[13] The rules of logic (*doct. chr.* 2.32.50), mathematics (*doct. chr.* 2.39.58), ethics (*doct. chr.* 2.40.60), and even rhetoric (*doct. chr.* 2.36.54) fall into the first category. As such, he argues, they cannot rightly be said to be "instituted by human beings" (*doct. chr.* 2.32.50). Rather, they are "observed and noted down by them" (ibid.). On the most basic level, Augustine thinks that we make signs to communicate truths we have discovered to one another.

[14] Augustine, *Teaching Christianity*, 154.

as signs, but in the end, it is a human decision that institutes the connection between a set of sounds and what they bring to mind.

On top of this, however, he is thinking of cultural convention. Again, the reason why the Roman culture has a certain set of conventions is because a certain set of Roman people along the way *chose* to introduce these customs into their societies; they used their agency to shape reality. In this way, the customs of a particular culture can be construed as one particular way of living socially, arising out of a specific context. One can even speak of a variety of ways of living socially that are, in theory, equally consonant with the original meaning of creation, though, Augustine suspects, most cultural conventions are "partly" in harmony with the world's original meaning and "partly not" (*doct. chr.* 2.19.29).[15] Insofar as they are harmonious, though, they are useful and creative responses to the human condition, contributing to the "necessary ordering of life" (*doct. chr.* 2.25.40).[16] The human creativity that the diverse expressions of social life reveals is part and parcel of our dignity as rational creatures. For Augustine, it is not *human creativity* that is troubling; it is the fact that we use signs in a way that contradicts and obscures their true meaning (*doct. chr.* 2.24.37).

Accordingly, when Augustine writes that "nothing that human beings derive from themselves is to be reckoned as more proper to them than any kind of falsehood and lie," what he is suggesting is that no thing, no subject of communication, that we derive from ourselves is really *from* ourselves except insofar as it breaks with the meaning of the Word (*doct. chr.* 2.25.29).[17] Recall that the main characteristic of the earthly city's speech is that it deviates from the whole truth for the sake of its own designs; it rewrites reality. Here, we are reminded of the logic of privation that we discussed toward the end of our first chapter. Sin, we saw there, is always a departure from something prior, and therefore, the sinful act always contains a vestige of what it could have been. We now see, similarly, that the speech of the earthly city is parasitic and distortive. Inducted into the earthly city's economy of *amor sui*, words become a vehicle for power, but they cannot help relying on some truth claims if they want to be credible. This makes it incredibly difficult to decipher what is true and what is a perversion. Confused by the cacophony, we need a divine standard.

While, to be sure, Augustine believes that the earthly city's worldview is perpetuated by an abuse of the power to communicate – we fashion,

---

[15] Ibid., 144.   [16] Ibid., 150.   [17] Ibid., 151.

promote, and reinforce the falsity of the earthly city's worldview every time we speak and act out of *amor sui* – he also believes that this tendency reaches the zenith of its pathology when human beings turn nature itself into a sign of the earthly city's dominance. This shuts off any possibility of creation conveying its original meaning and totalizes the dominant myth of a particular place and time. Furthermore, Augustine thinks, the "imaginary signs" that human beings impose upon nature only strengthen the illusion that the earthly city's economy of power is all that there is, and drive people further into it out of despair (*doct. chr.* 2.23.36).[18]

On one level, it is clear that when Augustine writes about imaginary signs, he is thinking of superstitious practices like astrology, augury, or haruspicy.[19] These he lambasts in a special way in *City of God* books 2–5, presenting them as convenient manipulations of a political audience for self-seeking purposes. The utility of such practices is obvious – one need only think of Romulus and Remus's respective interpretations of the birds at Rome's founding or Romulus's convenient apotheosis during an eclipse of the sun (*ciu.* 3.15).[20] Augustine sums it up well at *City of God* 4.32:

We need not seek further for the reason [why the Romans had so many myths about the gods] than the interest of the self-styled experts and savants in misleading the people in matters of religion. . . . The leaders of men (who were not men of integrity but the human counterparts of the demons) taught men as true, under the name of religion, things they knew to be false. By this means they bound them tighter, as it were, to the citizen community, so that they might bring them under control and keep them there by the same technique. (*ciu.* 4.32)

---

[18] Ibid., 148. What is more, any convention that bars our way to return to God, even if it seems to be merely human is, at least implicitly, a compact with demons. For the best article on this topic see, Robert Markus, "Augustine on Magic: A Neglected Semiotic Theory."

[19] According to Balthasar, "whereas sense impressions are 'true' at least to the extent that they announce states of affairs in the material world (which in turn are only striving for unity in time and space), the internal image-world of the imagination – and so human art as part of its domain, and also metaphysics in is far as it is dependent upon imagination and as it is un-Christian – is the source of all deception and the true *fabrica idolorum*" for Augustine. Balthasar, *Glory of the Lord II*, 124. Of course, the best treatment of Augustine's take on superstition is to be found in Markus's "A Neglected Semiotic Theory."

[20] Cf. Livy, *Ab urbe cond.*, 1.7. According to Livy, the brothers had asked the gods to communicate by augury "which of them should govern the town . . . Remus, the story goes, was the first to receive a sign – six vultures; and no sooner was this made known to the people than double the number of birds appeared to Romulus. The followers of each promptly saluted their master as king, one basing its claim upon priority, the other upon number." Livy, *The Early History of Rome*, 37.

In other words, Rome's leaders knew the importance of cultivating a vision of the cosmos that reinforced their own political power.[21] By filling their citizens' heads with stories about the Roman gods, they made participation in civil religion indispensable, and reshaped the cosmological horizon in the image of the political, if only to further their own political aspirations. We have already seen much of this in Chapter 3.

Underneath the machinations of the cunning, however, Augustine believes that there is a deeper source of the superstitions that arise in human communities. For him, the cultural development of superstition is concomitant with the fallen state. Stricken with anxiety and fragmented by multifarious desires, the fallen soul feels the necessity of participating in the earthly city's economy, and, seeing this necessity confirmed by *consuetudo*, comes to view the world in its terms. *Amor sui* becomes the hermeneutical key to the cosmos. Furthermore, because the fallen state cultivates a common set of symptoms in human beings, and in a particular culture, an even more particular set, it is easy for persons living in the same context to co-author, as it were, a superstitious worldview that seems particularly plausible to them. Systematizing their "erroneous guesses" about the meaning of events and things into a mythology, they entrap themselves in a tragic view of the universe (*doct. chr.* 2.24.37).[22] Any significance this new meaning has gains its traction from the minds of the interpreters themselves; its system of signs echoes their collective desires and fears back to them so that it increasingly closes in on itself, reflecting the narrowness of their hearts. In a community looking for proof that its "assumptions and ways of thinking" are true, the meaning of created things becomes constrained by the limited imagination of *amor sui* (*doct. chr.* 2.24.37).[23] Words break away from the Word.

Ultimately, then, Augustine's semiotic theory situates the dueling discourses of the two cities within an ontology that grounds one and

---

[21] In *City of God*, Augustine accuses the Roman empire of projecting a pantheon made in its own image onto the cosmos. Regarding this, John Cavadini writes, "The gods are pictured as an extension of the bureaucracy, a kind of projection onto nature of the body politic. . . . Nature is reduced to the status of the commonplace, subsumed under the realm of the commonwealth, where it will not be a competitor against the Empire for glory. The pantheon is nothing but the Empire writ large, divinized, and thus we recognize in the parody the accusation that the Roman religion represented nothing but the apotheosis of the Empire itself." Cavadini, "Ideology and Solidarity," 130.

[22] Augustine, *Teaching Christianity*, 148.   [23] Ibid.

deconstructs the other. In exploring Augustine's theory of signs, we have seen its intimate connection to his belief in *creation ex nihilo*. Because all human communication is set against the backdrop of an already spoken Word, the words that are "of" the earthly city are precisely those that deviate from this Word's meaning. They may deviate in a myriad of ways, but they cannot conceal their common root in *amor sui*. *Amor sui* inevitably narrows our read on the meaning of creation, so that we get caught in a world constructed by our own desires and fears – a world enticing for its glamor, but nihilistic at its core.

DUELING COSMOLOGIES IN *CITY OF GOD*

In the introduction to this chapter, I suggested that Augustine's semiotic theory in *De Doctrina* is the sacramental worldview of *City of God*, only viewed from another angle. To see this more clearly, it is necessary to return to *City of God*, where we find the dueling cosmologies of the two cities pitted against one another. Though Augustine addresses the pagan cosmology throughout the first ten books, it is his treatment of Porphyry's cosmology in book 10 that is the most illuminating for our purposes. We have already seen that Augustine uses particular philosophers' shortcomings as a sign that human beings cannot escape the earthly city on their own. Here, he uses Porphyry's cosmology and, in particular, his belief in theurgy to reinforce his message that human beings cannot escape the earthly city's enslavement to superstition on their own. Describing how Porphyry, a Platonist, was at once "in subjection to" the demonic powers and "at the same time ashamed of his subjection," Augustine presents his superstitious belief in theurgy as the tragic acceptance of a myth that only projected the ethos of the earthly city onto the cosmos as a whole (*ciu.* 10.24).

Making much of the fact that Porphyry could not discover "a universal way for the liberation of the soul," Augustine depicts him as a tragic figure much after the fashion of Varro and Seneca. Describing how he ruled out Christianity both for its teaching on the Incarnation and for the persecutions that seemed to spell its impending disappearance, Augustine again invokes his diatribe against philosophic pride, presenting Porphyry's pride as a blindness that prevents him from seeing the absurdity of theurgy (*ciu.* 10.32). Given that philosophic liberation was open only to the few, Porphyry considered theurgy, a form of ritual purification, to be at least something he could recommend to the many, capable, as it was, of raising unphilosophic souls "a little above the earth after death" (*ciu.* 10.9).[24] For Porphyry, like many others of his time, the distinction between angels and demons was one of rank: demons inhabited the lower air, while angels, whom the Platonists "prefer[red] to call" the gods, inhabited the ether (*ciu.* 9.23, cf. 10.9). According to the Platonists, the gods did not lower themselves to the realm of human beings, lest they be soiled by its materiality. Demons, therefore, acted as go-betweens, carrying men's supplications to the gods above.

Yet, in looking at the details of his cosmology more closely, Augustine reveals a number of absurdities in Porphyry's endorsement of theurgy. In the first place, Porphyry believed that the demons involved in relaying petitions to the gods begrudged the soul its true purification. Like Apuleius before him, he was of the opinion that the demons suffered from the same passions that human beings do. This is why they could be enticed into service, bribed by the right sacrifices or compelled with the right threats. Having already exposed the incongruities of Apuleius's position back in books 8 and 9, Augustine has only to draw out those of Porphyry. According to Augustine, Apuleius knew that the demons were not good. Like the worst of human masters, they were "prompted by anger," "influenced by gifts," and "mollified by honors" (*ciu.* 8.17). And yet, because they had finer bodies and lived in a higher region of the cosmos, he felt compelled to venerate them. They were, he thought, sadly indispensable in a cosmos where the "gods never mix with men" (*ciu.* 8.18). Augustine summarizes Apuleius's position somewhat sarcastically, writing, "For this is alleged as the principal mark of divinity, that the gods, in their sublimity, are aloof from human contact and cannot be contaminated by it" (*ciu.* 9.16). Just as in the earthly city's *saeculum*, in Apuleius's cosmos, the higher are untouchable, the lower are viewed as contaminants, and the middle men are sleazy.

Augustine, however, faults Porphyry for a greater aberration from the truth than this. While Apuleius "venerated" the demons, he at least went to great lengths to preserve the gods from slavery to passion – the bribed or coerced demons, on his telling, only relayed petitions, while the gods were free to grant requests as they saw fit (*ciu.* 10.27). Porphyry, on the other

---

[24] Cf. Robert Dodaro, "Theurgy," in *Augustine through the Ages*, 827–828. Augustine explains Apuleius's position regarding the philosophers' ability to ascend without the help of such rituals: "it is just possible for men of wisdom, when, through a strenuous effort of the soul, they have withdrawn themselves from the body as far as may be, to receive an apprehension of this God, and for this illumination to shine on them at intervals, like a sudden flash of dazzling light" (*ciu.* 9.15). Though Augustine explains this as Apuleius's position, it is likely close to what Porphyry thought as well.

hand, dragged "human weakness up into the exalted heights of the universe" by endorsing a cosmology in which even the gods were compelled to obey man, given the right rituals (ibid.).[25] Quoting a Chaldean astrologer, Augustine's Porphyry relates the complaint of a particular practitioner of the theurgic art who, despite his greatest efforts, could not purify the soul of a client because a more powerful practitioner "had been led by envy to conjure the powers with sacred spells and had bound them, to prevent their granting his requests" (*ciu.* 10.9). Because the gods could be "so terrified by the practitioner who demanded an evil result," the theurgist "who asked for a good result" was not able "to release them from their fear" (ibid.). Though Porphyry is clearly disturbed by this, he concludes that this is just the way theurgy works. If this were true, of course, the humble would be trapped in an unjust cosmos. Success would belong to those willing to do whatever it takes or else those brilliant enough to rise above the whole system.

This being the case, it is not obvious how Porphyry's endorsement of theurgy fits within his philosophic worldview. I think the best answer is that Porphyry simply accepts this state of affairs as part and parcel of a cosmos designed as a prison – a teaching he attributed to Plato (*ciu.* 12.27).[26] This belief, Augustine suggests, cultivated a complacency in Porphyry, whereby he considered anyone who did not yet wish to escape

---

[25] This, Augustine argues, Porphyry learned from the Chaldeans, which is significant because the Chaldeans were one of the nations most bound up with superstition in the Old Testament. See, e.g., *s.* 198.58 (Dolbeau 26). Glossing on Romans 1:21, Augustine argues that those who did not glorify God "went looking for a superstitious and sacrilegious defilement under the name of purification. Wishing to adhere, you see, to that thing which always is, which is always the same, abiding unchangeable, they were able to attain to it after a fashion by the acuteness of their wits, but refused to honor it with humble hearts. So they stumbled on that false mediator who is jealous of the human soul, and strives by all available means to prevent it passing from the labors and difficulties which he is in control of to that peace where there is one more sublime than he is himself. To him pertain all the sacrilegious rites and the wickedly deceitful machinations of the astrologers, fortune-tellers, soothsayers, Chaldeans." Augustine, *Sermons (Newly Discovered)*, trans. Edmund Hill, OP, series ed. John E. Rotelle, OSA (Hyde Park, NY: New City Press, 2002), 225. In a footnote, Edmund Hill adds, "Chaldeans were the magicians *par excellence.*" In modern terms he might just possibly have said "Gypsies." Ibid., 237. Cf. *exp. Ps.* 136:7.

[26] Augustine addresses the incongruities of this cosmology again in his discussion of Porphyry's student Origen, writing that "if there were any truth in the idea that the purpose of the world's creation was that souls should be enclosed in bodies, as in prisons, in accordance with their just desserts, the minor offenders receiving higher and lighter bodies, the greater sinners lower and heavier, then the demons, as the worst characters, ought to have the lowest and heaviest bodies . . . whereas in fact such bodies are the lot of men, even good men" (*ciu.* 11.23).

it by philosophical ascent to still be justly imprisoned. Because he set his own sights beyond the material world, he was susceptible to Chaldean superstition about the material world.[27] Unsure of how to read Porphyry's letter to the Egyptian priest Anebo, Augustine believes that, at the very least, it shows his unwillingness to condemn theurgy in his own voice. Contrasting the difficulty "so great a philosopher" had in censuring the demons with the confidence "any Christian old woman" would have had, Augustine again loops back to the pressures of worldly eminence and the fear of causing offense that follows from the desire to be esteemed (*ciu.* 10.11). Though Augustine thinks it likely that Porphyry suspected the theurgy gods were really demons, he presents Porphyry as afraid of offending his priestly interlocutor. He was incapable of questioning Anebo's teachings openly. Publicly, Porphyry endorsed a practice fraught with danger, and left the humble with no viable path toward salvation, just like Seneca.

In culminating with Porphyry's cosmology, it is clear that Augustine wants to show that any worldview generated by human lights cannot entirely transcend superstition. Yet, what is significant for our purposes is that Augustine presents all iterations of false cosmology, from the lowest of the poetic tradition to the highest of the philosophic as undergirded by the same, recurring falsehoods. Accordingly, in moving from the absurdities of the Roman pantheon to the cosmologies of the philosophers, Augustine might appear to be ascending the old divided line, moving from the cacophonous superstitions of the masses toward to an integrated, coherent, and true account of the universe. Yet, what he is actually doing is highlighting the way in which all humanity is weighed down by the same superstitions. Thus, what from one perspective looks like a ladder toward truth, from another looks like a ball and chain; it might give some a longer tether, but it ties them down just the same. By beginning with the agreed upon superstition of poetic myth, Augustine crafts his argument to draw the reader's eyes to the *continuities* between it and the cosmology of the philosophers. What we find is a recapitulation of the features of the earthly city's inner dynamics: the sense that power prevails, that virtue is not always expedient, and that, in order to survive, one may have to manipulate others. These are the shared presuppositions that Augustine thinks are "of" the earthly city.

---

[27] John Cavadini makes a similar point, suggesting that the Platonists lack of concern for the body led them to abandon it and therefore allowed Rome to resignify it as it wanted. Cavadini, "Ideology and Solidarity," 108.

For Augustine, Scripture allows us to see what undergirds these presuppositions: they all assume that God is nowhere to help. The sense of abandonment in an unfriendly universe, only magnified by superstition, exacerbates the human tendency to think that survival in the world necessitates participation in the economy of *amor sui*. Certainly, if God were disengaged from human affairs, either through indifference or fear of contamination, the world would be a place where the humble were abandoned to their weakness. However, as Augustine has told us in the preface, Scripture proclaims that the view from the heights misses the full story; it fails to see that humility has the secret power of allowing human beings to "soar above all the summits of this world" (*ciu.* 1.*praef*). Meditating on Scripture with the eyes of faith, we allow God to bring us to this vista beyond the heights, gradually realizing that the world, as it looks from the perspective of *amor sui*, is a dim and narrow apprehension of a world infused with *amor Dei*. By showing the *mysterium* of *amor Dei* hidden in the world, Augustine aims to dissolve the fears generated by the human condition and exacerbated by myth-making. He helps his readers soar above an alienated world in which humility cannot win.

Over and against the economy of *amor sui* projected onto the cosmos by the earthly city, books 11–13 of *City of God* present the cosmology revealed in Scripture. Significantly, this is a cosmology that recovers the original meaning of creation, reveals its original economy, and, thereby, unmasks all superstition. The first recovery has to do with the goodness of the material order. While Augustine does believe that God "arranged a scale of existences of various natures" so that different creatures have different powers, perfections, and gifts, he speaks of this hierarchy in a very different register than the Platonists (*ciu.* 12.2, cf. 11.16). This difference has a great deal to do with their respective accounts of the material order's origin (*ciu.* 12.25–27). Rather than a schema in which souls emanated from the One, only to be caught in a material prison designed by the lesser gods, in Scripture, Augustine finds a schema in which every creature has been created and intended by God himself (cf. *ciu.* 12.4–5, 12.27, and *ep.* 165, inter alia). In this light, he writes,

It would be ridiculous to regard the defects of beasts, trees and other mutable and mortal things which lack intelligence, sense, or life as deserving condemnation … These creatures have received their mode of being by the will of their creator, whose purpose is that they should bring to perfection the beauty of the lower parts of the universe by their alteration and succession in the passage of the seasons; and this is a beauty in its own kind. (*ciu.* 12.4)

Focusing on God's affirmation of the goodness of creation as the hermeneutical key of the biblical creation story, Augustine insists that even lower creatures have a value "in their own sphere and in their own nature" (*ciu.* 11.22). More than this, they have a special "position in the splendour of the providential order" such that they make a unique contribution "as to a universal commonwealth" (ibid.). The image of a commonwealth here is striking. It evokes a vision of fellowship among creatures, wherein each benefits from the particular gifts the others have to offer – a prescient description, perhaps, of the ecosphere. Fallen, we do not always see the special contribution that other creatures make, but Augustine insists that it is there (*ciu.* 12.4).

Lambasting Origen for his suggestion that the material order came into being through sin, Augustine writes, "I cannot express my astonishment that so learned and experienced a theologian should have failed to notice" that this idea is contrary to the authority of Scripture (*ciu.* 11.23). Origen could not bring himself to say that God created the material world since he himself could not see how it was good, and God only created good things. In arguing this, Origen alludes to the view of his teacher Porphyry: when souls withdrew from God, Porphyry had taught him, they came down to the earth and incurred the penalty of bodily imprisonment. Therefore, Origen believed, the purpose of "the world's creation was to restrain evil," and "the builders" of this prison were the gods, not God himself (ibid.; cf. *ciu.* 12.27). In believing this, Augustine thinks, Origen had not quite allowed Scripture to refashion his vision. Moreover, he contends, Origen's Porphyric account blots out God's providential care toward all his creatures. Contesting his claim that even the sun was crafted as a response to sin, Augustine instead insists that it was "due to the miraculous providence of the Maker in his concern for the health and beauty of his corporal creation" (*ciu.* 11.23). The God of Scripture, Augustine maintains, is a God who looks after the birds of the air and "the lilies of the field" (*ciu.* 10.14 citing Matt. 16:28).

Perhaps even more significant to Augustine's scriptural cosmology is what it implies for the relationship between angels (or gods) and men.[28] While Porphyry and those he represents envisioned a stratified universe, wherein only the highest beings had direct access to God, Augustine envisions an entire community of rational creatures intimately united to their Creator. Transforming the Platonic idea of participation from

---

[28] For an in-depth discussion of Augustine's angelology, see Elizabeth Klein, *Augustine's Theology of Angels* (Cambridge: Cambridge University Press, 2018).

a concept bound up with status to a concept bound up with love, Augustine does present the angels as superior, but not simply because they have a higher nature. If this were the case, the demons would also be superior to human beings. Yet, Augustine tells us, there were two truths that Christ revealed through his Incarnation: first, "that true divine nature cannot be polluted by the flesh," and second "that demons are not to be reckoned our superiors" (*ciu.* 9.17). In this way, the Incarnation reveals that the only significant criterion for superiority is nearness to God. Using his favorite example of fishermen and women, Augustine asserts that a holy person is closer to God to any demon. Just as humility allows the lowly to be drawn far above the reaches of worldly wisdom, "the devout man's hope" draws him far above the reaches of "the demon's despair" (*ciu.* 8.15). With the coming of Christ, the "scale according to the order of nature" has been superseded by the "criterion of righteousness" (*ciu.* 11.16).

With the revelation of God's accessibility, the whole cosmos becomes flushed with *amor Dei*. Because those nearer to God yearn for others to share in their fellowship, the cosmos is revealed to be animated by an economy of gift, or service, not an economy of power. Because the happiness of all rational creatures is constituted by the one act of clinging to God, Augustine's cosmology shifts the emphasis from the divisions of creaturely rank to the bond between rational creatures and their Creator. This is particularly evident in the way he discusses the city of God:

If we ask whence it arises, God founded it; if whence comes its wisdom, it receives light from God: if whence comes its bliss, it rejoices in God. It receives its mode of being by subsisting in God, its enlightenment by beholding him, its joy from cleaving to him. It exists; it sees; it loves. It is strong with God's eternity; it shines with God's truth; it rejoices in God's goodness. (*ciu.* 11.24)

This striking imagery of a single community of rational creatures cleaving to their God evokes a vision in which Christ is the bridegroom and the whole city of God is his bride.[29] Repeatedly referring to verse 28 of Psalm 73, "As for me, the true good is to cling to God," Augustine uses it as the refrain of the redeemed city throughout *City of God* 10–22, emphasizing that God is close to all those who love him, and not just the incorporeal angels.

In the end, the Scriptural account reveals, "only sins . . . separate men from God," and not their bodies (*ciu.* 10.22). With the Incarnation, the

---

[29] Goulven Madec explores this language in "Le Communisme Spirituel" in his *Petites Études Augustiniennes* (Paris: Institut d'Études Augustiniennes, 1994), 215–231. Cf. Cavadini, "Spousal Vision," esp. 140n41.

stratified system of demonic mediation is unmasked; anxiety over the necessary sacrifices to intermediary beings is no longer necessary. The angels, it turns out, need no incentive other than the "compassionate love" of *amor Dei* to draw their human confrères into their community of praise, knowing that "they themselves, together with us" are a "sacrifice" to God (*ciu.* 10.7). In presenting a cosmos in which God "condescends" to care for all directly, dwelling "in the union of all and in each person" Scripture liberates human beings from the deep-seated fears and superstitions generated by the Fall (*ciu.* 10.3). Brought into being through *amor Dei,* sustained by *amor Dei,* and arranged so that creatures help each other through *amor Dei,* the original meaning of the creation is *amor Dei.* The cosmos is governed by an economy of gift.[30]

REENTERING THE SACRAMENTAL WORLDVIEW

Of course, Augustine believes that this truth about the cosmos has become obscured by the dominance of the earthly city in the *saeculum.* We have examined the myriad of ways in which this dominance manifests itself in earlier chapters, so the question now is how Augustine expects humanity to recover a sacramental vision within an occupied world. There are manifold obstacles to this endeavor. On one level, the practices and behaviors animated by *amor sui* suggest that self-promotion is what leads to success in the world, discrediting the suggestion that humility could be a viable way of life. And yet, on another level, *amor Dei* is discredited by a myriad of counterfeit loves that arise within the confines of the earthly city itself.[31] To see this, we need only recall Rome's self-professed mission "to spare the humble and beat down the proud" (*ciu.* 1.*praef*). The latest in a series of powers who posture themselves as benevolent, Rome inscribes its plan to bring justice to a chaotic world in the annals of prophecy. The distortion contained in its mission presents itself in force, to be sure, but also in its use of language.

---

[30] In postmodern philosophy, the idea of gift as an antidote to economic logic has begun to circulate, but in this literature, economy is meant in the narrower modern sense, having to do exchange and trade. Here, I mean economy in the classical sense of *oikonomia*, such that it refers to the way God structures and manages the whole nexus of creatures for their good and the good of all. This literature also lacks the metaphysical underpinnings contained in Augustine's theology. For works exploring gift and economy in the postmodern context, see Jacques Derrida, *Given Time: I. Counterfeit Money,* trans. Peggy Kamuf (Chicago: University of Chicago Press, 1992), and Jean Luc Marion's responses to it, esp. Jean-Luc Marion, *Being Given: Towards a Phenomenology of Givenness,* trans. Jeffrey L. Kosky (Stanford, CA: Stanford University Press, 2002).

[31] Cf. Ward, *Cities of God,* 230.

For example, as Augustine points out in *City of God* 19.7, the Roman empire has feigned a *simulacrum* of unity within itself by imposing a common language on its provinces.[32] In one of his more cynical moments, Augustine portrays Rome's success on this front as the consequence of its utter superiority to other world powers such that it can enforce unity on the world under its dominion.[33] Yet, Augustine thinks that even Rome cannot entirely hide the link between pride and the fragmentation of language. That fact is that the bond of peace that its common language is supposed to ensure is never stable and its rule is always prone to insurrection. In arguing that fallen language will always be fundamentally fragmented, Augustine points us back to *De Doctrina,* where he refers to the story of the Tower of Babel. There he argues that the origin of the multiplicity of language was a punishment for pride, with God bestowing "discord in [pride's] speech as well as in its thoughts and its ambitions" (*doct. chr.* 2.4.5).[34] Thus, while pride seeks to unify those it has overcome, the fact that everyone grabs at first place consistently frustrates this project, and the attempt to see it through requires a high degree of force.

Significantly, it is also in this section of *De Doctrina* that Augustine proposes Scripture as a treatment for the "diseases of the human will" (*doct. chr.* 2.5.6).[35] For Augustine, the fact that God's salvific work is entirely unimperial is highly significant – Augustine's God does not tackle the problem of human disunity in such a domineering way as Rome. Rather, he initiates a relationship with an obscure people whose sacred writings were "able when the time came to be disseminated throughout the world, spreading far and wide through translation into a variety of other languages, and thus came to the knowledge of the nations for their salvation" (*doct. chr.* 2.5.6).[36] In this way, God allows the multiplicity of languages and culture to remain, giving them the means to be transformed at their root: at the level of the human will itself. Just as we saw in Chapter 2, here we see that the city of God does not come into the world as empire, destined to conquer political communities. Instead, it comes into the world as a wholly different kind of community; one that does not replace political communities, but that even encourages its members to "maintain and follow" the laws, customs, and institutions which they, in good conscience, can (*ciu.* 19.17).[37]

---

[32] Cf. Cochrane, *Christianity and Classical Culture,* 175.
[33] Cf. Rist, *Ancient Thought Baptized,* 226.   [34] Augustine, *Teaching Christianity,* 131.
[35] Ibid.   [36] Ibid.
[37] I have taken interpretive liberties in my construal here. To be more precise, Augustine says that they ought to follow the customs laws and institutions that do not provide a hindrance to "the religion which teaches that the one supreme and true God is to be

Before turning to Augustine's political advice more fully in the final chapter, it is important to give a brief sketch of Augustine's way of thinking about the Church's role in the retrieval of a sacramental worldview.[38] Since fallen human beings have lost the ability to read the sacramental meaning of the cosmos, it is fitting that God has founded a sacramental community designed to teach this meaning anew. This, in part, is why Augustine has written *De Doctrina*: to teach the clergy how to read Scripture and how to exposit it to their congregations. In this way, he envisions a kind of Christian pedagogy ordered toward the restoration of a worldview and way of life consonant with the original meaning of creation.

For the Church as a whole, this formation occurs in and through participation in the shared life of the ecclesial community. It is, for Augustine, the Church's participation in *latreia,* the worship due to God alone, that really forms the heart of this shared life. In remarking on Scripture's "many passages" on worshiping, or offering sacrifice to God, he explains that the purpose of such sacrifices has always been "that we may cleave to God and seek the good of our neighbour for the same end" (*ciu.* 10.5). "Thus," he explains, "the visible sacrifice is the sacrament, the sacred sign, of the invisible sacrifice" that God truly desires (ibid.).[39] The latter, of course, is the sacrifice of the heart. Existentially, this means the forsaking of our own fallen desires in order to do the will of God.

worshipped" (*ciu.* 19.17). The problem with this way of putting the caveat is that it could be construed narrowly, to include only religious laws that demanded pagan worship, or broadly, to include any law, custom or institution of which God would not approve. Markus tends in the former interpretive direction; Dodaro, Williams, Milbank in the latter.

[38] Harrison helpfully points out that Augustine considered the Church to be a body whose "distinctive emphasis upon the practice and rhetoric of live in its Scriptures and preaching enabled it to create a linguistic community in which the central message of faith could both be understood and communicated in such a way that it inspired and moved the hearer to love." Harrison, *Christian Truth and Fractured Humanity*, 67.

[39] A helpful treatment of sacrifice in book 10 is Eugene R. Schlesinger, "The Sacrificial Ecclesiology of City of God 10," *Augustinian Studies* 47, no. 2 (2016): 137–155; in it Schlesinger presents sacrifice as a central concept, linking Augustine's ecclesiology and Christology together: it is, he writes, "another locus for discussing the return of humanity to God through the incarnate Christ." Ibid., 139. For an overview of Augustine's position on sacrifice as a whole, see Gerald Bonner, "The Doctrine of Sacrifice: Augustine and the Latin Patristic Tradition," in *Sacrifice and Redemption: Durham Essays in Theology* (1991): 101–117, and Khaled Anatolios, "Sacraments in the Fourth Century," in *The Oxford Handbook of Sacramental Theology*, ed. Hans Boersma and Matthew Levering (Oxford: Oxford University Press, 2015), 140–155.

Metaphysically, it means the alignment of our will to God's will. Relationally, it means self-gift.[40]

Augustine's later exegesis of the story of Cain and Abel is illuminating on this point. The reason, Augustine theorizes, why Cain's sacrifice was rejected was that "he gave to God something belonging to him, but gave himself to himself" (*ciu.* 15.7). The practice of offering a bribe disguised as a sacrifice, he goes on, "is what is done by all those who follow their own will, and not the will of God. ... They suppose that with this gift God is being bought over to help them, not in curing their depraved desires, but in fulfilling them" (ibid.). For Augustine, then, sin's tendency is to try to align God's will to our own, rather than the other way around. True sacrifice, however, is always a gesture of *amor Dei* and is, thereby, undergirded by the desire to be united "to God in a holy fellowship" (*ciu.* 10.6). Because fallen human beings must learn to offer this kind of sacrifice anew, and must grow in *amor Dei* in order to do so, God gives his Church manifold opportunities to do good works in love. Indeed, under its tutelage, the human being is reintroduced into the economy of gift, coming to see that all of life can be incorporated into an offering to God, if it is lived rightly.

Just as Augustine reads the nature of created things as pointing human beings back to God as their origin, then, he reads *latreia* as a pedagogical activity designed to reintroduce humanity into *amor Dei*, the original economy of creation.[41] Another way of putting this is that the sacramental meaning of *latreia* orients human beings toward God as the one to whom they should cleave and to whom they should offer their lives. Notably, Augustine's discussion of *latreia* is both where he first introduces the refrain, "As for me, my true good is to cling to God" (Ps. 28:73) and also where he links "the sacrament of the altar" with the reintegration of humanity into the city of God (*ciu.* 10.6). Indeed, he suggests, the very purpose of the Church is to allow humanity to be reincorporated into *amor Dei's* economy of gift. Moreover, he writes, it is by participating in the sacrament of the altar that the Church learns her true identity. He explains,

---

[40] Because God's happiness is constituted by nothing other than *amor Dei*, or, the Fellowship of the Trinity itself, this self-offering is precisely what makes it possible for us to participate in it (ibid.).

[41] For recent studies of the connection between *latreia* and political life, see Cavadini, "Ideology and Solidarity," 101–105; Veronica Roberts, "Idolatry as the Source of Injustice in Augustine's *De ciuitate Dei*," *Studia Patristica LXXXVIII* 14, no. 1 (2017): 69–78; Ashleen Menchaca-Bagnulo, "Deeds and Words: Latreia, Justice, Mercy in Augustine's Political Thought," in *Augustine's Political Thought*, ed. Richard Dougherty (Rochester, NY: Rochester University Press, 2019), 74–104.

The whole redeemed community, that is to say, the congregation and fellowship of the saints, is offered to God as a universal sacrifice, through the great Priest who offered himself in his suffering for us – so that we might be the body of so great a head. ... This is the sacrifice which the Church continually celebrates in the sacrament of the altar, a sacrament well-known to the faithful where it shown to the Church that she herself is offered in the offering which she presents to God. (ibid.)

In learning that her essential identity lies in offering herself to God, wherein also lies her happiness, the Church is taught that her very existence is a divine gift.[42] Not only is she founded by a divine gift, by virtue of Christ, under "the form of a servant," giving himself as a sacrifice for her; she is also healed by participating in this selfsame gift, allowing Christ to offer her as the "whole sacrifice" for which he gave his life (ibid.).[43]

This sacrifice is ever expansive, always inviting new members in and spreading the hidden work of God more broadly. By participating in it in truth, members are progressively healed. Through this experience of God's love, they begin to see the *mysterium* of God at work in the world, becoming increasingly attentive to the way God uses his nexus of creatures to care for those whom he loves.[44] In addition, they come to face to face with their own shortcomings; beholding Love in its essence, the

---

[42] This gift draws a clear contrast to the theurgic world in which higher beings are contaminated by contact with humanity, thereby abandoning them to the demons; as Eugene Schlesinger argues, "Christ's sacrifice both cuts through the inchoate elitism of theurgy, and connects worshipers, in their entirety, to the true God." Schlesinger, "The Sacrificial Economy," 143.

[43] Another significant passage in book 10 that spells out Augustine's understanding of the true sacrifice is the following: "the true Mediator (in so far as he 'took the form of a servant' and was thus made the 'mediator between God and mankind, the man Christ Jesus') receives the sacrifice 'in the form of God, in union with the Father, with whom he is one God. And yet 'in the form of a servant' he preferred to be himself the sacrifice than to receive it, to prevent anyone from supposing that sacrifice, even in this circumstance, should be offered to any created being. Thus he is both the priest, himself making the offering, and the oblation. This is the reality, and he intended the daily sacrifice of the Church to be the sacramental symbol of this; for the Church, being the body of which he is the head, learns to offer itself through him. This is the true sacrifice; and the sacrifices of the saints in earlier times were many different symbols of it. This one sacrifice was prefigured by many rites, just as many words are used to refer to one thing, to emphasize the point without inducing boredom. This was the supreme sacrifice, and the true sacrifice, and all the false sacrifices yielded place to it" (*ciu.* 10.20). See also *s.* 227 for a detailed meditation on "the sacrament of the Lord's table." Augustine, *Sermons, (184–229Z) on the Liturgical Seasons*, trans. Edmund Hill, OP, series ed. John E. Rotelle, OSA (New Rochelle, NY: New City Press, 1993), 255–257.

[44] Though Romans 5:5 is one of Augustine's favorite verses to quote, he uses it in *City of God* only sparingly, most notably at *ciu.* 8.31.

distortions within their own attempts to love become visible. Coming to see that their own contribution to the sacrificial offering repeatedly falls short, they rejoice at being invited to participate just the same, joining in "the prayer of the whole City of God on pilgrimage," which asks for forgiveness (*ciu.* 19.27).

In connecting the prayer for forgiveness with the offering of true sacrifice, Augustine again presents the Church as imperfect in its humanity, though perfect and perfecting in its divinity, something he has been arguing for since the opening page of the work.[45] Here, perhaps surprisingly, we come to see that the Church itself is a sign with a teaching function: in being what it is, it teaches human beings that it is good to cling to God; in celebrating the sacrament of the altar, it bears witness to the divine standard of love, which gives humanity a way back to God; and in being at once sinful and purified, through being joined to a good God, it provides an antidote to pride. Ultimately, the role of the Church is to point humanity back to Christ, the Word through whom the world was made.

In this way, the Church also operates as a sign of contradiction against a world caught up in its own myths. By presenting the city of God as uniquely anchored in the truth, Augustine evokes the same sacramental worldview which we have just been exploring through his semiotic theory. Again, this is a worldview that grounds the discourse of the heavenly city in an ontology that deconstructs the discourse of the earthly city. Superstition, it suggests, is a mythology that reflects a certain people's desires and fears back to them, thereby denying the original meaning of the cosmos. Contrasting Rome's divinization of Romulus with the Church's proclamation of Christ's divinity to in order to make this point, he writes,

---

[45] For Augustine, the pilgrim church is always in the process of being healed by its head, Christ. In *s.* 137.1 he writes, "Our Lord Jesus Christ, who has already suffered and risen again for us, is the head of the Church; and that the Church is his body, and that in his body, as its very health, is to be found the unity of its members and the framework of love. Anyone who grows cold in love is sick in the body of Christ. But God, who has already raised our head on high, has the power to heal the sick members too, provided, that is, that they haven't amputated themselves by extreme wickedness, but stick in the body until they are healed. Whatever, you see, remains in the body need not despair of being restored to health; but any part that has been amputated can be neither treated nor healed." Augustine, *Sermons, (94A–147A) on the Old Testament*, 373. For an introduction to the *Totus Christus* concept in Augustine, see Tarsicius Van Bavel, "The 'Christus Totus' Idea: A Forgotten Aspect of Augustine's Spirituality," in *Studies in Patristic Christology: Proceedings of the Third Maynooth Patristic Conference*, ed. Thomas Finan and Vincent Twomey (Portland, OR: Four Courts Press, 1998), 84–94.

Rome believed Romulus to be a god because she loved him; the Heavenly City loved Christ because she believed him to be God. Thus Rome had already an object of her love, which she could readily turn from a loved object into a final good, falsely believed in; correspondingly, our City had already an object of her belief so that she might not rashly love a false good but with true faith might set her affection on the true good. (*ciu.* 22.6)

Here, Augustine presents Rome's divinization of Romulus as a reflection of her loves; resignifying the meaning of temporal events, Rome's mythology sprang from what she wanted the truth to be, and not the truth itself. Clearly, we see the earthly city's departure from reality at work. This, however, is only visible because of the heavenly city's contrasting fidelity to the truth.[46] Furthermore, because the Church allowed itself to be founded by the One it recognized as God, Augustine is able to see the significance of the fact that Rome was already founded when it decided to make Romulus into a god. By divinizing its founder, Rome denied the true Founder any prior claim on what its meaning in the world would be. This construal, of course, echoes his earlier remark about Adam, who abandoned the foundation upon which he should have been firmly fixed in order to make himself his own foundation. After the pattern of Adam, the Romans are "self-pleasers" (*ciu.* 14.13)

But this very freedom to pursue selfish interests is in itself a luxury, and one not afforded to all. Augustine notes how Rome spread her mythology to the broader world: having "attained a great empire ... she diffused, from that higher level, as it were, this belief among the other nations whom she dominated" (*ciu.* 22.6). These nations, he goes on, gave lip-service to this belief, fearing to offend the city to whom they were enslaved (ibid.). At any given time, then, the world dominated by the earthly city is a mélange of those invested in the dominant mythology, and those who lack the freedom to protest against it. The only reason that the city of God is capable of bearing witness against it is that she has "put Christ as the foundation of her faith" (*ciu.* 22.6). In other words, insofar as the members of the Church adhere to Christ, they bear witness to him, but insofar as they remain stricken with self-love, they stand in danger of descending into their own myth-making – a danger for all human beings.[47] True

---

[46] I follow Augustine in using the term *heavenly city* in this paragraph because it evokes the idea of the city of God triumphant, which the passage technically refers to. Nevertheless, for Augustine, there is one, and only ever one, city of God; in the *saeculum*, part of it is on pilgrimage, but the city of God *qua* city of God has always been faithful to the truth. It is just that the passage approaches the city from an eschatological perspective.

[47] In his best moments, Augustine strives to mitigate his own tendency toward this by cultivating a humble and charitable reading of Scripture. Perhaps the best example is

witness, Augustine concludes, is never a merely human achievement; it always requires the grace that comes through clinging to God (*ciu.* 22.7).

Zeroing in on the witness of the martyrs, Augustine highlights this point with vigor, arguing that no follower of Romulus would have received such strength as the martyrs did from his so-called god. Juxtaposing human weakness with divine strength, he writes that, while the nations under Roman rule were constrained by the "fear of hurting Roman feelings," the martyrs were miraculously undeterred by "the most terrible of all fears ... the fear of death itself" (ibid.). Even this "could not restrain a multitude of martyrs throughout the world from worshipping Christ as God, and, what is more, from proclaiming Him as God" (ibid.). In bearing witness to God, the martyrs are, for Augustine, the paradigmatic representatives of the Church's true identity. A sign of the original meaning of creation, they stand for a community that points to Christ, saying, "As for me, my true good is to cling to God" (*ciu.* 10.8, citing Ps. 73:28).

CONCLUSION

In this chapter, we have explored Augustine's theory of signs as an avenue into his sacramental worldview. Looking at the first two books of *De Doctrina*, we saw him argue that the world has been endowed by its Creator with an original meaning, though the earthly city strives to obscure it with its own mythology. We also saw how the superstitions affecting the earthly city all stem from the belief that *amor sui* is the only reality – that self-love undergirds the fundamental economy of the cosmos. Next, we focused on how the sacramental worldview presented in Scripture transforms our perception of the cosmos – how the humble trust that once seemed foolish is revealed to be the way out of the earthly city's tragic economy. Finally, we explored why Augustine thinks that the Church is the best place for the retrieval of a sacramental worldview, and how the Church *qua* sign unmasks the earthly city's mythologies.

---

trin. 1.2.4–1.3.5, where he writes, "What a wholesome regiment is provided for the faithful in holy Church whereby the observance of piety makes the ailing mind well for the perception of unchanging truth, and saves it from being plunged into opinions of noisome falsehood by the random whims of temerity. Nor will I for my part, wherever I stick fast be loath to seek, nor wherever I go wrong be ashamed to learn. Accordingly, dear reader, whenever you are as certain about something as I am go forward with me; whenever you stick equally fast seek with me; whenever you notice that you have gone wrong come back to me; or that I have, call me back to you. In this way let us set out along Charity Street together, making for him of whom it is said, *Seek his face always* (Ps 105:4)." Augustine, *The Trinity*, 68.

For our purposes, what is so significant about Augustine's sacramental semiotics is that it shows us how Augustine delegitimizes the earthly city's claim on the world without underestimating the hold the earthly city has on the world. Because Augustine's sacramental vision allows us to see the Son's hidden work of renewal already under way, it invites us to participate in this work here and now. The upshot of this is that Augustine is able to show us how to participate in our earthly communities without being beholden to the rules of the earthly city. Instead, we find, the earthly city's economy of power, as real and imposing as it is in the world, is a second-order reality, an economy overlaid on top of (and in opposition to) an ever-accessible and ever-fruitful economy of gift.

With all this laid out, we begin to see that politics cannot be the visible manifestation of the earthly city in the same way that the Church is the visible manifestation of the city of God. Rather, as with everything else, it parodies that relationship. While the city of God receives the visible Church as a gift, the earthly city grasps at the political community, claiming its power for its own designs. Thus, as I will argue in the next chapter, Augustine is aware of the earthly city's constant designs on political life, but he does not concede politics to the earthly city, nor does he make the Church the new realm of politics. Instead, the Church *as* sign of the city of God contradicts the message the earthly city sends about politics. It calls the earthly city's claim on politics into question.

Ultimately, while the earthly city might strive, and indeed, quite often succeed in making the world into an image (*imago*) of itself, for Augustine, its claim is neither legitimate nor is its hold on the world all-encompassing. Instead, he thinks, the possibility always remains of participating in our earthly communities in a way that taps into the economy of gift. Interpreting the world through sacramental vision, we can, with God's help, reject the necessity of participating in the scramble to gain leverage without rejecting the duty of participating in our political communities. Seeing *amor Dei* at work in the world, we can affirm that the earthly city does not have the last word on how we act in the world.

6

The Status of Politics

Rereading City of God 19 *in Light of Augustine's Sacramental Vision*

Having examined Augustine's semiotic theory in the previous chapter, we now know that Augustine views the entire cosmos sacramentally, endowed by its Creator with a very specific meaning: to bear witness to God's love and to draw rational creatures into fellowship with him. Furthermore, we have seen that Augustine's semiotic theory is deeply intertwined with his sacramental worldview; in neither do the two cities start out on an equal plane, one using signs for good, the other for ill. Rather, in both, the cosmos has an original meaning from which the earthly city is persistently falling away. In a world graffitied with millennia of fallen *consuetudines,* Augustine has to tackle the problem of how anyone can recover the original meaning of reality. To this end, he turns to Christian revelation. Pointing to Christ Incarnate as the hermeneutical key of the entire cosmos – the Word through whom the world was made – Augustine explains how Christ constituted the Church to help his members see and participate in the sacramental meaning of reality anew. By confessing its sins, participating in the sacrament of the altar, following God's commands, and meditating on Scripture, the Church becomes conformed to Christ, bearing witness to the *amor Dei* that constitutes it. In this way, it too becomes a sign of contradiction against the confusions of Babylon.

In this final chapter, our task is to unfold the implications of Augustine's sacramental vision for the status of politics in his thought. If, as I have argued, the earthly city lays claim to more than it ought, it would be a mistake to take the earthly city's encroachment on the political world as an indication that the latter is the realm of sin *tout court.* Moreover, if Augustine's retelling of Roman history is designed as an antidote to Rome's patriotic myth-making, it is unclear what conclusions it can yield about the status of politics in general. At most, it is fair to say that his indictment of the earthly city is also his indictment of Rome; both are the city that aims at domination; both are the city enslaved to its own *libido dominandi*.[1] And yet, does this mean that Rome is the earthly city? While some have concluded this, I am advocating a different relationship, namely, that of usurpation. For Augustine, Rome is coveted, besieged, by the earthly city.[2]

Indeed, given how Augustine's use of language reflects his participatory metaphysical framework, this relationship makes more sense than a strict or even partial identification of Rome with the earthly city. Rome, it is better to say, participates in the economy of *amor sui*. To put this another way, insofar as Roman citizens are motivated by *amor sui*, they live out and even institutionalize the patterns of behavior that the earthly city's foundational love fosters. They shape Rome into the kind of society that manifests these behaviors for all to see. Still, for as much as Augustine uses Rome to shed light on the earthly city, he leaves the question of the degree to which Rome participates in its dynamics unanswered: it remains to be seen whether Rome is wholly and irrevocably conquered by the earthly city. While it is true that Augustine essentially calls Rome the current capital of the earthly city, even this comment is best interpreted in light of his participatory metaphysics; Rome can fittingly be so called because it loves being the dominant power in his world, and empire is the apex of the earthly city's political aspirations (*ciu.* 15.5). Loving domination, it not only participates in, but epitomizes the ethos of the earthly city.

Accordingly, while Roman history lends us a window into the economy of the earthly city and its very real political effects, the key to the status of politics in Augustine's thought lies elsewhere, namely, in his sacramental semiotics and the ontology undergirding it. That is, if Augustine's deconstruction of the earthly city's way of speaking undermines its claims about the world and on the world, then it also undermines its claims about

---

[1] Michael Foley aptly describes the *libido dominandi* as "the pride that in its most aggravated condition seeks unity and absolute power over all things temporal." Foley, "The Other Happy Life," 175.

[2] I mean "besieged" in the general sense of being taken over. When a dominant force usurps power, it declares its rule legitimate, though the truth of the claim is dubious. Setting its eyes on the political realm as a prize worth having, the members of the earthly city have staged a coup, claiming the political sphere as their own and attempting to reshape the political community in their own image.

politics and on the political sphere – the other *ciuitas terrena*. The fact that
the two *ciuitates terrenae* are called by the same name only illustrates
Augustine's conviction that the earthly city gravitates toward the world.
Ultimately, to discover the status of politics in *City of God* we must
reconsider its key political passages in light of his sacramental vision,
especially those of book 19. Doing so in this chapter, I find that political
life is not merely a product of sin for Augustine, even though politics as we
know it is marred by sin.

Importantly, this means that there is a way of participating in political
life that is beyond the imagination of the earthly city. In the last section of
this chapter, I will explore what implications Augustine's sacramental
vision has for politics, and especially what sort of improvement our
political societies might expect to see as a result of having citizens animated by it. The answer is mixed; although Augustine's worldview does
suggest that true service of the political community can always be incorporated into *latreia*, it does not guarantee that this service will be successful
in worldly terms or that Christian citizens will inhabit it fully.
Nevertheless, by bearing witness to a political practice beyond the script
of the earthly city, Christians not only gain a way out of a political world
closed in on itself, they also sow the seeds necessary for genuine cultural
renewal. If these claims are true, then it again follows that politics cannot
merely be the realm of sin.

THE MEANING AND PLACE OF "POLITICS" IN CITY OF GOD

In arguing that politics is not, as Milbank puts it, the "realm of sin," but is
merely a natural project usurped by the earthly city, it is first necessary to
establish what politics means for Augustine.[3] In the first place, it is worth
noting that Augustine never speaks of "politics" in the abstract. Instead,
he always speaks of earthly cities, or, political communities. For
Augustine, the constitution of these communities reflects the ordering of
the cosmos as a whole: it is a nexus of creatures, arranged in particular
relationships. "Order," he writes, "is the arrangement of things equal and
unequal in a pattern which assigns to each its proper position"; substitute
the term "things" for "persons," and one has his vision of community
(*ciu.* 19.13). Augustine, in other words, thinks that human beings are
always arranged in a certain nexus such that they relate to one another
through their specific roles. One might connect this to his Trinitarian

---

[3] Milbank, *Theology as Social Theory*, 411.

theology, in which personhood is also role-based. These roles either constitute the bonds among persons, or the bonds among persons constitute these roles. Either way, Augustine thinks that humans, created in the *imago Dei,* naturally tend to form interpersonal bonds through which they adopt specific roles and engage in common projects. Some of these bonds, roles, and projects are political in nature, others familial, others, still, ecclesial. Regardless, they all reflect our social nature. As Augustine puts it, the human being is the most social creature there is; we only become the most "quarrelsome by perversion" (*ciu.* 12.28).

In trying to decipher whether political association is natural to human beings, Miikka Ruokanen, among others, has suggested that Augustine makes a conceptual distinction between the political and the social so that human beings are social by nature, but political only by perversion.[4] This would be a plausible assertion, but for the fact that the distinction rides on a modern conception of politics: one that views politics *as* coercion, and the institutional state as a man-made remedy against an anarchic state of nature. Augustine, however, comes at his study of politics from a premodern perspective. The Greek thought that influenced him through Cicero viewed politics as natural, and on top of this, did not focus on abstract institutions, but, again, on communities of persons. Consider the following Ciceronian passage that Augustine quotes in *City of God*:

> A community of different classes, high, low and middle, unites, like the varying sounds of music to form a harmony of very different parts through the exercise of rational restraint; and what is called harmony in music answers to concord in a community, and it is the best and closest bond of security in a country. And this cannot possibly exist without justice. (*ciu.* 2.21, citing *De Rep.* 2.42)

Here we see that Cicero conceives of the *res publica* in terms of its members, rather than its institutional branches. While America's own Founding Fathers divided the government into the Executive, Legislative, and Judicial branches, so that ambition might be made to counter ambition, Cicero observes that there are three classes in Roman society that must be brought into harmony – the high, the middle and the low.[5] In Cicero's political thought, then, and indeed, in ancient thought

---

[4] He writes, "Man is in his deepest essence *animal sociale,* a social creature, but not *animal politicum,* not a creature suited to live under the rule of other human beings." Ruokanen, *Theology of Social Life,* 101. Cf. Rist, *Ancient Thought Baptized,* 227, 253; Elshtain, *Augustine and the Limits of Politics,* 26; and Harrison, *Christian Truth and Fractured Humanity,* 215, inter alia.

[5] Cf. James Madison, "Essay 51," in *The Essential Federalist and Anti-Federalist Papers,* ed. David Wootton (Indianapolis, IN: Hackett, 2003), 245–250, 246.

more broadly, political science was about how a group of people lived together, and its concern stretched to the whole of that community's social life.[6] Though Augustine anticipated certain trends in modern political thought, he simply did not share its institutional focus. Throughout *City of God*, he follows Cicero in speaking about politics in classical terms – and the *polis* or *ciuitas* are not equivalent concepts to the state, despite the liberalities that some translators take.[7] Indeed, the only modification that Augustine makes to the classical paradigm is his naming of love as the binding force of the political community instead of *ius* or, as Cicero puts it, "a common sense of right and a community of interest (*coetum iuris consensu et utilitatis communione sociatum*)" (*ciu.* 2.21, cf. 19.21 and 19.24).[8]

Even with this departure from Cicero, Augustine remains influenced by Cicero's belief that when people come together to form a political community, they create a *res publica*, literally a "public thing," which they share, promote, and protect. This *res publica* is simultaneously the product of their bond and the common good that holds them together. Both also believe that this common good can wither away through vice, so that it becomes a mere shadow of what it ought to be. In other words, though Augustine disagrees with Cicero's contention that the Roman republic was once bound together by true justice, he does recognize that its increasing vice is what "corrupted and disrupted that ... unity which is ... the health of a people" (*ciu.* 19.24).

Moreover, Augustine shares Cicero's conviction that the true common good is more than the shared pursuit of material goods: it involves brotherhood. Lamenting the fratricide that founded the Roman *ciuitas* and the lack of fraternity it signified, he reflects, "Goodness is a possession enjoyed more widely by the united affections of partners in that possession in proportion to the harmony that exists among them," such that "anyone who refuses to enjoy this possession in partnership will not enjoy it at all";

---

[6] If anything, rather than distinguishing between the social and the political, the ancients distinguished between the public and the private. Arendt makes much, perhaps too much, of this distinction in ancient political thought. Hannah Arendt, *The Human Condition* (Chicago: University of Chicago Press, 1998), 22–78.

[7] Catherine Conybeare makes a similar argument in "The City of Augustine," 144–148. See also Dodaro, *Christ and the Just* Society, 8n10, and Peter Brown, "Saint Augustine and Political Society," in *The City of God: A Collection of Critical Essays* (New York: Peter Lang, 1995), 17–36, 18.

[8] CCSL 47.53. This distinction has significant ramifications in that it highlights the fallenness of most political communities. Some say that it cuts off the descriptive from the normative, but I would not agree.

anyone who does, however, "will find that he possesses it in ampler measure in proportion to his ability to love his partner in it" (*ciu.* 15.5). Here, Augustine captures the true recipe for a healthy *ciuitas*, and in doing so, sounds very Ciceronian.

Of course, given that he is in the middle of discussing the fratricides of Cain and Romulus, one could rightly argue that, unlike Cicero, Augustine thinks that political communities always fail to be authentically social. Rowan Williams has convincingly made this point.[9] The fratricides that mark the founding of the first city, on the one hand, and the founding of Rome on the other, both show *amor sui*'s resistance to sharing prestige and, indeed, its tendency to forget the primacy of those goods which make it possible to share the rest. Augustine's damning picture of Roman politics back in book 2 also highlights these failures. Mocking contemporary Romans who are "unconcerned about the utter corruption of their country," he writes,

> "So long as it lasts," they say, "so long as it enjoys material prosperity, and the glory of victorious war . . . why should we worry? What concerns us is that we should get richer all the time. . . . It is alright if the poor serve the rich, so as to get enough to eat and to enjoy a lazy life under their patronage; while the rich make use of the poor to ensure a crowd of hangers-on to minister to their pride; if the people applaud those who supply them with pleasures rather than those who offer salutary advice; if no one imposes disagreeable duties or forbids perverse delights; if kings are interested not in the morality but the docility of their subjects; if provinces are under rulers who are regarded not as directors of conduct but controllers of material things and providers of material satisfactions, and are treated with servile fear instead of sincere respect." (*ciu.* 2.20)

In depicting these citizens as selfishly using each other for their own private pleasures, Augustine echoes Cicero's lament that the Roman *res publica* has become a locus of shared utility instead of a truly common good.

Yet, does all this political pessimism indicate that political communities are, by definition, sinful? Like Cicero before him, Augustine is capable of imagining how a political community could be authentically social, writing that "if men were always peaceful and just, human affairs would be happier and all kingdoms would be small, rejoicing in concord with their neighbours" (*ciu.* 4.15).[10] Similarly, he celebrates moments where justice

---

[9] Williams, "Politics and the Soul," in *On Augustine*, 111.
[10] Cf. *ciu.* 2.19 and *ep.* 138.14. Here, I think, Augustine is not speculating about what politics might have been like if humanity had not fallen, but rather what politics *would* be

wins out, writing that "when victory goes to those who were fighting for the juster [*sic*] cause, can anyone doubt that the victory is a matter for rejoicing and the resulting peace is something to be desired? These things are goods and undoubtedly they are the gifts of God" (*ciu.* 15.4). At bottom, Augustine considers political life to be a proper manifestation of our social nature; it just perpetually misses the mark.[11]

This principle is also visible in his famous redefinition of the *res publica,* or, the commonwealth. Arguing that "a people is the association of a multitude of rational beings united by a common agreement on the object of their love," Augustine at first appears to be casting the commonwealth off from its anchor in justice (*ciu.* 19.24).[12] However, if this were true, he would not be able to assert that better and worse objects of love make for better or worse commonwealths. Though Augustine gives the name of "commonwealth" to political communities not bound together by justice, he never stops taking the just *res publica* *as* his measure – it is just that this *res publica* is now the Heavenly City, as *City of God* 2.21 makes clear. By shifting the emphasis from *ius* to *amor,* Augustine does not cast off the normative standard that *iustitia* provided; instead, he simply highlights what he regards as primary: love.[13]

---

like if all people decided to cooperate with grace, here and now. This is a theoretical possibility because each person has free will and is offered grace, even if it is virtually impossible because people refuse grace.

[11] In this way, I do not wholly agree that "politics is a mark of fallen society." Rist, *Ancient Thought Baptized,* 252.

[12] Cf. O'Donovan, "Augustine's City of God XIX and Western Political Thought," 96. O'Donovan suggests that Augustine anticipates modern political philosophy by separating society from virtue, but since I do not read Cicero as believing that all actual political communities are held together by justice, I do not see a large disjunct between his position and Augustine's. For both, there is a way in which it is true that the *res publica* requires justice – and, for both, there is a way in which it is not. Indeed, the fact that ancient political thought did not think that all de facto political communities were bound together by justice is evident from both its foundational texts: Aristotle's *Politics* and Plato's *Republic.* As Augustine himself argues, Cicero well knows that he is overstating the case for early Roman virtue (cf. *ciu.* 2.21). It is primarily because the position is salutary that he promotes it in *De Republica* – and, moreover, through the voice of a certain character. Just as Augustine knows that Cicero promotes a love of glory for its political utility (*ciu.* 5.13), so too, he knows, Cicero promotes the idea of the necessity of justice for its political utility; if he can convince his Roman readers that the republic cannot exist without justice, Cicero may well be able to conjure up the virtuous citizens that Rome needs to recover. After all, Cicero writes in exile as the Roman republic is falling apart.

[13] Given that in the Platonic tradition, *iustitia* is an order constituted by a harmonious agreement among the parts, wherein each plays its proper role, it is easy to see the

Importantly, for Augustine, love is really what binds any community together. *Amor Dei*, of course, does this in a robust way, so that the city of God is held together in God by God's Love, the Holy Spirit, dwelling in its members. Nevertheless, *amor sui* mimics this power such that it is capable of making a kind of unity out of diverse wills. Recall, as we saw in Chapter 1, *amor sui* causes human beings to approve of others' investment in a shared project insofar as that investment reinforces their own private ends. In politics, then, a people is formed whenever its members share a common love: that is, when they share a common investment in their political project. Because the citizens of Rome loved glory, for example, they cohered as a people; Americans, alternatively, love freedom and equality, and so forth.[14] Love, Augustine believes, undergirds all political community.

That said, it is important to point out that political love can take on nobler or baser forms. Augustine clearly asserts, for example, that the Roman love of glory took on better and worse forms over the course of its history. At times, it restrained the people from greater vices, at others, it stopped at nothing to achieve prominence. Here, then, Augustine's distinction between a love of praise that sought the approval of good men and a love of praise that did not "fear the disapprobation of sound judges" is apt (*ciu.* 5.19). The former "checked other appetites" (*ciu.* 5.12).[15] The

transference between the two concepts; Augustine has repeatedly depicted *amor Dei* as the root of all true order, and *amor sui* as the root of all disorder.

[14] In the early books, Augustine has unmasked love of glory as a fundamentally selfish love: there, he suggested that the Romans loved Rome because they loved being part such of a glorious empire and hoped to attain glory for themselves through it: this is what bound them to her and undergirded the heroes' great devotion. The question remains as to whether he thinks it is possible for a whole body of Romans to love Rome in Cicero's sense: to love it for the sake of true glory, and to serve the *patria* in gratitude for the flourishing it makes possible. His definition does leave room for this possibility, and such a community would certainly have a healthier civic life. Nevertheless, he also argues that there were only ever a few good men in Rome. In this way, it is most likely that citizens love their city in different ways for different reasons, coalescing in a coincidental approval of their common project that has something to do with the basic principle of the regime (glory, freedom, equality, and so forth).

[15] While this kind is certainly better, Augustine does not consider it to be true glory in the same way that Cicero does. In arguing this, I am parting ways with a certain emphasis in von Heyking's subtle and careful reading of Augustine's take on glory in *Politics as Longing in the World*, 152–157, namely, his claim that there Augustine holds "substantial agreement with the pagan philosophers' definition of glory." Ibid., 154. While the lover of God will find glory in God, it is terribly significant that, for Augustine, he seeks God's glory and not his own, and I would argue, this departure from the pagan vision is more significant than the similarity that comes from a shared belief that true glory requires virtue and a sound judge.

latter yielded "the most barefaced crimes" (*ciu.* 5.19). Returning to Augustine's selfish Romans in book 2, we see how the quality of a commonwealth's love shapes its shared perception of what is right, of *ius* itself. Out of wanton selfishness, these Romans declare,

> The laws should punish offenses against another's property, not offences against a man's own personal character. No one should be brought to trial except for an offence, or the threat against another person's property, house or person; but anyone should be free to do as he likes about his own or with his own, or with others, if they consent. (*ciu.* 2.20)

In other words, these citizens' *ius* is about protecting what is theirs and making sure they can do as they please. Accordingly, in Augustine's paradigm, *ius* only follows from *amor*: true *ius* from *amor Dei*, to be sure, but also the spectrum of parodic *iura* from the spectrum of fallen *amores* – and the latter is not monolithic. It makes for healthier or sicker political communities. While none will be wholly rooted in *amor Dei*, some retain a greater semblance to the kind of earthly peace that *amor Dei* could yield than others. Just as the shared sense of right (*ius*) depends on what a community loves, so too does its approximation of justice. Love, then, provides greater descriptive accuracy even as it provides the true normative standard.

Now, where things get tricky is in deciding how much Augustine thinks the earthly city is responsible for the existence of actual political societies. Must it be said, for example, that all political foundings are the work of the earthly city? Given Augustine's claim that God "granted [Constantine] the honour of founding a city," it would not appear to be so simple (*ciu.* 5.25). God, recall, gives good things to all alike, and the honor of political founding, it would seem, is one of those "rewards or consolations" that God gives "in accordance with his pleasure" (*ciu.* 5.24, 5.21). Importantly, then, Augustine does not think it intrinsically wrong to set up a political community, or even to find fame for doing so.[16] It is simply wrong to lust after it, for, he clarifies, "boasting is not something wrong with the praise of men; the fault is in a soul which perversely loves the praise of others and cares nothing for the 'witness of conscience'" (*ciu.* 12.8). Similarly, "pride is not something wrong in the one who loves power or the power itself; the fault is in the soul which perversely loves its own power, and has no thought for the justice of the omnipotent"

---

[16] In this way, I disagree that Augustine's focus on the two fratricides coinciding with political foundings means that "a political commonwealth cannot but be founded on the lust of rule and on violence." Ruokanen, *Theology of Social Life,* 112.

(ibid.). In short, one can have good reasons for founding a political community.

Nevertheless, it would seem that *amor sui* provides stronger motives for founding a political community than *amor Dei*, which suggests that the earthly city has a greater hand in shaping political communities as we know them. Indeed, read in light of his two cities ontology, *City of God* 19.17, Augustine's famous discussion of the two cities' attitudes toward earthly peace, lends itself to this conclusion. Much ink has been spilled over this chapter, both because of its frustrating ambiguities and because of its obvious importance for understanding Augustine's political thought. What is agreed upon is that the passage contrasts the two cities' ways of being in the world, such that the pilgrim who belongs to the heavenly city uses earthly goods for his journey, while the settler who belongs to the earthly city enjoys them. The contention lies in what this means for politics: can the two meet on political grounds as equals, as Markus argues in *Saeculum*, or is the political community always the terrain of the earthly city, as Milbank and O'Donovan retort?[17] *City of God* 19.7 does state that both cities share a need for earthly peace and, therefore, have reasons to be invested in the political project. Yet, it also seems to suggest that earthly cities belong more to the earthly city than to the city of God. The earthly city, after all, is the city that *settles*. Because its good is of this world, it has a greater incentive to get down to business and make life in the *saeculum* as enjoyable as possible.

What is more, Augustine works hard to give the pilgrim city an air of detachment in the passage, setting it apart from the city that is at home in the world. While, he argues, the city of God "defends" the peace of the political community and "seeks" to ensure that its members work together to preserve it, like its forerunner, it "leads a life of captivity in this earthly city as in a foreign land" (*ciu.* 19.17). By putting the tonal

---

[17] Most notably, the debate between O'Donovan and Markus is forefronted in "Augustine's City of God XIX and Western Political Thought," 97–99. There, O'Donovan writes, "It is the easiest mistake in the world for the casual reader to take the words rendered 'similarly' (*ita etiam*) to refer to what has gone immediately before: the City of God and the earthly city get on together by having a common use and differing ends." Ibid., 98. Demonstrating this is a misreading, and that, in fact, it is the earthly city that "has a common use but differing ends," he write that obscuring this, "is the single weakness of Markus's fine book." Ibid. Markus responds in *Christianity and the Secular*, 63–66. Gregory Lee has a helpful treatment of their debate in "Republics and Their Loves: Rereading *City of God* 19," *Modern Theology* 27, no. 4 (2011): 553–581. To my mind, Lee's treatment of book 19 is one of the best in the literature, especially its presentation of the relationship between books 18 and 19.

emphasis on the latter point, Augustine does not present the two cities as equal participants in a common project, but instead draws Old Testament parallels. Like Israel of old, the city of God is trapped in Babylon, an empire run on someone else's terms. The question we might ask here is, which earthly city is a foreign land to the city of God? Is it the political community or the community of *amor sui*? This is easier to answer once we remember that Augustine depicts the latter as a hegemon. In this way, the two meanings of "earthly city" come together as the confluence of the occupier and the occupied. Not only is the pilgrim not at home because her home is elsewhere, the earthly city has imposed itself on the world, making it all the more foreign to her. Perpetually besieged, the *ciuitas* is not a neutral space.

Even so, it remains to be seen whether 19.17 attributes politics wholly to the earthly city. I would argue that the key to this puzzle actually lies in an earlier part of the chapter, where Augustine writes that the earthly city "limits the harmonious agreement of citizens ... to the establishment of a kind of compromise between human wills about the things relevant to this life" (*ciu.* 19.17).[18] Three elements of this quote are noteworthy: first, that the earthly city limits the harmonious agreement, second that it limits it to a compromise, and third, that this compromise is only concerned with temporal goods. Having defined these temporal goods as the constitutive goods of earthly peace only chapters before – pointing to "bodily health ... fellowship with one's kind, and everything necessary to safe-guard [the two]" as its most important elements – Augustine need not elaborate on what he means by such "things" here (*ciu.* 19.13). What is of greater significance is that the earthly city *limits* the social enterprise to a consensus about them, and what this means in light of Augustine's sacramental worldview.

Recalling Augustine's teaching that sin is merely the refusal of the greater good for the sake of the lesser, it is clear that limiting "the harmonious agreement of citizens" to a "compromise ... about the things relevant to this life" has a very specific meaning (*ciu.* 19.17). First of all, it

---

[18] In context, it is clear that the earthly city he is referring to here is the city of *amor sui*. Just after discussing the city of self-love, Augustine writes, "*Ita etiam terrena ciuitas ... terrenam pacem appetit in eoque defigit imperandi oboediendique concordiam ciuium, ut sit eis de rebus ad mortalem uitam pertinentibus humanarum quaedam compositio, uoluntatum,*" which I would literalistically translate as saying, "And so also the earthly city desires earthly peace, and fixes the community's compromise about giving and obeying orders in it, so that this compact might be based on an agreement amongst human wills about the things that pertain to mortal life." (CCSL 48.684).

is written in light of his previous remark that only the Heavenly City has a "perfectly ordered and perfectly harmonious" agreement among its citizens because it alone is constituted by "mutual fellowship in God" (*ciu.* 19.13).[19] For Augustine, this agreement is the sole foundation for thinking well about earthly peace: heavenly peace sets its true parameters, even as it may not dictate all its details. This being the case, the earthly city's limitation of the visible community's agreement to a consensus is just another reflection of its age-old tendency to say "no," stopping the buck at the *Diktat* of the fallen will. Yet, by reserving the right to construe earthly peace however it wishes, the earthly city also obscures the goal of political societies in a way that cannot be superseded in the *saeculum*. By making itself something separate, the earthly city has irrevocably transformed the pursuit of earthly peace into a more difficult endeavor.

In other words, because human beings in the *saeculum* perpetually fail to cohere in *amor Dei*, achieving a harmonious agreement about the nature of earthly peace will always be difficult. In every age, "the wicked fight amongst themselves, and likewise the wicked fight against the good and the good against the wicked," and worse, because the good are still on their way to perfection, "there may be fighting among them" too (*ciu.* 15.5). In such a world, there is little hope for a stable and sustained consensus about how to achieve earthly peace or, indeed, what earthly peace entails: human beings are too invested in their own interests and too shaped by distorted notions of *ius* and *iustitia*. In the world as we know it, aligning a community in a shared vision of earthly peace often deteriorates into a battle of wills. Consensus becomes a euphemism for the will of the stronger.

Nevertheless, there is a way in which the political community's pursuit of earthly peace can only be based on consensus. This, counterintuitively, is because the political community is a natural community.[20] Like Cicero, Augustine conceives of nature in the teleological sense, which means that

---

[19] Similarly, because Augustine conceives of peace as a kind of "tranquility of order," wherein lower modes of peace are perfected and sustained by higher modes, he thinks that "obedience to God" provides a much more perfect ground for human peace, the "ordered agreement of mind with mind," than mere consensus does (ibid.). Because of the cacophony of human desires, it is difficult to find stable and deeply held consensus in a household, let alone a city or an empire (*ciu.* 19.5–8). This is why *consuetudo* is so often conscripted into forming it.

[20] A number of other scholars have also argued that politics is a natural good in Augustine. See, e.g., Combès, *La Doctrine Politique de Saint Augustin*; Fortin, "Political Idealism and Christianity," 52; Rosemary Radford Reuther, "Augustine and Christian Political Theology," *Interpretation* 29, no. 3 (1975): 252–265, 260; and von Heyking, *Politics as Longing in the World*, 51–109.

because the political community is oriented toward a natural good, it too is natural.[21] Accordingly, it is important to distinguish between the inherent sinfulness of the earthly city's insurrection and the ambiguity of the political foundings we have been discussing. On the one hand, we can talk about how the earthly city makes itself its own foundation, so that its social life is necessarily unmoored from the love of God. On the other hand, we can talk about how human beings must found political communities because it is in their nature to seek earthly peace together (*ciu.* 19.12, inter alia). There is, therefore, a difference between the earthly city's demand that politics be limited to a consideration of earthly peace on its terms, and nature's plan that human beings come together to pursue earthly peace. The latter does not require earthly peace to become unmoored from *amor Dei*. Thus, while the founding of any actual political community is a product of human agency, it is so only in the same way that every convention springs from human agency. Just as the neutral sense of *consuetudo* is ontologically prior to its perversion, so too, politics in its integrity, is ontologically prior to its perversion. Though the political community perennially falls short, it is not founded on sin in the same way that the earthly city is.

Ultimately, Augustine thinks, the only community that is not founded by human beings is the Church: the visible manifestation of the city of God.[22] This being the case, one might ask whether Augustine would be a proponent of integralism. While integralism may seem to solve the

---

[21] In *De Republica*, Cicero argues, "It is impossible to live well except in a good common-wealth." Cicero, *De Re Publica, De Legibus*, trans. Clinton Walker Keyes (Cambridge, MA: Harvard University Press, 2006), v.iii.7. Giving an account of all the natural appe-tites in *De Officiis* i.iv.11–xliv.159, Cicero first notes the inclination toward self-preservation and reproduction, common to all living creatures. Then, he notes the human being's special affection for family, shared with some animals. Finally, he points out the desires particular to humans; those for truth, independence, order, and propriety. The most noteworthy of these, indeed the "deepest feeling in our nature," is the desire for society. Cicero, *De Officiis*, trans. Walter Miller (Cambridge, MA: Harvard University Press, 1913), i.xliv.159. For Cicero, the institution of political life is a natural response to these various inclinations. Of the many kinds of things necessary for life, Cicero notes that a great many are produced by human labor. Yet, it is only through human cooperation that these discoveries become beneficial to all. In this way, *civitates* are the culmination of human ingenuity; laws, customs and other institutions allow for civilized life to form and a humane spirit to be cultivated in a people. Through this humane spirit, cities become the forum for "giving and receiving," and through this "mutual exchange of commodities and conveniences," people are able to meet all their wants and needs (ibid., i.iv.15). While Augustine might not believe, like Cicero, that the city is the realm of human *perfection*, he can follow Cicero on the natural quality of political society.

[22] For Augustine, the Church is founded by Christ, in Christ, and on Christ. Cf. *en. Ps.* 103.5.17.

political problem, reintegrating the political community's understanding of earthly peace into a vision shaped by heavenly peace, for the *City of God*'s Augustine, this is too idealistic. As Markus has well established in his work, *Saeculum*, the fact that Augustine passes over Constantine's Christianization of the empire in silence speaks volumes; having been disillusioned by the post-Constantinian era, he no longer uses the term *tempora Christiana* with a positive political meaning.[23] Given the dis-ordering effects of the Fall, this Augustine has concluded that it is one thing for an individual to join herself to Christ, and quite another to expect such a conversion across a whole society. Accordingly, though he does praise the emperor Theodosius for his faith and good works, he persistently presents him as a son of the Church, and not as a unifier of two realms. To praise a particular emperor for "help[ing] the Church" with "just and compassionate legislation" is a far cry from recommending that statecraft and soulcraft be melded into one project (*ciu.* 5.26).[24]

Again, as Markus persuasively points out, Augustine is not willing to speak of a Christian Empire or of the conversion of political rule (*regna*) to Christianity.[25] Indeed, as we will see below, all that he seems to advocate in *City of God* is a proper ordering of loves, encouraging Christian emperors to love God more than status and to use their position as a means of service, interpreting the responsibilities with which they are charged in light of the true good.[26] Though the goods that the political community pursues can be

---

[23] See Markus, *Saeculum*, 38–39. In his history of the emperors of the 300s, Cochrane also has a helpful discussion of Eusebius and Lactantius's very different take on Constantine – the one from which Augustine departs. Cochrane, *Christianity and Classical Culture*, 202–205. Cf. Rist, *Ancient Thought Baptized*, 208, 216, 228.

[24] The question, of course, can be raised as to whether Augustine is whitewashing Theodosius's rule. Cochrane's history of his reign, for example, is less than rosy: *Christianity and Classical Culture*, 354–371. McLynn attempts to account for this discrepancy with an interesting appeal to Augustine's autobiography: Neil McLynn, "Augustine's Roman Empire," *Augustinian Studies* 30, no. 2 (1999): 32. Responding to worries about Augustine's praise of Theodosius, Fortin argues that Augustine "stresses their private virtues to the virtual exclusions of their political virtues. Ernest Fortin, "Augustine's 'City of God' and the Modern Historical Consciousness," *The Review of Politics* 41, no. 3 (1979): 338; Dodaro, along with Williams on the other hand, disagrees with this claim, arguing that "Augustine is not interested in extolling private virtue." Dodaro, "Augustine's Revision of the Heroic Ideal," 154; cf. Williams, "Politics and the Soul," in *On Augustine*, 120. For them, Theodosius's public penance is the most significant antidote to the disease affecting the Roman empire.

[25] See Markus, *Saeculum*, 38, esp. note 4.

[26] There is admittedly ambiguity in what the latter would entail: does it, for example, require that one use one power to suppress pagan practices? Liberal Augustinianism might not want to go all the way with Augustine on this point – or, at least the way he

integrated into the pursuit of a higher end, the community that pursues them *qua* community is the Church, and, as we have already seen, Augustine does not consider the Church to be a new political community. It is, rather, "a society of aliens, speaking all languages":

> She takes no account of any difference in customs, laws and institutions, by which earthly peace is achieved and preserved – not that she annuls or abolishes any of those, rather, she maintains and follows them (for whatever divergences there are among the diverse nations, those institutions have one single aim – earthly peace). (*ciu.* 19.17)

Thus, just as Christ's coming did not nullify the diversity of languages, it seems that the coming of the Church does not nullify political communities. Instead, it invites its members to integrate their service to the political community into their service of God, and so bear witness to an alternative economy at work in the world.

Before we turn to our discussion of this service and its implications for our political communities, it is important to elaborate further on what political life looks like after the Fall. Politics, we have just seen, is not fundamentally "of" the earthly city for Augustine. Instead, the earthly city has co-opted a natural project for its own ends, reinterpreting the goal of earthly peace through the lens of *amor sui*. While, therefore, the earthly city *qua* political community is "earthly" because it is oriented toward earthly peace, and the earthly city *qua* city of self-love is also "earthly" because it is oriented toward earthly peace, these two statements mean different things. The former means that the political community pursues an interim peace; the latter means that *amor sui* refuses an eternal peace. Because the city of self-love only wants happiness in the world, it hijacks the political project for its own ends, which are legion. Becoming a fraught endeavor as a result, the besieged city's pursuit of earthly peace is perpetually marked by the earthly city's attempt to limit the construal of earthly peace to something grounded in its own will. Striving to ground itself in *amor Dei*, the pilgrim city struggles against the very same tendency in itself. While Augustine's history of Rome has given us a window into what politics becomes when it is reduced to such strife, it remains to be seen how politics is transformed in response to sin. This is where we can start talking about what we call political institutions, but what Augustine would conceive of in terms of dominion, or rule.

---

seems to in contexts beyond *City of God* – and could even make Augustinian arguments as to why it is an imprudent tactic to do so. Many have written on this contentious topic, but I will not venture into it in the current project, given its particular scope.

DOMINION REIMAGINED

In the previous section of this chapter, I argued that, for Augustine, the political community is not "of" the earthly city; it is merely besieged by the earthly city. To demonstrate this, I showed that Augustine primarily conceives of politics in classical terms, which means that his political thought, if it can properly be so called, focuses on communities before institutions. Indeed, many have noted that Augustine's institutional thinking is not strongly developed: he is simply not concerned with the project of crafting institutions or examining how different institutional arrangements might better achieve certain political goals.[27] Instead, when he does talk about institutions, he speaks of them simply as the practices that human communities have instituted, reflecting his overall contention that human beings either participate in or cover over the original meaning of reality with their customs.[28] One of the few times he mentions *instituta* in a strictly political context is in *City of God* 19.17, where he uses the term as a vague catch-all for the means that political communities devise to promote earthly peace, listing them alongside the laws and customs that members of the pilgrim city are happy to follow, so long as they do not hinder *latreia*. In reality, then, Augustine does not discuss political institutions to a significant extent. However, in the latter part of *City of God* 19, he does consider how political communities approximate earthly peace in a fallen world, and the roles and responsibilities that their members take on as a result.

In discussing the social order as we know it, Augustine distinguishes between "what was required by the order of nature and what was demanded by the desert of sinners" (*ciu.* 19.15). Importantly, his use of the term "order of nature" shows that he conceives of nature in its

---

[27] O'Donovan, "Augustine's City of God XIX and Western Political Thought," 99; Williams, "Politics and the Soul," in *On Augustine*, 110.

[28] Examples include the institution of the rules of war (*ciu.* 2.2); the institution of particular church communities (*ciu.* 2.6); the practices of the many (*ciu.* 2.7, 21); the institution of the Roman priesthood (*ciu.* 2.8, 15; 3.9); the institution of the Jewish priesthood (*ciu.* 17.5); the calling of the disciples (*ciu.* 18.54); the founding of the Academic school (*ciu.* 19.1); the institution of the secular games (*ciu.* 2.8; 3.18; 18.2); man-made, rather than natural, occurrences (*ciu.* 12.10); God's creation, particularly of human beings (*ciu.* 12.1, 11–13, 24; 13.3; 14.27; 20.8; 22.24, inter alia); political founding (*ciu.* 15.5); the institution of laws and courts (*ciu.* 18.3; 19.17); and once, the institution of political offices (*ciu.* 5.12). The most frequent reference, however, relates to the institution of superstitious practices and the erection of false gods (*ciu.* 4.10, 26; 6.4–6; 7.1, 34; 8.24–27; 18.12–13, 24, inter alia). Most of these occur in verb form, rather than speaking of "institutions" per se.

integrity; unlike the moderns, his version is hardly anarchic. Instead, it is marked by a divinely appointed order.[29] On top of this order, we will also see, is the order of dominion, ordained by God as a punishment for sin. Indeed, Augustine's culminating insight that men were not originally intended "to have dominion over any but irrational creatures (*inrationabilibus*)" follows from his judgment that the earthly city does violence to the natural order (*ciu.* 19.15).[30] We see this, for example, in his presentation of the earthly city's peace. Pride's peace, he has famously argued, "hates a fellowship of equality under God and seeks to impose its own dominion on fellow men, in place of God's rule" (*ciu.* 19.12). True peace, on the other hand, "is the perfectly ordered and completely harmonious fellowship in the enjoyment of God and of each other in God" (*ciu.* 19.17). Having not yet arrived at the latter, humanity is left to deal with the fallout of the former. This requires that the proud be constrained – though unfortunately, they are often the ones doing the constraining.

Noticing in Scripture that "the first just men were set up as shepherds of flocks, rather than as kings of men," Augustine takes this as evidence that God did not originally wish human beings to have dominion over one another (*ciu.* 19.15). There is, he seems to suggest, a dignity in being made in God's image that renders it unfitting. The difficulty, then, is in discovering what counts as dominion (*dominium*) in this sense. Distinguishing, as I have mentioned, between the order of nature and the desert of sinners, he traces the origin of slavery (*servitus*) to sin (ibid.). By making slavery the ultimate example of interpersonal dominion, Augustine shows that its essence lies in the constraint of freedom: the slave is obligated to obey the master's will because he is wholly subject to him. He lacks any choice. Associating such slavery with the slavery to sin that followed from the Fall, Augustine presents both as a just punishment devised by God, the latter worse for its interiority. The result of sin, therefore, is a new "order of peace in which men are subordinate to other men" (ibid.). Leaving his

---

[29] John Rist argues that, by the time Augustine writes the *City of God*, "the natural order" only refers to "the physical world" and that "the operations of human and angelic wills are not included in it." Rist, *Ancient Thought Baptized*, 214–215. I, however, do not agree that this is the case; for example, in *City of God* 11.16, Augustine writes that in the order of nature, the angels are higher than all the other creatures (*tantum ualet in naturis rationalibus quoddam ueluti pondus uoluntatis et amoris, ut, cum ordine naturae angeli hominibus, tamen lege iustitiae boni homines malis angelis praeferantur*) (*ciu.* 11.16; CCSL 48.336). Accordingly, I read the order of nature as referring to the whole of God's providential design.

[30] " '*dominetur*,' inquit, '*piscium maris et uolatilium caeli et omnium repentium, quae repunt super terram*' " (*ciu.* 19.15; CCSL 48.682).

justification of slavery to the side, we can conclude that Augustine views all institutions in which some people are subject (*subderetur*) to others as postlapsarian modifications to the order of nature. The Fall has thrust human beings into positions of command and obedience.

The difficulty, however, arises at the beginning of the chapter we have been discussing. There, Augustine deems a certain relationship to be "prescribed by the order of nature (*hoc naturalis ordo praescribit*)" (*ciu.* 19.15).[31] At first glance, it appears that the "this" (*hoc*) he is referring to is the domestic arrangement exposited in the previous chapter. Yet, this, too, seems to be marked by dominion: "wives obey husbands, the children obey parents, the servants (*seruis*) their masters" (*ciu.* 19.14).[32] What is the difference? While it might seem that Augustine is merely deeming the domestic hierarchy natural, and the political hierarchy unnatural, this is not exactly his point and cannot be, since he is about to deem servitude a postlapsarian phenomenon. Instead, I will argue, it is the special concern that a *paterfamilias* has toward the members of his household which is prescribed by the order of nature.

The order of nature, Augustine has just explained, dictates that there ought to be peace among all human beings (*ciu.* 19.14). This, he goes on, is why God gave them two commandments: love God and love your neighbor. By following these commandments, human beings are brought back into proper relation with God and with one another, learning to have concern for their neighbor's well-being and wishing their neighbor to have concern for theirs – this being a sign that their neighbor, too, loves God. Depicting peace among men (*pace hominum*) as a product of such right relation among persons, Augustine roots its "ordered harmony (*ordinata concordia*)" in the "observance of two rules: first ... do no harm," and second, "help everyone whenever possible" (ibid.).[33] While demanding good will toward all, Augustine's order of nature also subscribes to the principle of subsidiarity. That is, each person has a special responsibility toward his or her own (*ei suorum*): those to whom he or she is closest.[34] This, Augustine explains, is because "he [or she] has easier and more immediate contact with them" (ibid.). Yet, importantly, he adds that this is true "both in the order of nature and in the framework of human society (*uel naturae ordine uel ipsius societatis humanae*)" (ibid.).[35]

This being the case, then, we cannot conclude that everything that follows in 19.14 is strictly based on the order of nature. Instead, the

[31] CCSL 48.682.   [32] CCSL 48.681.   [33] CCSL 48.681.   [34] Ibid.
[35] CCSL 48.680–681.

arrangement of the passage shows that Augustine is writing about the household as he knows it: in the framework of Roman society. Read in context, it is clear that the passage presents a model of domestic dominion redeemed, arguing that the exercise of fatherly authority (*imperium*) should be a form of service.[36] The passage, in other words, is Augustine's correction of the model offered by the *paterfamilias*-robber only two chapters before. Describing in 19.12 how that *paterfamilias* is "delighted" to have his wife, children, and servants "obedient to his beck and call," and how he is "indignant" when they are not, Augustine decries his *libido dominandi* (*ciu.* 9.12).[37] Enslaved in soul, the robber convinces himself that peace cannot exist unless all are subject to his will. To bring such peace about, "he employs savage measures," imposing harsh punishments on all those who countermand his will (ibid.). Effectively, he reigns as a tyrant.

In *City of God* 19.14, then, Augustine is trying to show that domination (*dominatio*) is not the only form of dominion.[38] Upending the expectations laid in place by the economy of the earthly city, Augustine claims that true heads of household (*iusti*) "give orders (*imperant*)," not out of pride or *libido dominandi*, "but from a dutiful concern for the interest of others," such that they are, in reality, "the servants of those whom they appear to command" – or, to quote the Latin in its entirety: "*etiam qui imperant seruiunt eis, quibus uidentur imperare*" (ibid.).[39] Importantly, he is showing his readers how it is possible to participate in the social order without yielding to the ways of the earthly city. More will be said about this below; for now, our purpose is to discover whether paternal dominion is prescribed by the order of nature. Spelling out the answer two chapters later, Augustine confirms what we might have guessed. It is in accord with the order of nature that the *paterfamilias* be concerned for the eternal well-being of all in his household (*ciu.* 19.16).[40]

---

[36] Cf. Elshtain, *Augustine and the Limits of Politics*, 39–40.

[37] Note that the *libido dominandi* (literally, the lust for dominion) yields domination, as Augustine points out in *City of God* 12.8. In other words, it is a disordered love for ruling that results in perverse rule.

[38] More often than not, *dominatio* carries with it a pejorative tone in *City of God*. Used when one political community crushes another, or a tyrannical leader dominates a people, in the early books on Roman history, it frequently evokes the *libido dominandi* or sometimes a synonym thereof, such as *dominationis cupiditas*. Significantly, the term is closely related to the participle Augustine uses to talk about demonic oppression, *dominatus*.

[39] CCSL 48.681.

[40] On this point, John Rist wonders if Augustine reads the duty to love one's neighbor too restrictively. Rist, *Ancient Thought Baptized*, 239. It is true that Augustine does not flesh out the obligations one has to care for another's bodily needs in *City of God*, and this is

The fact that he must give orders to them is not. Instead, Augustine considers *imperium* to be a burden: a "necessary duty" brought about by the disorder of the world as we know it (ibid.). Returning to the end of 19.14, then, we find that the relationships and roles wherein people express "concern for the interests of others" are actually what Augustine is referring to at the opening of the subsequent chapter (*ciu.* 19.14). For him, God's economy of gift puts human beings in relationship so that they can serve one another in *amor Dei*: this nexus of bonds constitutes the true order of nature.

In arguing that dominion within the household is also a product of the Fall, however, I am not suggesting that Augustine denies the existence of natural hierarchies. This would contradict what we have already seen in his cosmology. Instead, I am suggesting that there is a difference between a hierarchy defined by agency and a hierarchy defined by dominion. As we have already seen, Augustine does not think that the natural superiority of the angelic beings leads to a situation in which they rule over human beings.[41] Instead, they point human beings to God, seeking to help them however they can. In the economy of gift, then, the superior beings are in a higher position, but ultimately as a position of service – and, I have argued, this economy demarcates the original order of creation.

Accordingly, while Augustine might well see a natural stratification of agents within the family, such that the children naturally need looking after by their parents, and wives need looking after by their husbands because they are "the inferior of the human pair," he still does not think this necessitates dominion or rule until sin enters the picture (*ciu.* 14.11). Thus, in Augustine's order of nature, there is no need for a total equality to avoid a situation of dominion; for him, every community is naturally made up of weaker and stronger members, and this is for the good. While we may disagree with him about the nature of the stratification that he sees among human beings, it is important to stress that his understanding of the order of nature is one that puts those with greater agency at the service of those with lesser without creating a situation of dominion. The economy of gift is an economy of service, but not naturally one of rule – at least among rational creatures.

---

arguably a lack. Yet, for Augustine, love of neighbor is a fruit of love of God, such that, if a person were to love God rightly, she would know how to love her neighbor well – that is, as she loves herself. Of course, Augustine has many sermons that highlight the importance of giving alms, and the presence of Christ in the poor. See, for example, *s.* 359A.11, *s.* 399.7, *s.* 345.2, *s.* 389.4, inter alia.

[41] Cf. Klein, *Augustine's Theology of Angels*, 75.

Ultimately, the reason why the dominion of some human beings over others is only a postlapsarian phenomenon is because it implies coercion, or a human person being made to do something regardless of, and potentially against, his or her own volition.[42] With the alignment of all wills to God, the latter was an impossibility before the Fall, and the former was simply unfitting (*ciu.* 14.12, 14.15, inter alia). As we have already seen, Augustine believes that all rational creatures were created with a good will (*ciu.* 12.5–9, 14.10–11). This meant that they adhered directly to God by their own volition. Because of this harmony of orientation among their wills, and the dignity they each had in being able to offer themselves to God, freely and fully, there was no need for the higher ones to rule the lower.[43] Thus, while one can imagine direction or counsel occurring within Augustine's prelapsarian order, he never expressly discusses this. He simply makes it clear that dominion

---

[42] Katherine Chambers has argued that servitude, for Augustine, meant "to exist in a state of dependence on another's will." Katherine Chambers, "Slavery and Domination as Political Ideas in Augustine's City of God," *Heythrop Journal* (2013): 14. Her main thesis is that, against Petit and Skinner's interpretation of Augustine's views on slavery and what she calls domination, Augustine did not think the enslaved person was necessarily subject to arbitrary power, just another's power per se. Though I do not agree with every aspect of her reading, her article contains a careful exegesis of Augustine's treatment of women and slavery.

[43] There is rule, generally speaking within the order of nature – however, I am arguing, not amongst rational agents. Just as human beings naturally rule the beasts in Augustine, the mind naturally rules the body: this is according to the order of nature. Yet, it does not follow that interpersonal rule is according to the order of nature. While a case could be made for rule of children that have not reached the age of reason, I am skeptical that he regards women as so below rational capacity that they need ruling in the same way as the beasts or the body. Indeed, he often characterizes the subjection of Eve as a punishment for her sin. See, e.g., *ciu.* 15.7 and *Gn. litt.* 11.37.50, where Augustine writes, "It was God's sentence, you see, that gave this position to the man, and it was by her own fault that the woman deserved to have her husband as her lord, not by nature (*hoc enim uiro potius sententia dei detulit et maritum habere dominum meruit mulieris non natura, sed culpa*)." (CSEL 28.372). Notice that he does not describe this lordship as *dominationem*. Moreover, differentiating between the "kind of service, by which human beings later on began to be the slaves of other human beings" and the kind of service that love bids by its very nature, he categorizes the kind of service that a wife must give her husband as the former, describing it as a matter of "social status (*cuiusdam condicionis*)." Augustine, *On Genesis*, trans. Edmund Hill, OP, ed. John E. Rotelle, OSA (Hyde Park, NY: New City Press, 2002), 458; CSEL 28.372. To me, this aligns the introduction of dominion in the political world with its introduction in the home. Both are punishments for sin. Chambers reads this passage differently in "Slavery and Domination as Political Ideas in Augustine's City of God," 16–17. Her take is that Eve's servitude was natural, but only became a hardship after the Fall.

belongs to God alone (*ciu.* 12.16).[44] The angels who continued in *amor Dei*, of course, remain in this original order, while the rational creatures who fell away from it became subject to the consequences of its loss. For human beings, this meant our subjection to sin and to one another.

However, while all coercive institutions are postlapsarian, they are not all sinful – that is, they are not necessarily "of" the earthly city. To be sure, Augustine argues, "unjust institutions" (*iniqua hominum constituta*) are not to be considered legitimate (*ciu.* 19.21).[45] The question could be raised as to what institutions he has in mind here: at the very least, idolatrous ones. Nevertheless, he is clear that political communities must consider both what is "required by the order of nature" and what is "demanded by the deserts of sinners" when they are trying to achieve peace (*ciu.* 19.15). In a world where some have no better reason to keep the peace than for fear of punishment, this is simply a matter of prudence. Affirming that coercion and punishment have an important role to play in the world as we know it, Augustine tells one Roman magistrate that "the power of the sovereign, the judge's right over life and death, the executioner's instruments of torture, the weapons of the soldier, the discipline of the ruler, and the severity of a good father," were all instituted for a reason: "All these have their limits, causes, reasons, and utility. When these are feared, the evil are held in check and the good live more peaceful lives among the evil" (*ep.* 153.16).[46] His affirmation of all of the methods that communities use to achieve earthly peace in *City of God* 19.17 echoes the same sentiment.

In this way, Augustine thinks of coercion and punishment as necessary tools for maintaining social order in a fallen world and endorses them as such, both in *City of God* and elsewhere. In describing the duty of a *paterfamilias* in 19.16, for example, Augustine argues that he must reprove members of his household who have committed wrongdoing both for their

---

[44] In Augustine's description of pre-lapsarian life, God's rule is not tantamount to coercion because Adam and Eve have good wills and naturally lived according to God's will (*ciu.* 14.10–11). Nevertheless, God is sovereign. Augustine can argue this because he defines true freedom as the state one is in when one's will is "not subservient to faults and sins" (*ciu.* 14.11). That is, the rational creature's freedom is *in* obedience to God (*ciu.* 14.12). For Augustine, this obedience is an act of love, made possible by God's love working in us, even as it is also free. As he explains, if the pre-lapsarian will "had remained unshaken in its love of God, God would have continued to "who shed on it light to see and kindled in it fire to love" (*ciu.* 14.13). The good will, in other words, is naturally sustained by God in its freedom. This freedom has been lost with the Fall, but Christ has the power to restore it in us.

[45] CCSL 48.688.

[46] Augustine, *Letters 100–155*, trans. Roland Teske, ed. Boniface Ramsey (Hyde Park, NY: New City Press, 2003), 398.

own good and for the sake of mending the domestic peace that they have damaged. Recalling that Augustinian peace is rooted in right relationship, it follows that wrongdoing sunders a person from the community's peace, and so damages its social fabric. As such, it is the responsibility of the one in authority to see if it can be repaired.

Yet, even from this brief example, we see that it is not so simple as to say that Augustine views *imperium*, the command involved in dominion, as "damage control."[47] Instead, the duty with which Augustine charges leaders is better described as healing the damage from the root, rather than plugging holes in a faulty dam. The dam, to be sure, is faulty, but as *City of God* 19.6 suggests, the *paterfamilias'* objective is actually of one restoration and healing; whether through punishment or clemency, he must discern the best way to "readjust [the offender] to the domestic peace from which he had broken away" (*ciu.* 19.16). Returning to his depiction of Theodosius in book 5, we see that here too Augustine praises such peace-making. Celebrating Theodosius's ability to make peace after civil war with the kidnapped sons of his enemies, he notes that Theodosius "did not deprive them of their property ... and never allowed victory to be followed by the satisfaction of private feuds" (*ciu.* 5.20). In this way, he not only controlled the negative effects of strife, but created a set of conditions that allowed for the reconciliation of former enemies; he made his political society more authentically social than it was before. For Augustine, the ability to bring about the restoration of peace is a positive power, and even a way of participating in God's healing work.

Moreover, it is significant that in writing that the coercive tools of the sovereign, the judge, the soldier and the father were all instituted for a reason, Augustine is making a concession to further a different point; his actual purpose in letter 153 is to justify his own practice of interceding in capital cases. Yet, to make room for this clemency, Augustine must defend a specifically Christian approach to administering legal punishments: it will not do to assume that the good judge should apply the maximum penalty. Now that Christians have been "taught to pardon," he argues, it hardly "counts as a failure in their office" if judges "act mercifully ... towards those over whom they have the legitimate power of life and death" (*ep.* 153.17).[48] Mercy, therefore, has a significant role in true service, and can be the source of great healing for all parties.

---

[47] Kaufman, *Incorrectly Political*, 69.
[48] Augustine, *Letters 100–155*, 394. For a wide-ranging treatment of Augustine's letters to political figures, see Joseph Clair, *Discerning the Good in the Letters & Sermons of*

Importantly, Augustine stresses, leniency and mercy are not the same thing. Mercy is ordered toward the correction of the offender; leniency simply ignores the crime. Writing that it is neither a kindness to ignore a wrongdoing nor to punish it too harshly, he points to the importance of the judge's attitude in discerning what is most merciful:

> For just as at times mercy punishes, so cruelty also pardons. After all, to set forth something obvious as an example, who would not more correctly call him cruel who gave in to a boy who was most insistent about wanting to play with snakes? But who would not call a person merciful who forbade such actions and chastised even with a beating the boy who scorned his words? And for this reason discipline should not be carried to the point of death in order that the person may still live who can benefit from it. (*ep.* 153.17)[49]

Significantly, we see the same perspective defended in *City of God* 19.16, though his point there is not to argue for mercy – recall, he is trying to show that the good *paterfamilias* gives orders out of duty, and not out of the *libido dominandi*. Even so, in writing that it is not a kindness "to spare a man, when by so doing you let him fall into a greater sin," Augustine displays the same sense of responsibility toward persons that animates his plea for clemency in the above-quoted letter (*ciu.* 19.16). Justice and mercy, it turns out, are not at odds. For him, being charged with the care of others involves steering them in the right direction, whatever that might be: coercion, he thinks, is for the sake of correction.[50]

Augustine (Oxford: Oxford University Press, 2016), 107–129. For my own extensive treatment of letter 153, see Ogle, "Sheathing the Sword," 737–741.

[49] Augustine, *Letters 100–155*, 399.

[50] According to Lewis and Short, *coerceō* can mean "*to hold some fault, some passion*, etc., or *the erring* or *passionate person in check, to curb, restrain, tame, correct*, etc." Charlton T. Lewis et al., *A Latin Dictionary Founded on Andrews' Edition of Freund's Latin Dictionary* (Oxford: Clarendon Press, 1879), 359. It is frequently used in this sense by Cicero, Sallust, and Livy, among others, and is not coincidentally the term used to describe the pruning of plants. The language of pruning immediately conjures up biblical imagery, such as Jn. 15:2, where Christ explains that he is the Vine and his Father prunes all his branches so that they might bear more fruit. Augustine, for his part, certainly considers such pruning to be a benevolent and corrective activity and urges Christians in positions of authority to engage in it. See, e.g., *ep.* 22, 93, 134, 177. Augustine's understanding of coercion as a benevolent practice has become somewhat notorious because of his attitude toward the Donatists. Indeed, we can see how it could so easily go wrong. Nevertheless, recent studies have helpfully contextualized his policies in this particular case: John von Heyking, *Augustine and Politics as Longing in the World*, 222–257; Eric Gregory, *Politics and the Order of Love*, 297–306; Gregory Lee, "Using the Earthly City: Ecclesiology, Political Activity, and Religious Coercion in Augustine," *Augustinian Studies* 47, no. 1 (2016): 41–63; and Michael Lamb, "Augustine and

Significantly, the *paterfamilias* on whom we have been focusing happens to be the model Augustine uses to convey this message to those in authority. Writing to a different Roman magistrate, for example, he pleads,

Carry out, O Christian judge, the duty of a loving father. Be angry at wickedness in such a way that you remember to be humane, and do not turn the desire for revenge upon the atrocities of sinners, but apply the will to heal to the wounds of sinners. (*ep.* 133.2)[51]

By imploring his interlocutor to inhabit the benevolent posture of a father instead of the detached posture of a Stoic, Augustine again presents the authority-figure as a healer. Recognizing, of course, that not everyone will be filled with contrition after wrongdoing, he nevertheless hopes for its possibility, following the mantra we have already seen: "punishing and pardoning are done well only in order to correct the life of human beings" (*ep.* 153.19).[52]

In this passage, we also find a helpful articulation of Augustine's position back in *City of God*: for him, the bounds of coercion are always defined by one's responsibility toward others: both toward the person one is correcting and the community at large – but never the latter at the expense of the former. In this way, we see that what we conceive of in terms of institutional structures, Augustine conceives in terms of interpersonal bonds.[53] Because coercive offices always involve responsibilities to concrete persons and communities, Augustine cannot conceive of coercion in the abstract; instead, he thinks of it as a tool for mending broken bonds and healing broken persons.

Ultimately, Augustine's all too brief political counsel in *City of God* 19 is to look upon whatever authority one has as an opportunity for service; as he famously puts it, a bishop who seeks the glory of office is no bishop at all – and likewise with any position of authority (*ciu.* 19.19). Theorizing about the function of office, he explains that what is to be valued in any such position is the task that is capable of being achieved by means of its power: "if that achievement is right and helpful, that is, if it serves to

---

Republican Liberty: Contextualizing Coercion," *Augustinian Studies* 48, no. 1–2 (2017): 119–159.

[51] Augustine, *Letters 100–155*, 203.   [52] Ibid., 400.

[53] This is arguably related to his Roman context, wherein the social hierarchy was conceived of as a vast nexus of human bonds, and experienced in the form of patron-client relationships. Cf. Peter Brown, *Power and Persuasion in Late Antiquity* (Green Bay: University of Wisconsin Press, 1992), 56–57; Lendon, *The Empire of Honour*, 211, 236.

promote the well-being of the common people," then it is rightly valued (ibid.). In this way, good rulers discern punishment in relation to the common good, punishing "wrong because of the necessity to direct the state (*rei publicae*), and not to satisfy their personal animosity" (*ciu.* 5.24). Yet, they also balance this concern with care for the well-being of those under judgment. Clearly, then, Augustine accepts postlapsarian hierarchy for what it is, and calls on the Christian to use his or her social position, whatever it might be, as an opportunity for service. This, in turn realigns his or her actions with the animating principle of the order of nature: *amor Dei*. In this way, dominion can be baptized. What cannot be baptized is domination.

While Augustine does not theorize about what came first: domination as a political ailment, or dominion as a political remedy, it is clear that both are the consequences of the Fall. While, therefore, the political community and even the political project can properly be called natural, the coercive institutions with which moderns tend to associate politics are postlapsarian, introduced as a way to approximate earthly peace in a fallen world. To put this another way, the political project is ontologically prior to both dominion and domination. However, given that earthly city has essentially effected a political coup, politics as we know it has always been marred by its economy. While the coercive remedies that Augustine endorses mitigate the effects of *amor sui* among the ranks, some remain beyond its grasp. The lower, he laments in more than one letter, have a hard time bringing justice to bear on the higher.[54] Dominion, in other words, does not solve the political problem of domination on its own. Ever a radical thinker, Augustine thinks that the only solution for the problem of domination is one that gets at the root of the problem: one that targets *amor sui*. While we tend to think of radicality as that which is revolutionary – that which overthrows unjust structures – Augustine thinks that new versions will only grow back if the root of the problem is not faced.[55]

Some, of course, have argued that Augustine's lack of interest in amending institutional structures derived from his sense that the hierarchies of the Roman world were fixed – a hierarchical world was all he had ever known and all he could imagine.[56] There is a certain truth to this. Yet, what is also true is that Augustine primarily conceives of institutions as

---

[54] Cf. *ep.* 9*.3–4; *ep.* 153.25.
[55] We saw this in his treatment of the Gracchi in Chapter 4.
[56] Rist, *Ancient Thought Baptized*, 210.

arrangements enshrined by human beings. In this way, it is first and foremost hearts that yield institutions and customs, even as institutions and customs also shape hearts. Because Augustine has this conviction, he thinks that there is no use in attacking unjust institutions as the source of the problem when the love animating human beings is the real issue.[57] As long as human hearts are not fixed in *amor Dei*, injustice will arise in some form or another. This being so, Augustine presents the offices wielding coercive authority as both useful and necessary in the world as we know it, even as they are so frequently inhabited badly. Distinguishing between dominion and domination, he is able to show his readers that it is possible to serve others well through *imperium*, striving to bring healing to the wounded communities and persons they rule.

Stepping back, we see that over the course of the past two sections, I have sought to address three questions in our search for the status of politics: To what extent does Augustine think about politics institutionally? Is his conception of political institutions proto-modern? Are political institutions natural, postlapsarian, or purely sinful? Doing so, I have argued that Augustine does not primarily think of politics in terms of institutions, but in terms of communities. These communities, which remain the focus of his thought, generate practices and social orders designed to help them in their pursuit of earthly peace. It is only in this context – of subjects initiating conventions in accord with or in opposition to the original meaning of creation – that Augustine is concerned with institutions.

Nevertheless, if we shift focus to the order of nature and the order responding to the desert of sinners, Augustine's treatment of what we think of as political institutions begins to emerge. This is his discussion of the postlapsarian tools designed to approximate order in a fallen world. Augustine's view of these institutions is proto-modern insofar as he views *imperium*, the power of coercive office, as a way of restraining human wickedness. Yet, he also views *dominium* as a means of healing and serving others. This complicates the picture a bit.

Finally, when it comes to the status of these coercive institutions, I have argued that they are decidedly postlapsarian. This, however, does not

---

[57] This is not to say that there is no use in attacking injustice, just that there is no use acting as if it were the source of the problem. There are many letters that document Augustine's own attempt to remedy injustices, ep. 10* being a primary example. Cf. Robert Dodaro, "Between Two Cities: Political Action in Augustine of Hippo," in *Augustine and Politics*, ed. John Doody, Kevin Hughes, and Kim Paffenroth (Lanham, MD: Lexington Books, 2005), 99–116.

mean that the offices themselves are sinfully undertaken – it is only the love of wielding their power that is sinful. This suggests that there is a way of participating in the social order that resists participating in the economy of the earthly city. That said, Augustine does not promise that, by so serving their communities, Christian leaders will be able to heal them entirely; there are a number of caveats that render this virtually impossible. In the last section of this chapter, therefore, our main task will be to consider what implications Augustine's vision does have for the amelioration of our political communities.

LATREIA IN POLITICS AND THE TENSIONS IT CREATES BETWEEN THE TWO CITIES

In the previous chapter, I argued that Augustine's sacramental vision calls the claims made by the earthly city into question. Essentially, by making conceptual space between the antisocial practices presented by the earthly city as political, and the underlying social endeavor that is truly political, Augustine opens up a new way of viewing our political communities: they are wounded, stunted by antisocial self-love, but nonetheless capable of being improved by rightly ordered service. As such, he offers a way of participating in our political communities that resists participation in the economy of *amor sui*.

However, to argue this is not to claim that Augustine's sacramental vision actually brings the participation of which it speaks about. Instead, it only points to those things that make it possible. This caveat reveals an important distinction between philosophic and Christian pyschagogy. Augustine thinks that everything he writes is auxiliary; he can argue for a worldview, but cannot instill *amor Dei* in his reader's heart. Significantly, as we will see below, Augustine puts the same limitation on political communities, regarding their ability to cultivate virtuous citizens. They can hold up virtues as laudable or condemn vices as shameful, but they can only ever encourage appearances.

Even so, conversion to a sacramental worldview bears the only hope for cultural renewal that Augustine really trusts. Because the political community is of human origin, Augustine considers it to be just as incapable of healing its own wounds as its fallen members. Unable to see beyond the horizon of *amor sui* by its own power, its solutions to strife involve more antisocial practices: in particular, the manipulation of the weak. Deploying private desires to meet public ends, the many are misled in the name of stability, becoming addicted to their games, their superstitions, and their luxuries. Community is not what it ought to be. For this reason, Augustine regards a life rooted in *latreia* – the offering of oneself and one's works to God in love – as the singular antidote to the problem of fallen *consuetudo*.

Simply put, Augustine thinks that *amor Dei* stands in opposition to the economy animating fallen *consuetudo* and so bears witness against it. Insofar as a life rooted in *latreia* grows in *amor Dei,* it will become increasingly capable of embodying this witness. Such a witness is foreshadowed by those humane women of book 2, whose tears recast the scenes in which they found themselves; both the Horati sister who wept at the death of her betrothed and the Sabine women who pleaded for peace between their fathers and husbands bore witness against a glory that ignored the bonds of kinship. By so doing, they revealed the price of fallen *consuetudo* in a way that was not previously visible.

It is worth noting, therefore, that Augustine's sacramental vision makes room for any humane acts to bear witness against the inhumanity that so often influences politics. Contrasting Caesar's compassion with Stoic *apatheia,* Augustine calls the former "far more credible, more humane (*humanius*), and more in harmony with the feelings of true religion" (*ciu.* 9.5).[58] Applauding Cicero's view that compassion is the most admirable of the virtues, he muses, "What is compassion but a kind of fellow-feeling in our hearts for another's misery, which compels us to come to his help by every means in our power?" (ibid.).[59] This fellow-feeling is in accord with human nature and can be experienced and acted upon rightly by anyone.

Even so, Augustine believes that the only solid foundation for a sustained resistance to the economy of *amor sui* is *amor Dei*. Though human beings are naturally capable of fellow-feeling, given our fallen condition, these impulses are frequently prevented from being what they could by the pull of self-love – a pull that is exacerbated and exploited by fallen *consuetudo*. As we saw in Chapter 3, even great men like Cicero, Varro, and Seneca experienced a lack of freedom in the face of their besieged city's customs. Fearing to offend the people or to disturb the status quo, they fell into the trap of unintentionally proposing solutions that reinforced the earthly city's fundamental economy.

---

[58] CCSL 47.254.

[59] Clarifying that this emotion is properly considered the "servant of reason," he explains that it is praiseworthy only when it is shown "without detriment to justice"; sometimes emotional reactions can be wrong-headed (ibid.). Yet, since mercy and justice are not in opposition for Augustine, this does not mean compassion violates justice whenever it pardons and forgives. Instead, it only does so when it forsakes the true good.

The lack of freedom that these philosopher-statesmen experienced, Augustine thinks, makes perfect sense. Without God, the only fulfillment human beings can find in doing the right thing derives from human praise, and as a result, what society does not esteem is frequently left undone and unsaid. As proof of this "general and universal" disposition in human beings, Augustine quotes Cicero's adage: "It is honour that nourishes the arts; it is glory that kindles men to intellectual effort. All pursuits lose lustre when the fall from general favour" (*ciu.* 5.13). There is truth in Cicero's observation. Nevertheless, he stresses, insofar as our actions are undergirded by the desire either to please others or to please ourselves – another form of the same phenomenon – we lack the resources necessary to step outside of the worldview in which we are imprisoned.[60] Because the human imagination is imitative, it cannot itself generate better practices for its political community without importing some distortions from the besieging city into them. This, we have seen, is his point in lambasting Rome's philosopher-statesmen.

Significantly, those who did manage to get beyond the earthly city's worldview were not great minds; they were human beings who saw the risen Christ with their own eyes. Describing the Apostles as "men of humble birth, without position, [and] without education," Augustine explains the significance of these attributes; they reveal that all the Apostles did was really due to Christ, who was "present ... and acting in them" (*ciu.* 18.49). This, however, does not negate the indispensability of their free response: when they saw the Word Incarnate, they loved him, clung to him, and followed him. Again we see the power of humility, which alone allows human beings to "soar beyond the summits of this world" (*ciu.* 1.*praef*).

Thus, while Cicero was convinced that glory alone motivated virtuous action, the Apostles stand as evidence of a deeper economy than the one in which this is so. While, Augustine admits, love of praise cannot be wholly rooted out from the heart in this life, the Apostles reveal what grace can do to human hearts in the *saeculum*. Pointing out that Cicero's truism cannot account for their behavior, he writes,

They preached the name of Christ where that name was not in "general favour." ... They preached in places where, in fact, Christ's name was held in

---

[60] In *City of God* 5.20, Augustine argues that those who pride themselves on not being enslaved to the opinions of others are dependent on human praise in another way. It is only that they value their own judgment and good opinion more than that of others. This, Augustine argues, leads to a different kind of blindness.

utter detestation. .... Amidst curses and slanders, amidst the severest persecutions and the harshest punishments, all the clamorous hostility of men did not stop them from preaching men's salvation. (*ciu.* 5.14)

Unlike the captives of the besieged city, then, the Apostles overcame the pressures generated by fallen *consuetudo*. Simply put, they found God's approval more desirable than human praise, and found his strength stronger than their weakness.

Though the Apostles, to be sure, were not political figures, Augustine's treatment of them does illuminate the effect *amor Dei* can have on political service. Citing the "divine quality" of their words, acts and lives, Augustine describes how they won over many (*ciu.* 5.14). Here, we see the most significant parallel: acting well in political life, one is bound to find favor with others, at least for a period. Nevertheless, upon finding such favor, the Apostles "did not rest on that glory as if they had attained the goal of their own virtue. They ascribed it all to the glory of God who made them what they were" (ibid.). This recognition and the truth behind it make political service rooted in *amor Dei* superior and sustainable.

Indeed, as Augustine exclaims only a few chapters later, when a man "endowed with true piety," who lives a good life, and who is "skilled in the art of government" happens to wield political power, nothing can be better for the political life (*ciu.* 5.19). Because this kind of man "has his virtues from the Spirit of God," he is able to resist the pressures put in place by the earthly city (ibid.). Because glory is not his greatest good, he can love his enemies regardless of what they say about him. Similarly, he can love those who approve of him without taking "account of their applause" (ibid.). Imagining such a person in a position of leadership, one can immediately see how he (or she) is freer to seek the true good than the one compelled to say whatever it takes to gain approval. Motivated by *amor Dei*, his greatest desire is that God be praised, and he knows he can only praise God by living a good life and rooting his service of others in *latreia*.

Crowning his approval for such persons in leadership, Augustine highlights what makes them good rulers and statesmen. It is humility:

Such men attribute to the grace of God whatever virtues they may be able to display in this present life, because God has given those virtues to them in response to their wish, their faith, and their petition. At the same time, they realize how far they fall short of perfect righteousness, such as is found in the fellowship of the angels for which they strive to fit themselves. (*ciu.* 5.19)

Because *amor Dei* points these men beyond the political realm, it relativizes the political horizon for them and thereby contextualizes the pressures of its customs. Significantly, it also transforms the terms upon which political decision-making is made. While convention deploys the tools of praise and blame to elicit sought-after behavior from citizens, *amor Dei* provides a new foundation for political service; now, only that which can harmonize with God's will is permitted. No longer, in other words, can it be counted necessary to do evil for the sake of a greater good; no longer can it be counted as necessary to subdue others for the sake of status; and, no longer can it be counted necessary to lie to others for the sake of political stability.

Notably, however, Augustine points out the difficulty of refusing to countenance the earthly city's opinions on these matters, especially when one is in a position of power. One finds that the inner compulsion to please others is reinforced by the culture at large. In the besieged city, it is paradoxically the higher who are more constrained by their positions than the lower; the whole system of honor mitigates against their freedom.[61] Describing the reign of Theodosius, for example, Augustine recounts the disaster at Thessalonica; when a mob there murdered the governor, Theodosius's supporters "drove him to avenge the crime" (*ciu.* 5.2). Describing the pressure they put on him as a kind of clamoring of various voices, he contrasts it with the one voice of the Church which advocated for clemency. Presenting political life as being filled with such clamoring voices, Augustine seems to think that any time a leader manages to rise above the anxiety they induce with good judgment, it is a miracle.

Theodosius, however, famously caved in and ordered a massacre to avenge the murder. Hardly perfect, the reason why he nevertheless stands as Augustine's model for a good leader is precisely because he later admitted the wrongness of the deed.[62] Though Augustine's Theodosius does have many other good qualities – he is generous, peace-seeking, and honest – the one that Augustine highlights the most is his "religious humility" (*ciu.* 5.26). Rather than making excuses, Theodosius owned up to his mistake and so overcame all the forces tempting him to think of

---

[61] Because it showers them with so much praise, it acclimatizes them to honour. This practice of treating leaders as if they were gods, Augustine suggests is born either of excessive "humility or noisome flattery (*siue humilitate nimia siue adulatione pestifera*)" (*ciu.* 10.4; CCSL 47.276).

[62] Cf. Dodaro, *Christ and the Just Society*, 191–193, inter alia.

himself as beyond reproach. This, after all, was a society where men of status were "said to be worthy of homage and veneration," and in Theodosius's own case, even "of adoration" (*ciu.* 10.4). To see himself as "a member of the Church" under such conditions, Augustine believes, is the true fruit of *amor Dei* (*ciu.* 5.26).

Moreover, it is in Theodosius's penance that Augustine gives the clearest example of how service rooted in *latreia* can sow the seeds for genuine cultural renewal. Describing the scene in which Theodosius submitted to Church discipline, Augustine writes that "the people of Thessalonica, as they prayed for him, wept at seeing the imperial highness thus prostrate, with an emotion stronger than their fears of the emperor's wrath at their offence" (*ciu.* 5.26). Strikingly, here is a scene in which an act of humility does not undermine a statesman's power, but instead draws a community together in genuine healing.

Despite hoping for the possibility, Augustine does not guarantee that such humiliating actions, or even virtuous actions in general, will bear this kind of fruit in the public sphere. The one who despises glory might well be taken to be an attention-seeker, aspiring to win even greater praise (*ciu.* 5.19). Likewise, the one who asks for forgiveness faces the real possibility of being shunned by an angry *populus*. This, of course, is one reason why such actions are so rarely taken. For Augustine, the visible fruit of virtuous action is radically contingent upon how it is received by the community. Spurius Maelius was killed and then immortalized as a traitor because he distributed free corn during a famine – he was said to be vying for the throne (*ciu.* 3.17). The Horatii's sister was killed for her tears – she was said to be unpatriotic. Augustine's own dear friend Marcellinus, to whom *City of God* is dedicated, was executed unjustly – he was said to be involved in a rebellion. Cultural renewal, in other words, is contingent upon free will. Its invitation can easily be rejected.

This being the case, we again see the importance of Augustine's sacramental vision for sustained Christian service; it is only if God truly sees and reward our good actions that it is possible to swim against the current consistently and without despairing, especially in the face of our own weakness. In his passage on the Apostles, Augustine explains how significant Christ's counsel is for them in this regard (*ciu.* 5.14). He points them upward, to an eternal reward while still encouraging them to bear public witness. Remarking that the martyrs followed the examples of the Apostles – who themselves followed the example of Christ – Augustine highlights how they "endured what was inflicted upon them" because of their trust in God, and how their witness ultimately multiplied their numbers (ibid.). Returning to the martyrs in a later book, he describes how, when given the choice between submitting to a worldly power's wrongful desire and death, the martyrs were miraculously able to choose the latter (*ciu.* 13.4). Quoting Paul, he concludes that the pressure the earthly city places on human beings has great power to do harm when grace is not there to help, but promises that God's grace is strong enough to overcome its pressure whenever it is sought (*ciu.* 13.5).

Ultimately, then, Augustine's sacramental worldview does not guarantee that Christian citizens will act out of *amor Dei* consistently or even at all, nor does it guarantee that acts truly rooted in *amor Dei* will have visible political benefits. It does, however, claim that *amor Dei* alone gives human beings strength to consistently bear witness against the *ethos* of the earthly city in the *saeculum*. For Augustine, this witness is itself a vital political service. Paradoxically, this is because it creates tension within the political community. As we have seen in earlier chapters, a political culture can all too easily close in on itself. Without a higher motive and a truer vision of love, citizens lack the wherewithal to address the problem of fallen *consuetudo* at its root; they do not know what to throw out or what to introduce. They have no perspective on their culture and the besieged city becomes an echo chamber.

When *amor Dei* comes on the scene, then, it introduces a new voice into this echo chamber. Because sacramental vision casts political decision-making in a new light, it is liable to conflict with the earthly city's ideas about what is best for the political community.[63] When this happens, the refusal to follow the status quo comes across as disloyalty – a complaint that Augustine frequently challenges in the aftermath of the sack. For him, the Christian citizen is not out to be a revolutionary. Instead, he is peace-seeking:

[The pilgrim city] does not hesitate to obey the laws of the earthly city by which those things which are designed for the support of this mortal life are regulated; and the purpose of this obedience is that, since this mortal condition is shared by both cities, a harmony may be preserved in them in things that are relevant to this life (*legibus terrenae ciuitatis, quibus haec administrantur, quae sustentandae mortali uitae adcommodata sunt, obtemperare non dubitat ut, quoniam communis est ipsa mortalitas, seruetur in rebus ad eam pertinentibus inter ciuitatem utramque concordia*). (*ciu.* 19.17)[64]

---

[63] Thomas W. Smith goes into great detail on this point in his discussion of what he calls resident alienship. Smith, "The Glory and Tragedy of Politics," in *Augustine and Politics*, 199–205.

[64] CCSL 48.684. Examining the passage, we can note that the "earthly city" whose laws are in question is the occupied city. The passage, in other words, states that obedience to the

This being the case, from Augustine's perspective, the tension between the two cities has far more to do with the earthly city's response to the pilgrim city than the other way around. Augustine's pilgrim does not want to be difficult; like England's Thomas More, he sees what laws and customs he can obey and does so. He does not strive to be a martyr, simply to do his job well.

In presenting the pilgrim city this way, Augustine hearkens back to his discussion of the *paterfamilias* at the end of the previous chapter. There, he argued that the *paterfamilias* ought to "take his rules from the law of the city, and govern his household in such a way that it fits with the peace of the city" (*ciu.* 19.16). For Augustine, domestic peace contributes to political peace because it mirrors the "ordered harmony" that structures the political community; the latter is an order shaped by convention, and so varies from place to place (ibid.). By following his own community's arrangements regarding the giving and obeying of orders, the *paterfamilias* takes his cue from the larger whole and integrates his household into it.

Yet, as we have seen, the true *paterfamilias* takes his cue from his city with regard to the nature and scope of his responsibility, not how he should inhabit it. Because Augustine thinks that one can work within a postlapsarian order without inhabiting one's role in the manner the earthly city suggests, it makes sense that he thinks the pilgrim can follow a besieged city's laws – that is, its just laws – without issue. Its customs, on the other hand, remain questionable; some, Augustine will argue a few chapters later, are indecent and immoderate and can only be inhabited in *amor sui* (*ciu.* 19.19).[65] Like laws that are unjust, these are out of the question.

While Augustine's pilgrim does not seek to make a fuss, she does follow her conscience. She hopes for peace and seeks to find avenues to work for it that are in harmony with *latreia*. From her perspective, this should be enough. Yet, as Augustine's ontology of the earthly city clearly shows, *amor sui* hates anything that calls its narratives into question, and this is exactly what loyalty to *latreia* does. Insofar as a pilgrim's life is truly

---

occupied city's laws is designed to cultivate harmony (*concordia*) between *the* two cities – the earthly and the heavenly.

[65] Moreover, when Augustine does promote acquiescence to customs alongside laws and institutions in 19.17, he is trying to make a case that the pilgrim city is not tied to any particular set of conventions. *Whichever* achieve and preserve earthly peace are welcome, provided that they do not interfere with true religion. Again, because the city of God has a transpolitical *patria*, it can be detached about human things in a way that the earthly city cannot.

rooted in *latreia*, everything she does stems from a different origin. Her very way of using earthly peace is shaped by her alien hope. This is why her adherence to some of the besieged city's laws is not enough; her very existence calls the coherence of its worldview into question. Thus, while Augustine's pilgrim hopes for harmony between the two cities, Augustine does not guarantee such a harmony. Indeed, he writes, when the pilgrim city's dissented from Rome's religious laws, it "proved a burdensome nuisance" to those who "thought differently" (*ciu.* 19.17).

Nevertheless, as I began to argue above, when *amor Dei* does create conflict between the two cities, it is paradoxically salutary; it bears witness to the difference between the two loves, and as a result, has the capacity to broaden the political horizon for the citizen body. Notably, for example, in the passage we have just been examining, Augustine attributes the Christianization of his culture to the witness of the martyrs, writing that their bravery and sheer number wore the Romans down (*ciu.* 19.17). After seeing so many martyrs, in other words, the Romans could no longer dismiss their witness. Their motive could not be ascribed to anything the Roman culture understood. Calling their whole worldview into question as a result, the martyr's witness began to make an impact, ultimately affecting the whole society through the conversion of Constantine. Thus, we see that cultural renewal occurs through the response of individual human beings to *amor Dei*, flowing outward as their witness touches others in the same way. Eventually, this can yield a cultural shift.

Be that as it may, the witness of *amor Dei* only ever serves as an invitation, and any movement it engenders in a culture is only sustainable in and through individuals being struck by what they see. As such, any political community in the throes of Christianization needs authentic conversions, predicated on authentic encounters with *amor Dei*, to prevent its version of Christianity from becoming distorted. While Christian Rome might have adopted better laws and more humane practices as a result of the martyrs' witness, Augustine never describes the Christian empire as a converted political body in *City of God*. He knows that it is all too easy to adopt the appearance of Christian virtue without moving beyond a love of human praise. In this way, any society, even one ruled by Christians, can quickly become a parody of what it ought to be.

Indeed, given that Augustine presents all political communities as perpetually besieged, we must ask what sort of amelioration we can expect to see in them. Ultimately, Augustine's answer is both liberating and sobering. While God is undeniably at work in the world, drawing human beings back to him through his love, much of the political fruit we would hope to see as a result remains unripened. While the faithful Christian can strive to inhabit her role with love, repenting when she fails, the world she strives to heal is constantly in the process of being wounded anew. This is why no progress can truly be had in the *saeculum*. For Augustine, the health of political communities is ever contingent upon the health of the human beings that make them up. Good citizens, especially those whose service is rooted in *latreia*, can be a healing presence, at least for a time, but it is not guaranteed that this will last.

While this may appear to be a position of pessimism, for Augustine it is actually rooted in Christian hope; while the worldly success of true witness is predicated upon others recognizing what they see as valuable, this is true of every action in the *saeculum*. What makes Christianity hopeful is that every action incorporated into *latreia* is allowed to participate in God's work of healing the world. While the pilgrim might not see the fruit their actions, they can trust that God knows how to bring good fruit about. While any true witness to *amor Dei* is perpetually vulnerable to misunderstanding and condemnation, the belief that God has hidden plans for all he inspires liberates the Christian to act in hope. This is the best foundation for cultural renewal that Augustine can conceive.

CONCLUSION

In this chapter, we have explored the status of politics in Augustine's sacramental vision. Importantly, this is a vision in which the political project is merely co-opted by the earthly city; it is not the earthly city's project *per se*. Instead, politics is a natural endeavor: a proper manifestation of our social nature. The dominion that holds our besieged cities together, however, is merely postlapsarian; it would have been unnecessary in our unfallen state. Distinguishing between dominion and domination, Augustine's fundamental political advice is that we learn to inhabit our roles of responsibility in a spirit of service. By offering us a vision that allows us to participate in our political communities without participating in the economy of *amor sui*, he liberates us from the worldview of *amor sui* and points toward the One who can liberate us from *amor sui* altogether.

Ultimately, in writing *City of God*, Augustine wants to help his readers see the world as part of a created order that is good, but that, nonetheless, points to a greater good. Resituating politics within an eschatological worldview, therefore, fits into his project. Nevertheless, it can hardly be called the whole of it; what Augustine writes about politics in *City of God*, he writes as a bishop, and what he has to offer in his episcopal capacity is a sacramental worldview.

Happily for his patriotic readers, this sacramental worldview does provide a kind of political education. It helps us see that there are two opposing economies at work in the world, one a parody of the other. It teaches us that the earthly city is not itself responsible for the natural good it seeks and effects, only the good that it fails to bring about and the evil that comes in its stead. It reminds us that we are all born into the earthly city, and that this city's economy is strengthened every time we act out of *amor sui*. It cautions us that it is not possible to escape the earthly city on our own, and that any virtue we hope to acquire must be rooted in humility. It points us toward the Church as the community in which humility's font, *amor Dei*, is best nurtured. It admonishes us to offer all things in sacrifice to God, imitating his mercy and extending his friendship. Above all, it offers us liberation in Christ, stressing that the earthly city need not have the last word on how we act in the world.

Perhaps all these lessons might seem prepolitical to a statesman. Yet, insofar as Augustine's sacramental worldview teaches these things, it suggests a way of participating in political life that is beyond the imagination of the earthly city. Indeed, unless these lessons are learned, such participation is hardly sustainable. They are, therefore, indispensable aspects to any real political education. While Augustine does not promise that the participation this education fosters will heal our wounded communities entirely, he does argue that it is the best thing for them and, more importantly, for the citizens that inhabit them.

Conclusion

In this book, I have taken a closer look at Augustine's sacramental vision in order to understand the status of politics in the *City of God*. Throughout, I have argued that the *City of God* is really an attempt to persuade the proud, all of us, of the virtue of humility. He does this by showing us the ugliness of the dynamics of the earthly city in a way that renders us complicit in its patterns of behavior even when we try to escape them by ourselves. If he can dispose us to see our need for the Mediator, Augustine hopes, we will realize that we have been interpreting the city of God through the eyes of the earthly city – as a community bound together by *its* love for a common object, rather than by God's love for humanity, which human beings receive and grow in. For Augustine, the world has always been cradled by God's love, we have just forgotten this.

In helping his readers have this "Copernican turn," through which we come to see that the world of self-sufficiency is counterfeit – a self-constituted kingdom that denies its situatedness in God's universe – Augustine also prepares us to see politics with new eyes. In detaching us from an immanent perspective, he allows us to see that the political sphere has been claimed, *besieged*, by the hegemonic earthly city who covets this world as if it were its own. By revealing this, Augustine implies that political life has a natural purpose that the earthly city obscures: it is designed to be a nexus of service. While some philosopher-statesmen have glimpsed this, Augustine thinks that we cannot see the extent to which politics has been renarrated by the earthly city and by our own self-love unless we let God show us.

Furthermore, by stressing that the earthly city will be with us until the end of time and reminding that we have and to some degree continue to participate in its dynamics, Augustine gives us a reason to guard against presumption and false hope. He also gives us a way forward, inviting us to break free of the cycles of behavior dictated by the rules of the earthly city. Namely, we can introduce *humanitas* into our world. This mission, however, should not just come from our own good intentions – insofar as we insist that it does, it will be restricted, less humane than it could be. To participate in the healing dynamic of God's city to the greatest extent possible, Augustine argues, our lives of service must flow out of an ongoing encounter with Christ in the life of the Church.

Essentially, in my reading of the *City of God*, Augustine seeks to liberate his readers from an inappropriate attachment to "the world." This is why he seems to be a pessimist. In reality, I argue, his goal is to help us see creation, to see politics *anew*. This is not to say that he shows us an idealized future where earthly politics will be liberated from the shackles of self-love. Rather, by unmasking the illegitimate claims of the earthly city, he helps us to see our world as wounded and in perpetual need of healing. *City of God*, then, constitutes a call to bear witness to a relationality that is beyond the imagination of the earthly city: to heal our communities here and now insofar as we can.

Thus, in the end, Augustine's political teaching is not proto-modern; it is not realist; it is not idealist; it is not institutional. It is not simply reducible to a classical exhortation to good citizenship. It is sacramental. By detaching his readers from the world, Augustine does not ask us to abandon the world, but invites us to work for an earthly peace understood in light of *amor Dei*. In this way, he gives us a foundation for thinking about earthly peace properly, which is to say, in light of the needs of concrete human persons.

Bibliography

WORKS IN TRANSLATION BY AUGUSTINE

Augustine. *City of God*. Translated by Henry Bettenson. London: Penguin, 2003.
    The Confessions. Vol. I/1. Introduction, translation, and notes by Maria
    Boulding, OSB. Series edited by John E. Rotelle, OSA. Hyde Park, NY:
    New City Press, 1997.
    Expositions of the Psalms, 121–150. Vol. III/20. Translation and notes by Maria
    Boulding. Edited by Boniface Ramsey. Hyde Park, NY: New City Press, 2004.
    Homilies on the First Epistle of John. Vol. I/14. Translation and notes by
    Boniface Ramsey. Edited by Daniel E. Doyle, OSA, and Thomas Martin,
    OSA. Hyde Park, NY: New City Press, 2008.
    Homilies on the Gospel of John 1–40. Vol. 1/12. Translation and notes by
    Edmund Hill, OP. Edited and with an introduction and notes by
    Allan Fitzgerald, OSA. Hyde Park, NY: New City Press, 2009.
    Letters 1–99. Vol. II/1. Translation and notes by Roland Teske. Edited by John
    E. Rotelle. Hyde Park, NY: New City Press, 2001.
    Letters 100–155. Vol. II/2. Translation and notes by Roland Teske. Edited by
    Boniface Ramsey. Hyde Park, NY: New City Press, 2003.
    Letters 156–210. Vol. II/3. Translation and notes by Roland Teske. Edited by
    Boniface Ramsey. Hyde Park, NY: New City Press, 2004.
    Letters 211–270. Vol. II/4. Translation and notes by Roland Teske. Edited by
    Boniface Ramsey. Hyde Park, NY: New City Press, 2005.
    On Genesis. Vol. I/13. Translation and notes by Edmund Hill, OP. Edited by
    John E. Rotelle, OSA. Hyde Park, NY: New City Press, 2002.
    Sermons (51–94) on the Old Testament. Vol. III/3. Translation and notes by
    Edmund Hill, OP. Series edited by John E. Rotelle, OSA. Brooklyn, NY: New
    City Press, 1991.
    Sermons (94A–147A) on the Old Testament. Vol. III/4. Translation and notes
    by Edmund Hill, OP. Series edited by John E. Rotelle, OSA. Brooklyn, NY:
    New City Press, 1992.

Sermons (148–183) on the New Testament. Vol. III/5. Translation and notes by Edmund Hill, OP. Series edited by John E. Rotelle, OSA. New Rochelle, NY: New City Press, 1992.

Sermons (184–229Z) on the Liturgical Seasons. Vol. III/6. Translation and notes by Edmund Hill, OP. Series edited by John E. Rotelle, OSA. New Rochelle, NY: New City Press, 1993.

Sermons (273–305A) on the Saints. Vol. III/8. Translation and notes by Edmund Hill, OP. Series edited by John E. Rotelle, OSA. Hyde Park, NY: New City Press, 1994.

Sermons (Newly Discovered). Vol. III/11. Translation and notes by Edmund Hill. Edited by John E. Rotelle. Hyde Park, NY: New City Press, 1997.

Teaching Christianity. Vol. I/11. Introduction, translation, and notes by Edmund Hill, OP. Series edited by John E. Rotelle, OSA. Hyde Park, NY: New City Press, 1996.

The Trinity. Vol. I/5. Introduction, translation, and notes by Edmund Hill, OP. Series edited by John E. Rotelle, OSA. Brooklyn, NY: New City Press, 1991.

SECONDARY LITERATURE AND OTHER SOURCES

Anatolios, Khaled. "Sacraments in the Fourth Century." In *The Oxford Handbook of Sacramental Theology*, edited by Hans Boersma and Matthew Levering, 140–155. Oxford: Oxford University Press, 2015.

Ando, Clifford. "Augustine on Language." *Revue d'Études Augustiniennes et Patristiques* 40, no. 1 (1994): 45–78.

"Signs, Idols, and the Incarnation in Augustinian Metaphysics." *Representations* 73, no. 1 (2001): 24–53.

Angus, S. *The Sources of the First Ten Books of Augustine's City of God*. Princeton, NJ: Princeton University Press, 1906.

Arendt, Hannah. *The Human Condition*. Chicago: University of Chicago Press, 1998.

Love and Saint Augustine. Chicago: University of Chicago Press, 1996.

Arquillière, Henri-Xavier. *L'Augustinisme Politique: Essai sur la Formation des Théories Politiques du Moyen Âge*. Paris: Librairie Philosophique J Vrin, 1933.

Avramenko, Richard. "The Wound and Salve of Time: Augustine's Politics of Human Happiness." *The Review of Metaphysics* 60, no. 4 (2007): 779–811.

Balot, Ryan K. "Truth, Lies, Deception and Esotericism: The Case of St. Augustine." In *Augustine's Political Thought*, edited by Richard Dougherty, 173–199. Rochester, NY: Rochester University Press, 2019.

Balthasar, Hans Urs von. *The Glory of the Lord: A Theological Aesthetics*, vol. 2. Edinburgh: T&T Clark, 1982.

Bathory, Peter Dennis. *Political Theory as Public Confession the Social and Political Thought of St. Augustine of Hippo*. New Brunswick, NJ: Transaction Books, 1981.

Bonner, Gerald. "Augustine's Conception of Deification." *The Journal of Theological Studies* 37, no. 2 (1986): 369–386.

"The Doctrine of Sacrifice: Augustine and the Latin Patristic Tradition." In *Sacrifice and Redemption: Durham Essays in Theology*, edited by S. W. Sykes, 101–117. Cambridge: Cambridge University Press, 1991.

Brown, Peter. *Augustine of Hippo*. London: Faber and Faber Ltd, 1967. Reprinted by Berkeley: University of California Press, 2000.

Authority and the Sacred, Cambridge: Cambridge University Press, 1995.

Power and Persuasion in Late Antiquity. Green Bay, WI: University of Wisconsin Press, 1992.

"Saint Augustine and Political Society." In *The City of God: A Collection of Critical Essays*, 17–36. New York: Peter Lang, 1995.

Bruggisser, Philippe. "City of the Outcast and City of the Elect: The Romulean Asylum in Augustine's City of God and Servius's Commentaries on Virgil." *Augustinian Studies* 30, no. 2 (1999): 75–104.

Bruno, Michael. *Political Augustinianism: Modern Interpretations of Augustine's Political Thought*. Minneapolis, MN: Fortress Press, 2014.

Burnaby, John. *Amor Dei: A Study of the Religion of St. Augustine*. New York: Harper & Row, 1972.

Burnell, Peter. "The Problem of Service to Unjust Regimes in Augustine's City of God." *Journal of the History of Ideas* 54, no. 2 (1993): 177–188.

"The Status of Politics in St. Augustine's City of God." *History of Political Thought* 13, no. 1 (1992): 13–29.

Burns, Daniel. "Augustine on the Moral Significance of Human Law." *Revue d'Études Augustiniennes et Patristiques* 61, no. 2 (2015): 273–298.

Burt, Donald X. "Courageous Optimism: Augustine on the Good of Creation." *Augustinian Studies* 21 (1990): 55–66.

Burton, Phillip. "Augustine and Language." In *A Companion to Augustine*, edited by Mark Vessey, 113–124. Malden, MA: Wiley-Blackwell, 2012.

Byers, Sarah. *Perception, Sensibility, and Moral Motivation in Augustine: A Stoic-Platonic Synthesis*. New York: Cambridge University Press, 2013.

"The Psychology of Compassion: Stoicism in City of God." In *Augustine's City of God: A Critical Guide*, edited by James Wetzel, 130–148. Cambridge: Cambridge University Press, 2012.

Cameron, Michael. "Augustine and Scripture." In *A Companion to Augustine*, edited by Mark Vessey, 200–214. Malden, MA: Wiley-Blackwell, 2012.

Carrié, Jean-Michel. "Developments in Provincial and Local Administration." In *The Cambridge Ancient History*, vol. 12, edited by A. Bowman, A. Cameron, and P. Garnsey, 269–312. Cambridge: Cambridge University Press, 2005.

Cary, Phillip. *Outward Signs: The Powerlessness of External Things in Augustine's Thought*. Oxford: Oxford University Press, 2008.

Cavadini, John. "Ideology and Solidarity." In *Augustine's City of God: A Critical Guide*, edited by James Wetzel, 93–110. Cambridge: Cambridge University Press, 2012.

"Feeling Right." *Augustinian Studies* 36, no. 1 (2005): 195–217.

"Spousal Vision: Text and History in the Theology of Saint Augustine." *Augustinian Studies* 43, no. 1/2 (2013): 127–148.

"Trinity and Apologetics in the Theology of St. Augustine." *Modern Theology* 29, no. 1 (2013): 48–82.

Cavanaugh, William. "The City: Beyond Secular Parodies." In *Radical Orthodoxy: A New Theology*, edited by John Milbank, Catherine Pickstock, and Graham Ward, 182–200. London: Routledge, 2002.

"From One City to Two: Christian Reimagining of Political Space." *Political Theology* 7, no. 3 (2006): 299–321.

Chambers, Katherine. "Slavery and Dominion as Political Ideas in Augustine's City of God." *The Heythrop Journal* 54, no. 1 (2013): 13–28.

Cicero. *De Officiis*. Translated by Walter Miller. Cambridge, MA: Harvard University Press, 1913.

De Re Publica, De Legibus. Translated by Clinton Walker Keyes. Cambridge, MA: Harvard University Press, 2006.

Clair, Joseph. *Discerning the Good in the Letters & Sermons of Augustine*. Oxford: Oxford University Press, 2016.

Clark, Gillian. "*Imperium* and the City of God: Augustine on Church and Empire." *Studies in Church History* 54 (2018): 46–70.

Cochrane, Charles. "Augustine and the Problem of Power." In *Augustine and the Problem of Power: The Essays and Lectures of Charles Norris Cochrane*, edited by David Beer, 26–102. Eugene, OR: Wipf and Stock, 2017.

Christianity and Classical Culture. Indianapolis, IN: Liberty Fund, 2003.

Combès, Gustave. *La Doctrine Politique de Saint Augustin*. Paris: Plon, 1927.

Conybeare, Catherine. "The City of Augustine: On the Interpretation of *Civitas*." In *Being Christian in Late Antiquity: A Festschrift for Gillian Clark*, edited by Carol Harrison, Caroline Humfress, and Isabella Sandwell, 139–155. Oxford: Oxford University Press, 2014.

Cornish, Paul J. "Augustine's Contribution to the Republican Tradition." *European Journal of Political Theory* 9, no. 2 (2010): 133–148.

Cranz, F. Edward. "The Development of Augustine's Ideas on Society before the Donatist Controversy." *Harvard Theological Review* 47, no. 4 (1954): 255–316.

Cress, Donald A. "Augustine's Privation Account of Evil: A Defense." *Augustinian Studies* 20 (1989): 109–128.

Cutrone, E. J. "Sacraments." In *Augustine through the Ages: An Encyclopedia*, edited by Allan Fitzgerald and John C. Cavadini, 741. Grand Rapids, MI: Eerdmans, 1999.

Deane, Herbert. "Augustine and the State: The Return of Order upon Disorder." In *City of God: A Collection of Critical Essays*, 51–74. New York: Peter Lang, 1995.

The Political and Social Ideas of St. Augustine. New York: Columbia University Press, 1963.

Derrida, Jacques. *Given Time: I. Counterfeit Money*. Translated by Peggy Kamuf. Chicago: University of Chicago Press, 1992.

Dodaro, Robert. "Augustine's Revision of the Heroic Ideal." *Augustinian Studies* 36, no. 1 (2005): 141–157.

"Augustine's Secular City." In *Augustine and His Critics: Essays in Honor of Gerald Bonner*, edited by Robert Dodaro and George Lawless, 231–259. New York: Routledge, 2000.

"Between Two Cities: Political Action in Augustine of Hippo." In *Augustine and Politics*, edited by John Doody, Kevin Hughes, and Kim Paffenroth, 99–116. Lanham, MD: Lexington Books, 2005.

Christ and the Just Society in the Thought of Augustine. Cambridge: Cambridge University Press, 2004.

"*Ecclesia* and *Res Publica*: How Augustinian Are Neo-Augustinian Politics?" In *Augustine and Postmodern Thought: A New Alliance Against Modernity?*, edited by L. Boeve, M. Lamberigts, and M. Wisse, 237–271. Leuven: Peeters, 2009.

"Eloquent Lies, Just Wars and the Politics of Persuasion." *Augustinian Studies* 25 (1994): 77–137.

"The Secret Justice of God and the Gift of Humility." *Augustinian Studies* 34, no. 1 (2003): 83–96.

"Theurgy." In *Augustine through the Ages: An Encyclopedia*, edited by Allan Fitzgerald and John C. Cavadini, 827–828. Grand Rapids, MI: Eerdmans, 1999.

Ebbeler, Jennifer. *Disciplining Christians: Correction and Community in Augustine's Letters*. Oxford: Oxford University Press, 2012.

Ellul, Jacques. *The Humiliation of the Word*. Translated by Joyce Main Hanks. Grand Rapids, MI: Eerdmans, 1985.

Elshtain, Jean Bethke. "Augustine." In *The Blackwell Companion to Political Theology*, edited by Peter Scott and William T. Cavanaugh, 35–47. Oxford: Blackwell, 2004.

Augustine and the Limits of Politics. Notre Dame, IN: University of Notre Dame Press, 1998.

"The Other Happy Life: The Political Dimensions to St. Augustine's Cassiciacum Dialogues." *The Review of Politics* 65, no. 2 (2003): 165–183.

"Why Augustine? Why Now?" *Theology Today* 55, no. 1 (1998): 5–14.

Figgis, John Neville. *The Political Aspects of St. Augustine's "City of God."* London: Longmans, 1921.

Fitzgerald, Allan D. "Christ's Humility and Christian Humility in the De Civitate Dei." *Mayéutica* 40 (2014): 241–261.

Fortin, Ernest. "Augustine and the Problem of Christian Rhetoric." *Augustinian Studies* 5 (1974): 85–100.

"Augustine's 'City of God' and the Modern Historical Consciousness." *The Review of Politics* 41, no. 3 (1979): 323–343.

"Political Idealism and Christianity in the Thought of St. Augustine." In *Classical Christianity and the Political Order*, edited by Brian J. Benestad, 31–64. Lanham, MD: Rowman and Littlefield, 1996.

"The Political Thought of St. Augustine." In *Classical Christianity and the Political Order*, edited by Brian J. Benestad, 1–30. Lanham, MD: Rowman and Littlefield, 1996.

"St. Augustine." In *History of Political Philosophy*, edited by Leo Strauss and Joseph Cropsey, 3rd ed., 176–205. Chicago: University Of Chicago Press, 1987.

Geary, Patrick. "Barbarians and Ethnicity." In *Late Antiquity*, edited by Peter Brown, Glen Bowersock, and Andre Grabar, 106–129. Cambridge MA: Cambridge University Press, 1999.

Gregory, Eric. *Politics and the Order of Love: An Augustinian Ethic of Democratic Citizenship*. Chicago: University of Chicago Press, 2008.

Hadot, Pierre. *Philosophy as a Way of Life: Spiritual Exercises from Socrates to Foucault*. Malden, MA: Blackwell, 1995.

Harmon, Thomas P. "The Few, the Many, and the Universal Way of Salvation Augustine's Point of Engagement with Platonic Political Thought." In *Augustine's Political Thought*, edited by Richard Dougherty, 129–151. Rochester, NY: Rochester University Press, 2019.

Harrison, Carol. *Beauty and Revelation in the Thought of Saint Augustine*. Oxford: Oxford University Press, 1992.

Christian Truth and Fractured Humanity. Oxford: Oxford University Press, 2000.

Hermanowicz, Erika. "Catholic Bishops and Appeals to the Imperial Court: A Legal Study of the Calama Riots in 408." *Journal of Early Christian Studies* 12, no. 4 (2004): 481–521.

Heyking, John von. *Augustine and Politics as Longing in the World*. Columbia: University of Missouri Press, 2001.

Hollingsworth, Miles. *The Pilgrim City: St. Augustine of Hippo and His Innovation in Political Thought*. London: T&T Clark International, 2010.

Isaac, Benjamin. "The Barbarian in Greek and Latin Literature." In *Empire and Ideology in the Graeco-Roman World: Selected Papers*, 197–220. Cambridge: Cambridge University Press, 2017.

Jackson, B. D. "The Theory of Signs in St. Augustine's De Doctrina Christina." *Revue d'Études Augustiniennes* 15 (1969): 9–49.

Jordan, Mark D. "Words and Word: Incarnation and Signification in Augustine's *De Doctrina Christiana*." *Augustinian Studies* 11 (1980): 177–196.

Kamimura, Naoki. "Scriptural Narratives and Divine Providence: Spiritual Training in Augustine's *City of God*." *Patristica*, suppl. vol. 4 (2014): 43–58.

Kaufmann, Peter I. *Incorrectly Political: Augustine and Thomas More*. Notre Dame, IN: University of Notre Dame Press, 2007.

"Patience and/or Politics: Augustine and the Crisis at Calama, 408–409." *Vigiliae Christianae* 57, no. 1 (2003): 22–35.

Keys, Mary. "Augustinian Humility as Natural Right." In *Natural Right and Political Philosophy: Essays in Honor of Catherine Zuckert and Michael Zuckert*, edited by Ann Ward and Lee Ward, 97–116. Notre Dame, IN: University of Notre Dame Press, 2013.

Klein, Elizabeth. *Augustine's Theology of Angels*. Cambridge: Cambridge University Press, 2018.

Kolbet, Paul. *Augustine and the Cure of Souls: Revising a Classical Ideal*, Christianity and Judaism in Antiquity 17. Notre Dame, IN: University of Notre Dame Press, 2010.

Kries, Douglas. "Augustine's Response to the Political Critics of Christianity in the *De Civitate Dei*." *American Catholic Philosophical Quarterly* 74, no. 1 (2000): 77–93.

Lamb, Michael. "Augustine and Republican Liberty: Contextualizing Coercion." *Augustinian Studies* 48, no. 1–2 (2017): 119–159.

"Between Presumption and Despair: Augustine's Hope for the Commonwealth." *American Political Science Review* 112, no. 4 (2018): 1036–1049.

"Beyond Pessimism: A Structure of Encouragement in Augustine's City of God." *Review of Politics* 80 (2018): 591–624.

Lavere, George. "The Political Realism of Saint Augustine." *Augustinian Studies* 11 (1980): 135–144.

"The Problem of the Common Good in Saint Augustine's *Civitas Terrena*." *Augustinian Studies* 14 (1983): 1–10.

Lee, Gregory. "Republics and Their Loves: Rereading *City of God* 19." *Modern Theology* 27, no. 4 (2011): 553–581.

"Using the Earthly City: Ecclesiology, Political Activity, and Religious Coercion in Augustine." *Augustinian Studies* 47, no. 1 (2016): 41–63.

Lee, James K. "Babylon Becomes Jerusalem: The Transformation of the Two Cities in Augustine's *Enarrationes in Psalmos*." *Augustinian Studies* 47, no. 2 (2016): 157–180.

Le Fort, Gertrud von. *The Eternal Woman*. San Francisco: Ignatius Press, 2010.

Lendon, J. E. *The Empire of Honour: The Art of Government in the Roman World*. Oxford: Oxford University Press, 2001.

Lienhard, Joseph T. "The Glue Itself Is Charity: Ps. 62: 9 in Augustine's Thought." In *Collectanea Augustiniana: Presbyter Factus Sum*, edited by J. Lienhard, E. Mueller, and R. Teske, 375–384. New York: Peter Lang, 1993.

Livy. *The Early History of Rome*, books I–V, translated by Aubrey de Selincourt. London: Penguin Classics, Penguin, 1960.

The War with Hannibal, books XXI–XXX, edited by Betty Radice and translated by Aubrey de Selincourt. London: Penguin Classics, 1965.

MacCormack, Sabine. "Cicero in Late Antiquity." In *The Cambridge Companion to Cicero*, edited by C. E. W. Steel, 251–305, 274–282. Cambridge: Cambridge University Press, 2013.

The Shadows of Poetry: Vergil in the Mind of Augustine, The Transformation of the Classical Heritage 26. Berkeley: University of California Press, 1998.

MacQueen, D. J. "The Origin and Dynamics of Society and the State According to St. Augustine." *Augustinian Studies* 4 (1973): 73–101.

Madec, Goulven. *Petites Études Augustiniennes*. Paris: Institut d'Études Augustiniennes, 1994.

Madison, James. "Essay 51." In *The Essential Federalist and Anti-Federalist Papers*, edited by David Wootton, 245–250. Indianapolis, IN: Hackett, 2003.

Manent, Pierre. *The City of Man*. Translated by Marc LePain. Princeton, NJ: Princeton University Press, 2000.

Metamorphoses of the City. Translated by Marc LePain. Cambridge, MA: Harvard University Press, 2013.

Manetti, Giovanni. *Theories of the Sign in Classical Antiquity*. Translated by Christine Richardson. Bloomington: Indiana University Press, 1993.

Marion, Jean-Luc. *Being Given: Towards a Phenomenology of Givenness*. Translated by Jeffrey L. Kosky. Stanford, CA: Stanford University Press, 2002.

Markus, Robert. "Augustine on Magic: A Neglected Semiotic Theory." *Revue d'Études Augustiniennes et Patristiques* 40, no. 2 (1994): 375–388.

Christianity and the Secular. Notre Dame: University of Notre Dame Press, 2006.

Saeculum: History and Society in the Theology of St. Augustine. Cambridge: Cambridge University Press, 1970.

"St. Augustine on Signs." *Phronesis* 2 (1957): 60–83.

Marrou, Henri-Irénée. *Saint Augustin et La Fin de la Culture Antique*. Paris: E. De Boccard, 1938.

Mathewes, Charles. "A Worldly Augustinianism: Augustine's Sacramental Vision of Creation." *Augustinian Studies* 41, no. 1 (2010): 333–348.

Mathisen, Ralph W. "Peregrini, Barbari, and Cives Romani: Concepts of Citizenship and the Legal Identity of Barbarians in the Later Roman Empire." *The American Historical Review* 111, no. 4 (2006): 1011–1140.

McCarthy, Michael C. "An Ecclesiology of Groaning: Augustine, the Psalms, and the Making of Church." *Theological Studies* 66, no. 1 (2005): 23–48.

McLynn, Neil. "Augustine's Roman Empire." *Augustinian Studies* 30, no. 2 (1999): 29–44.

Meconi, David. "Becoming Gods by Becoming God's: Augustine's Mystagogy of Identification." *Augustinian Studies* 39, no. 1 (2008): 61–74.

The One Christ: St. Augustine's Theology of Deification. Washington, DC: Catholic University of America Press, 2018.

"Ravishing Ruin." *Augustinian Studies* 45, no. 2 (2014): 227–246.

Menchaca-Bagnulo, Ashleen. "Deeds and Words: Latreia, Justice, Mercy in Augustine's Political Thought." In *Augustine's Political Thought*, edited by Richard Dougherty, 74–104. Rochester, NY: Rochester University Press, 2019.

Milbank, John. *Theology as Social Theory: Beyond Secular Reason*. Oxford: Oxford University Press, 2006.

Miles, Gary B. *Livy: Reconstructing Early Rome*. Ithaca, NY: Cornell University Press, 1997.

Murphy, Andrew R. "Augustine and the Rhetoric of Roman Decline." *History of Political Thought* 26, no. 4 (2005): 586–606.

Niebuhr, Reinhold. "Augustine's Political Realism." In *The Essential Reinhold Niebuhr*, edited by Robert McAfee Brown, 123–141. New Haven, CT: Yale University Press, 1986.

Nygren, Anders. *Agape and Eros*. Translated by Phillip Watson. Chicago: University of Chicago Press, 1982.

O'Daly, Gerard. *Augustine's City of God: A Reader's Guide*. Oxford: Oxford University Press, 2004.

"Thinking through History: Augustine's Method in the City of God and Its Ciceronian Dimension." *Augustinian Studies* 30, no. 2 (1999): 45–57.

O'Donovan, Oliver. "Augustine's City of God XIX and Western Political Thought." *Dionysius* 11 (1987): 89–110.

The Problem of Self-Love in Augustine. Eugene, OR: Wipf and Stock, 1980.

Ogle, Veronica Roberts. "Sheathing the Sword: Augustine and the Good Judge." *Journal of Religious Ethics* 46, no. 4 (2018): 718–747.

"Therapeutic Deception: Cicero and Augustine on the Myth of Philosophic Happiness." *Augustinian Studies* 50, no. 1 (2019): 13–42.

Oort, J. van. *Jerusalem and Babylon: A Study into Augustine's City of God and the Sources of His Doctrine of the Two Cities.* Supplements to Vigiliae Christianae 14. Leiden: E. J. Brill, 1991.

Pickstock, Catherine. "Music: Soul, City and Cosmos after Augustine." In *Radical Orthodoxy: A New Theology*, edited by John Milbank, Catherine Pickstock, and Graham Ward, 243–277. London: Routledge, 2002.

Plato. *The Republic of Plato.* Translated by Allan Bloom. New York: Basic Books, 1991.

Pollmann, Karla. "Moulding the Present: Apocalyptic as Hermeneutics in *City of God* 21–22." *Augustinian Studies* 30, no. 2 (1999): 165–181.

Puffer, Matthew. "Retracing Augustine's Ethics: Lying, Necessity and the Image of God." *Journal of Religious Ethics* 44, no. 4 (2016): 685–720.

Radford Reuther, Rosemary. "Augustine and Christian Political Theology." *Interpretation* 29, no. 3 (1975): 252–265.

Ratzinger, Joseph. *Jesus of Nazareth: The Infancy Narratives.* New York: Image Press, 2012.

Richardson, J. "Roman Law in the Provinces." In *The Cambridge Companion to Roman Law*, edited by D. Johnston, 45–58. Cambridge: Cambridge University Press, 2015.

Rist, John. *Augustine: Ancient Thought Baptized.* Cambridge: Cambridge University Press, 1995.

Roberts, Veronica. "Augustine's Ciceronian Response to the Ciceronian Patriot." *Perspectives on Political Science* 45, no. 2 (2016): 113–124.

"Idolatry as the Source of Injustice in Augustine's *De Ciuitate Dei*." *Studia Patristica LXXXVIII* 14, no. 1 (2017): 69–78.

Ruokanen, Miikka. *Theology of Social Life in Augustine's De Civitate Dei.* Göttingen: Vandenhoeck & Ruprecht, 1993.

Sallust. *Cataline's War, the Jugurthine War, Histories.* Translated by A. J. Woodman. New York: Penguin Classics, 2007.

Schall, S. J., and V. James. "The 'Realism' of Augustine's 'Political Realism': Augustine and Machiavelli." *Perspectives on Political Science* 25, no. 3 (1996): 117–123.

Schlesinger, Eugene R. "The Sacrificial Ecclesiology of City of God 10." *Augustinian Studies* 47, no. 2 (2016): 137–155.

Scheil, Andrew. *Babylon under Western Eyes: A Study of Allusion and Myth.* Toronto: University of Toronto Press, 2016.

Schindler, David C. "Freedom beyond Our Own Choosing: Augustine on the Will and Its Objects." In *Augustine and Politics*, edited by John Doody, Kevin Hughes, and Kim Paffenroth, 67–98. Lanham, MD: Lexington Books, 2005.

Sehorn, John. "Monica as Synecdoche for the Pilgrim Church in the Confessiones." *Augustinian Studies* 46, no. 2 (2015): 225–248.

Smith, Thomas W. "The Glory and Tragedy of Politics." In *Augustine and Politics*, edited by John Doody, Kevin Hughes, and Kim Paffenroth, 187–216. Lanham, MD: Lexington Books, 2005.

Sorabji, Richard. *Emotion and Peace of Mind: From Stoic Agitation to Christian Temptation*. Oxford: Oxford University Press, 2000.

Stewart-Kroeker, Sarah. *Pilgrimage as Moral and Aesthetic Formation in Augustine's Thought*. Oxford: Oxford University Press, 2017.

"Resisting Idolatry and Instrumentalisation in Loving the Neighbour: The Significance of the Pilgrimage Motif for Augustine's Usus–Fruitio Distinction." *Studies in Christian Ethics* 27, no. 2 (2014): 202–221.

"A Wordless Cry of Jubilation: Joy and the Ordering of the Emotions." *Augustinian Studies* 50, no. 1 (2019): 65–86.

"World-Weariness and Augustine's Eschatological Ordering of Emotions in *enarratio in Psalmum* 36." *Augustinian Studies* 47, no. 2 (2016): 201–226.

Strand, Daniel. "Augustine's *City of God* and Roman Sacral Politics." In *Augustine's Political Thought*, edited by Richard Dougherty, 222–244. Rochester, NY: Rochester University Press, 2019.

Swift, Louis. "Pagan and Christian Heroes in Augustine's *City of God*." *Augustinianum* 27, no. 3 (1987): 509–522.

Taylor, Charles. "The Politics of Recognition." In *Multiculturalism: Examining the Politics of Recognition*, edited by Amy Guttmann, 25–73. Princeton, NJ: Princeton University Press, 1994.

Testard, Maurice. *Saint Augustin et Cicéron*. Paris: Études Augustiniennes, 1958.

Trainor, Brian T. "Morality: Why Augustine Did, and Milbank Didn't Quite, Get It Right." *New Blackfriars* 93, no. 1047 (2012): 524–543.

Trout, Dennis. "Re-textualizing Lucretia: Cultural Subversion in the *City of God*." *Journal of Early Christian Studies* 2, no. 1 (1994): 53–70.

Van Bavel, Tarsicius. "The 'Christus Totus' Idea: A Forgotten Aspect of Augustine's Spirituality." In *Studies in Patristic Christology: Proceedings of the Third Maynooth Patristic Conference*, edited by Thomas Finan and Vincent Twomey, 84–94. Portland, OR: Four Courts Press, 1998.

Ward, Graham. *Cities of God*. London: Routledge, 2000.

Warner, John M., and John T. Scott. "Sin City: Augustine and Machiavelli's Reordering of Rome." *The Journal of Politics* 73, no. 3 (2011): 857–871.

Weithman, Paul J. "Augustine and Aquinas on Original Sin and the Function of Political Authority." *Journal of the History of Philosophy* 30, no. 3 (1992): 353–376.

"Augustine's Political Philosophy." In *The Cambridge Companion to Augustine*, edited by Eleonore Stump, 234–252. Cambridge: Cambridge University Press, 2001.

Webb, Melanie. " 'On Lucretia Who Slew Herself': Rape and Consolation in Augustine's *De ciuitate dei*." *Augustinian Studies* 44, no. 1 (2013): 37–58.

Wetzel, James, ed. *Augustine's City of God: A Critical Guide*. New York: Cambridge University Press, 2012.

"Splendid Vices and Secular Virtues: Variations on Milbank's Augustine." *Journal of Religious Ethics* 32, no. 2 (2004): 271–300.

"A Tangle of Two Cities." *Augustinian Studies* 43, no. 1/2 (2012): 5–23.

Augustine and the Limits of Virtue. Cambridge: Cambridge University Press, 1992.

Williams, Rowan. "Augustine on Creation." In *On Augustine*, 59–79. London: Bloomsbury, 2016.

"Insubstantial Evil." In *On Augustine*, 79–106. London: Bloomsbury, 2016.

"Language, Reality and Desire: The Nature of Christian Formation." In *On Augustine*, 41–58. London: Bloomsbury, 2016.

"Politics and the Soul: A Reading of the City of God." *Milltown Studies* 19, no. 20 (1987): 55–72. Reprinted in *On Augustine*, 107–130. London: Bloomsbury, 2016.

Index